I WILL ALWAYS PLACE THE
MISSION FIRST.

I WILL
NEVER ACCEPT DEFEAT.

INTRODUCTION TO LEADERSHIP

I WILL NEVER QUIT.

MSL I

REVISED EDITION

I WILL NEVER LEAVE
A FALLEN COMRADE.

Custom Publishing

New York   Boston   San Francisco
London   Toronto   Sydney   Tokyo   Singapore   Madrid
Mexico City   Munich   Paris   Cape Town   Hong Kong   Montreal

Interior figures, maps, photos, and tables courtesy of the US Army, unless otherwise indicated.
Excerpts taken from many sources, which are referenced at the end of each section.

Printed in the United States of America

10   9   8   7   6

2008420010

RG/RH

**Pearson
Custom Publishing**
is a division of

www.pearsonhighered.com

ISBN 10: 0-536-56317-9
ISBN 13: 978-0-536-56317-0

CONTENTS

Introduction   viii

Overview of the BOLC I: ROTC Curriculum   ix

Military Science and Leadership (MSL) Tracks   ix

MSL 101 Course Overview: Leadership and
  Personal Development   xi

MSL 102 Course Overview: Introduction to
  Tactical Leadership   xii

The Role of the MSL I Cadet   xii

Academic Approach   xiii

How to Use This Textbook   xiii

Cadet Resources   xiv

Leadership Track

Section 1   Introduction to Army Leadership   2

What Is Leadership?   4

The *Be, Know, Do* Leadership Philosophy   5

Levels of Army Leadership   9

Leadership vs. Management   10

The Cadet Command Leadership Development
  Program   11

Section 2   Army Leadership—Character   16

Seven Core Army Values   18

Empathy   26

The Warrior Ethos   27

Character Development   29

Section 3   Army Leadership—Presence   32

Military Bearing   34

Physical Fitness   35

Confidence   36

Resilience   36

Section 4 Army Leadership—
Leader Intelligence 40
Leader Intelligence 42
Mental Agility 43
Sound Judgment 44
Innovation 44
Interpersonal Tact 45
Domain Knowledge 48

Section 5 Army Core Leader Competencies 54
Leading 56
Developing 61
Achieving 65

Personal Development Track

Section 1 Time Management 70
The Process for Effective Time Management 71
Barriers to Time Management 71
SMART Goals 72
The POWER Model 73

Section 2 Health and Fitness 76
Components of Fitness 78
Principles of Exercise 78
Frequency, Intensity, Time, Type (FITT) 79
Safety and Smart Training 80
Nutrition and Diet 81

Section 3 Introduction to Stress Management 86

Defining Stress 87

Causes of Stress 88

Symptoms of Distress 88

Managing Stress 89

Depression 90

Suicide 91

Section 4 Goal Setting and Personal Mission Statement 94

Defining a Vision 96

Writing a Personal Mission Statement 96

Writing SMART Goals to Support a Vision
and Mission 97

Section 5 Introduction to Effective Army Communication 100

The Communication Process 102

Five Tips for Effective Communication 102

Four Tips for Effective Writing 105

Three Tips for Effective Speaking 107

Values and Ethics Track

Section 1 Introduction to the Warrior Ethos 110

The Warrior Ethos Defined 112

The Soldier's Creed 113

The Four Tenets of the Warrior Ethos 113

Officership Track

Section 1 ROTC Rank Structure 120
The Purpose of Army Ranks 121
The Cadet Ranks 121
The Cadet Unit Structure 122
The Cadet Chain of Command 123

Section 2 US Military Customs and Courtesies 128
Military Customs and Courtesies: Signs of Honor and Respect 129
Courtesies to Colors, Music, and Individuals 129
Military Customs: Rank and Saluting 131
Reporting to a Superior Officer 133

Section 3 Officership and the Army Profession 136
The Concept of a Profession 138
The Three Characteristics of a Profession 138
Professionalism and the Military 141

Tactics and
Techniques Track

Section 1 Orienteering 144
Understanding Orienteering 146
Using a Map 147
Finding Your Way 150
Orienteering Terms and Techniques 152

Section 2 Introduction to Tactics I 156
The Elements of a Fire Team 158
The Elements of a Rifle Squad 165

Section 3 Introduction to Tactics II 168
The Three Individual Movement Techniques 169
The Two Fire Team Movement Formations 173

Section 4 Introduction to Map Reading 178
Marginal Information 180
Topographic Symbols 184
Terrain Features 185
Using Four- and Six-Digit Grid Coordinates 189

Section 5 Introduction to Land Navigation 198
Understanding Azimuths 200
Converting Azimuths 204
Determining Elevation 206
Calculating Distance on a Map 208

Index 214

INTRODUCTION

Key Points

1 Overview of the BOLC I: ROTC Curriculum

2 Military Science and Leadership (MSL) Tracks

3 MSL 101 Course Overview: Leadership and Personal Development

4 MSL 102 Course Overview: Introduction to Tactical Leadership

5 The Role of the MSL I Cadet

6 Academic Approach

7 How to Use This Textbook

8 Cadet Resources

Leadership is intangible, and therefore, no weapon ever designed can replace it.

General of the Army Omar N. Bradley

Overview of the BOLC I: ROTC Curriculum

Being an officer in the US Army means being a leader, a counselor, a strategist, and a motivator. Officers must lead other Soldiers in all situations and adjust to environments that are always changing. To prepare prospective officers to meet this challenge, the Army ROTC program is designed to develop confident, competent, and adaptive leaders with the basic military science and leadership foundation necessary not only to lead small units in the Contemporary Operating Environment (COE) but also to evolve into the Army's future senior leaders.

The ROTC program is the first, or pre-commissioning, phase of the Army's Basic Officer Leader Course (BOLC). The goal of BOLC is to develop competent and confident leaders imbued with a warrior ethos, grounded in fieldcraft, and skilled in leading Soldiers, training subordinates, and employing and maintaining equipment. BOLC is designed to ensure a tough, standardized, small-unit leadership experience that flows progressively from the pre-commissioning phase (BOLC I, one source of which is ROTC) through the initial-entry field leadership phase (BOLC II) to the branch technical phase (BOLC III). This progressive sequence will produce officers with maturity, confidence, and competence who share a common bond—regardless of whether their branch is movement and maneuver, intelligence, fires, sustainment, command and control, or protection—and who are prepared to lead small units upon arrival at their first unit of assignment.

The basis of the Army ROTC curriculum is the BOLC common core task list, which represents the foundation of competencies a second lieutenant needs upon arrival at his or her first unit. ROTC Cadets receive education and training BOLC I common core tasks, as do officers produced by other commissioning sources (the United States Military Academy and Officer Candidate School). Then, in BOLC II and III, all second lieutenants, regardless of commissioning source, participate in more advanced, field- and branch-oriented education and training events that are also part of the BOLC common core task list.

Like the BOLC model, ROTC's Military Science and Leadership (MSL) courses are sequential and progressive; that is, the content and expectations placed on you as the student increase as you progress through the ROTC Program. Your courses are organized into five tracks: the Leadership, the Personal Development, the Values and Ethics, the Officership, and the Tactics and Techniques Tracks. Each succeeding year will treat each MSL track in greater depth in order to teach you all the knowledge, skills, and attitudes essential for commissioning, success at BOLC II, and the establishment of a sound foundation for a career as a commissioned Army officer.

In addition to classroom instruction, your MSL I year will provide you with multiple opportunities to apply military science and leadership concepts in field environments, including leadership labs, battalion or joint field training exercises (FTX), and any battalion situational training exercises (STX) training that your professor of military science (PMS) may direct. Contracted Cadets must participate in physical training (PT) to build their fitness ethos and maintain Army Physical Fitness Test (APFT) standards. Crucial to the ROTC program is Cadet attendance at the Leader Development and Assessment Course (LDAC), normally between the MSL III and MSL IV years. The primary focus at LDAC is to evaluate each Cadet's officer potential in a collective garrison and field training environment. The secondary purpose of LDAC is to validate specific skills taught on campus and to impart selective individual and collective skills.

Military Science and Leadership (MSL) Tracks

Each of the five learning tracks in the Army ROTC Military Science and Leadership curriculum has subcategories that are reiterated and developed progressively through the MSL courses. The US Army has long recognized the importance of the effective leader who fully embodies the leadership ethos, who is fully committed to being a lifelong learner of leadership as a process and journey rather than a destination; a person who has the professional acumen to put this leadership into action in an effective, value-added manner regardless of the challenge of the situation faced in the fast-paced, ever-changing COE.

Leadership

- *Leader Attributes* from FM 6-22 are used throughout the curriculum as a graphic organizer for developing a basic knowledge of leader dimensions. The implicit focus throughout the curriculum is on the importance of personal discipline in becoming a leader of character, a leader with presence, and a leader with intellectual capacity.

- *Core Leader Competencies* are centered around what an Army leader does. These competencies are defined and illustrated as they apply to direct (tactical), organizational (operational), and strategic levels of leader responsibility. The course of study as a whole is designed to challenge and develop the leader's ability to lead (demonstrate competence, communicate, and motivate), develop self and others (adapt, learn, and mentor), and achieve (prioritize, plan, and execute).

Personal Development

- *Character Development* is an implicit aspect of the ROTC curriculum. Cadets are challenged throughout the course of study to recognize and model the Army Values of loyalty, duty, respect, selfless service, honor, integrity, and personal courage; to empathize with their peers, subordinates, and others; and to live the Warrior Ethos.

- *Physical Presence* is foundational for Army leader development. Every Cadet who seeks to become an officer must be able to demonstrate an exceptional level of physical fitness, composure, confidence, and resilience.

- *Intellectual Capacity* has always been and continues to be an imperative characteristic for officers serving in the US Army. Those serving in the Contemporary Operating Environments of Iraq and Afghanistan are learning firsthand the value of mental agility and innovation to Army leadership. Vignettes and case studies from these environments are used to challenge Cadets to examine nonlinear situations, to hone their judgment, and to increase their tactical, technical, cultural, and geopolitical knowledge.

Values and Ethics

- *Army Values.* While it is important for Cadets to be able to articulate the seven Army Values, it is even more imperative that they be able to demonstrate these values in their daily interactions with others. Values form the foundation for Army leadership.

- *Professional Ethics.* In addition to the Army Values, military codes and regulations govern ethical behavior and decision making. Cadets apply the ethical decision making process during case studies and historical vignettes.

- *Warrior Ethos* is embedded in case studies and historical vignettes throughout the curriculum. Cadre members discuss the four basic principles of the Warrior Ethos whenever possible. Cadets apply the Warrior Ethos to increasingly complex situations as they progress through the ROTC program.

Officership

- *Military Heritage.* Cadre members teach and model military heritage through daily performance and contact, lab exercises, ceremonies, and interpersonal interactions throughout the ROTC curriculum.

- *Military History.* Cadets review vignettes and case studies, which provide opportunities for critical reasoning in evaluating tactics, leadership styles, problem solving, and decision making.

- *Management and Administration.* Cadets learn Army programs, policies, and procedures related to areas such as organization, human resources, management, administration, training, and facilities in order to support Army operations.

Tactics and Techniques

- *Tactical Operations.* Cadets develop a practical understanding of the basics of map-reading, land navigation, and tactical maneuvering at the individual, team, and squad levels.

MSL 101 Course Overview: Leadership and Personal Development

MSL 101 introduces Cadets to the personal challenges and competencies that are critical for effective leadership. Cadets learn how the personal development of life skills such as critical thinking, goal setting, time management, physical fitness, and stress management relate to leadership, officership, and the Army profession. The focus is on developing basic knowledge and comprehension of Army leader attributes and core leader competencies while gaining a big-picture understanding of ROTC, its purpose in the Army, and its advantages for the student. Cadets must meet the following objectives for MSL 101:

Leadership

- Describe the relationship between leader character and competence
- Identify the leader attributes and core leader competencies of the Army Leadership Requirements Model.

Personal Development

- Define standards for the Army Physical Fitness Test (APFT)
- Write short-term and long-term goals to prepare for APFT
- Define the basic elements of time and stress management.

Values and Ethics

- Explain the Warrior Ethos
- List and define the seven Army Values.

Officership

- Explain the importance of being a model citizen as an Army officer
- React to passing colors, national music, and approaching officers.

Tactics and Techniques

- Find on-campus locations by reading a campus map.

MSL 102 Course Overview: Introduction to Tactical Leadership

MSL 102 overviews leadership fundamentals such as setting direction, problem solving, listening, presenting briefs, providing feedback, and using effective writing skills. Cadets explore dimensions of leadership values, attributes, and competencies in the context of practical, hands-on, and interactive exercises. Continued emphasis is placed on recruitment and retention of Cadets. Cadre role models and the building of stronger relationships among the Cadets through common experience and practical interaction are critical aspects of the MSL 102 experience. Cadets must meet the following objectives for MSL 102:

Leadership

- Distinguish between leadership values, attributes, and competencies
- Illustrate leader leading, developing, and achieving actions.

Personal Development

- Develop personal mission statement and goals
- Explain the basic elements of Army communication.

Values and Ethics

- Explain how values impact leadership
- Describe the importance of the Warrior Ethos for effective leadership.

Officership

- Explain the importance of personal development for officership.

Tactics and Techniques

- Describe the components of a fire team and squad
- Describe the three individual movement techniques
- Identify symbols and colors on a military map.

The Role of the MSL I Cadet

LEADS—The MSL I year is the time to master the basics of being an ROTC Cadet—Army Values, customs and courtesies, physical fitness, and school success or "life skills" such as goal setting and time management. As a potential Army officer, you will be challenged to study, practice, and evaluate Army leadership and values as you become more familiar with the Army.

DEVELOPS—To learn the skills required of a quality officer and leader, you must participate actively in learning through critical reflection, inquiry, dialogue, and group interactions. MSL 101 and 102 will teach you the specific leadership values, skills, and actions described in FM 6-22 as they relate to your development as a future Army lieutenant. Your instruction in small-unit tactical operations will be the foundation for future, more challenging tactical exercises. Everyone is responsible for contributing to the success of the learning experience.

ACHIEVES—Extensive small-group discussions and exercises are integrated throughout the MSL 101 and 102 courses. Emerging officers are encouraged to work together as a team and with their instructors in modifying assignments, suggesting agendas, and raising questions for discussion. Collaborative learning is enhanced when students apply what they learn in class by describing relevant lessons learned through experiences outside the ROTC classroom.

Academic Approach

The MSL curriculum is outcomes based and designed to focus on Cadet learning, rather than on any specific subject matter. Focusing on the Cadet requires student-centered objectives and conscious attention to how Cadets react to the instruction received. For effective instruction, Cadets need the opportunity to apply the knowledge received from instruction by experienced cadre. Too often, academic instruction is limited to the delivery of information, either through reading assignments, lectures, or slide presentations. Active, student-centered learning, in contrast, is founded on the belief that interaction is central to the learning process. Learning occurs during class in the same way it does outside the classroom: through unstructured and structured experiences in which the Cadet interacts with cadre, with the instructional material, and with other Cadets. Helpful synonyms for ROTC's student-centered approach to learning are experiential learning, direct experience, discovery learning, experience-based learning, and participatory learning. All of these approaches center around five basic steps:

1. Readiness for and openness to the experience
2. The experience itself
3. Reflection upon the experience
4. Analysis, application of theory, or additional explanation of information to clarify the relationship between theory and actions, with an understanding of lessons learned regarding needed changes
5. The opportunity to reexperience (practice in new situations/practical exercises).

The emphasis must first be on the Cadet's preclass preparation. Cadets must come to class with a foundation of knowledge from their preclass readings. This allows the cadre to apply the Socratic model of reflective learning during the 50 minutes of classroom instruction. During this limited contact hour, the cadre can focus on explaining the concepts or material that needs clarifying.

> *Helpful synonyms for ROTC's student-centered approach to learning are experiential learning, direct experience, discovery learning, experience-based learning, and participatory learning.*

How to Use This Textbook

The readings in this textbook have been compiled to prepare the Cadet to participate actively and productively in MSL classes and labs. The chapters are divided into the five MSL curriculum tracks as follows:

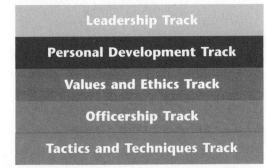

Leadership Track

Personal Development Track

Values and Ethics Track

Officership Track

Tactics and Techniques Track

To be most effective, MSL class sessions are best sequenced to coincide with leadership lab schedules, which may vary from campus to campus due to weather, academic calendars, and other local variables. Thus, class sessions may not necessarily follow the same sequence as textbook chapters. *Cadets must follow the reading assignments given by their instructors to ensure they are adequately prepared for each class session.*

The first page of each chapter orients the Cadet to the key points to be covered in the reading assignment. At the end of each chapter, learning assessment questions serve as "checks on learning" for the Cadet to ensure he or she understands the key points of the chapter. Additionally, vignettes, scenarios, case studies, and critical-thinking questions are dispersed throughout the chapters to help the Cadet build critical-thinking skills and to apply the coursework to real-world situations. The learning assessment questions at the end of each chapter are aligned with the learning objectives for each coinciding lesson.

Cadet Resources

Cadet Textbook. This textbook contains the readings that support the MSL 101 course, Leadership and Personal Development, and the MSL 102 course, Introduction to Tactical Leadership.

Blackboard (Bb). The Blackboard course website, **http://rotc.blackboard.com**, contains MSL course materials.

CONCLUSION

The Basic Officer Leader Course (BOLC) common core task list forms the foundation of competencies a second lieutenant needs to know upon arrival at his or her first unit. Today's Army officer develops through a progression of BOLC sequential learning programs designed for pre-commissioning (BOLC I), common tactical training that is focused on warrior tasks and battle drills (BOLC II), and basic branch-specific training (BOLC III). The ROTC program is the implementation of BOLC I in a university setting. Today's ROTC Cadet represents the future leadership of this great nation. Such responsibility must be carried by officers well versed in the principles and practices of effective leadership, military operations, and personal development. A future officer must be a leader of character, of presence, and of intellectual capacity—a professional who is able to think critically and ready to lead Soldiers in the Contemporary Operating Environment (COE). The MSL I year of ROTC forges this officer through a challenging curriculum of leader development, Army operations, and personal development.

Although this course prepares you for this challenge, it is your responsibility to live the leader attributes while adopting and demonstrating Army Values at all times—both on and off campus. The qualities of an Army officer are not words professed for an exam or exercise. At the MSL I level, these qualities are the expression of a Cadet who has learned and looks for opportunities to apply the fundamentals of Army officership in preparation to "support and defend the Constitution of the United States against all enemies, foreign or domestic." Your commitment to excellence through personal development, learning and living the Soldier's Creed and the Warrior Ethos, and improving your capability for leadership is essential to the success of the Army of the future.

References

Cadet Command Reg. 145-3, *ROTC Precommissioning Training and Leadership Development*. 20 September 2006.

Field Manual 6-22, *Army Leadership: Competent, Confident, and Agile*. 12 August 2006.

INTRODUCTION TO ARMY LEADERSHIP

Key Points

1 What Is Leadership?

2 The *Be, Know, Do* Leadership Philosophy

3 Levels of Army Leadership

4 Leadership Versus Management

5 The Cadet Command Leadership Development Program

All my life, both as a soldier and as an educator, I have been engaged in a search for a mysterious intangible. All nations seek it constantly because it is the key to greatness — sometimes to survival. That intangible is the electric and elusive quality known as leadership.

GEN Mark Clark

Introduction

As a junior officer in the US Army, you must develop and exhibit character—a combination of values and attributes that enables you to see what to do, decide to do it, and influence others to follow. You must be competent in the knowledge and skills required to do your job effectively. And you must take the proper action to accomplish your mission based on what your character tells you is ethically right and appropriate. This philosophy of *Be, Know, Do* forms the foundation of all that will follow in your career as an officer and leader. The *Be, Know, Do* philosophy applies to all Soldiers, no matter what Army branch, rank, background, or gender. SGT Leigh Ann Hester, a National Guard military police officer, proved this in Iraq and became the first female Soldier to win the Silver Star since World War II.

Silver Star Leadership

SGT Leigh Ann Hester of the 617th Military Police Company, a National Guard unit out of Richmond, Ky., received the Silver Star, along with two other members of her unit, for their actions during an enemy ambush on their convoy. Hester's squad was shadowing a supply convoy [in March 2005] when anti-Iraqi fighters ambushed the convoy. The squad moved to the side of the road, flanking the insurgents and cutting off their escape route. Hester led her team through the "kill zone" and into a flanking position, where she assaulted a trench line with grenades and M203 grenade-launcher rounds. She and Staff SGT Timothy Nein, her squad leader, then cleared two trenches, at which time she killed three insurgents with her rifle.

When the fight was over, 27 insurgents were dead, six were wounded, and one was captured. Being the first female soldier since World War II to receive the medal is significant to Hester. But, she said, she doesn't dwell on the fact.

"It really doesn't have anything to do with being a female," she said. "It's about the duties I performed that day as a soldier." Hester, who has been in the National Guard since April 2001, said she didn't have time to be scared when the fight started, and she didn't realize the impact of what had happened until much later.

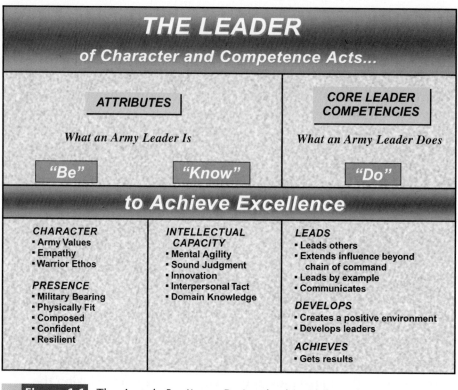

Figure 1.1 The Army's *Be, Know, Do* Leadership Philosophy

What Is Leadership?

Leadership is the process of influencing people by providing them with *purpose, direction,* and *motivation* while you are operating to accomplish a mission and improve the organization.

An *Army leader* is anyone who, by virtue of assumed role or assigned responsibility, inspires and influences people to accomplish organizational goals. Army leaders motivate people both inside and outside the chain of command to pursue actions, focus thinking, and shape decisions for the greater good of the organization.

Being a leader is a lot more complex than just giving orders. Your influence on others can take many forms. Your words and your deeds, the values you talk about, the example you set, every action you take—on or off duty—are all part of your influence on others.

Providing Purpose and Vision

By providing purpose, you enable your Soldiers to see the underlying rationale for a mission; you provide them the reason to act in order to achieve a desired outcome. Leaders should provide clear purpose for their followers; they do that in a variety of ways. They can use direct means through requests or orders. As time goes on, your subordinates will notice that you communicate in a consistent style of **command** and decision making that builds their trust and confidence. Your Soldiers will eventually be able to read a situation and anticipate your intentions and actions. This trust in turn leads to a cohesive, integrated, and effective unit.

Vision is another way that leaders provide purpose. Vision refers to an organizational purpose that may be broader or have less immediate consequences than other purpose statements. Higher-level leaders carefully consider how to communicate their vision.

Providing Direction

When giving direction, you make clear how you want your Soldiers to accomplish a mission. You prioritize tasks, assign responsibility for completing them (delegating appropriate authority), and make sure subordinates understand the Army standard for the tasks. You decide how to accomplish a mission with the available people, time, and resources. It is your subordinates' job to carry out your orders. But to do that, they need clear direction. Give just enough direction to allow Soldiers to use their initiative, abilities, and imagination—and they will surprise you with the results.

Providing Motivation

Motivation is the will to accomplish a task. By learning about your Soldiers and their capabilities, you will soon be able to gear the team to the mission. Once you have given an order, don't micromanage the process—allow your Soldiers to do their jobs to the best of their abilities. When they succeed, praise them. When they fail, give them credit for the attempt, and coach them on how to improve. Remember that it takes more than just words to motivate. The example you set is at least as important as what you say and how well you manage the work. Stay involved and motivate yourself to attain the best mission result, and your enthusiasm will carry over. A leader's role in motivation is to understand the needs and desires of others, to align and elevate individual drives into team goals, and to influence others and accomplish those larger aims. You'll find that some people have high levels of internal motivation to finish a job, while others need more reassurance and feedback. Motivation spurs initiative when something needs to be accomplished.

The *Be, Know, Do* Leadership Philosophy

The characteristics of an effective Army leader make up the **Be, Know, Do** philosophy. As you have already seen, leadership involves influencing others to take appropriate action. But becoming a leader involves much more. Embracing a leadership role involves developing all aspects of yourself: your character, your competence, and your actions. You learn to lead well by adopting the Army Values, learning military skills, and practicing leadership actions. Only by this self-development will you become a confident and competent leader of character. Figure 1.1 will help you correlate the *Be, Know, Do* philosophy of Army leadership with the *leader attributes* and *core leader competencies*.

Be, Know, Do

the key characteristics of an Army leader that summarize the leader attributes and core leader competencies

TABLE 1.1	The Seven Key Army Values	
L	**Loyalty**	Bear true faith and allegiance to the US Constitution, the Army, your unit, and other Soldiers
D	**Duty**	Fulfill your obligations
R	**Respect**	Treat people as they should be treated
S	**Selfless Service**	Put the welfare of the nation, the Army, and subordinates before your own
H	**Honor**	Live up to all the Army Values
I	**Integrity**	Do what is right—legally and morally
P	**Personal Courage**	Face fear, danger, or adversity (physical or moral)

Attributes—What an Army Leader Is

BE: Who You Are—A Leader of Character and a Leader With Presence
Army leadership begins with what the leader must *Be*—the values and attributes that shape character. It may be helpful to think of these as internal and defining qualities you possess all the time. As defining qualities, they make up a leader's identity. Your character is *who you are* and informs everything you do and ask others to do. You demonstrate your commitment to character and to a leadership role in the Army by adopting and living the seven Army Values and the leader attributes. These values form the foundation of your character as a military officer and will guide you in your career. By living the Army Values, you will teach your subordinates by example and help them develop leader attributes.

TABLE 1.2a	The Leader Attributes

1. A Leader of Character *(Identity)*
Factors internal and central to a leader, that which makes up an individual's core

Army Values

- Values are the principles, standards, or qualities considered essential for successful leaders
- Values are fundamental to help people discern right from wrong in any situation
- The Army has set seven values that must be developed in all Army individuals: loyalty, duty, respect, selfless service, honor, integrity, and personal courage.

Empathy

- The propensity to experience something from another person's point of view
- The ability to identify with and enter into another person's feelings and emotions
- The desire to care for and take care of Soldiers and others.

Warrior Ethos

- The shared sentiment internal to Soldiers that represents the spirit of the profession of arms.

2. A Leader With Presence
How a leader is perceived by others based on the leader's outward appearance, demeanor, actions, and words

Military Bearing

- Possessing a commanding presence
- Projecting a professional image of authority.

Physically Fit

- Having sound health, strength, and endurance that support one's emotional health and conceptual ability under prolonged stress.

Composed

- Demonstrating composure and an outward calm through steady control over one's emotions.

Confident

- Projecting self-confidence and certainty in the unit's ability to succeed in whatever it does.

Resilient

- Showing a tendency to recover quickly from setbacks, shock, injuries, adversity, and stress while maintaining a mission and organizational focus.

TABLE 1.2b	The Leader Attributes (continued)

3. A Leader With Intellectual Capacity

The mental resources or tendencies that shape a leader's conceptual abilities and impact effectiveness

Mental Agility

- Flexibility of mind
- The tendency to anticipate or adapt to uncertain or changing situations; to think through second- and-third-order effects when current decisions or actions are not producing the desired effects
- The ability to break out of mental "sets" or habitual thought patterns; to improvise when faced with conceptual impasses
- The ability to quickly apply multiple perspectives and approaches to assessment, conceptualization, and evaluation.

Sound Judgment

- The capacity to assess situations or circumstances shrewdly and to draw sound conclusions
- The tendency to form sound opinions and make sensible decisions and reliable guesses
- The ability to make sound decisions when all facts are not available.

Innovation

- The tendency to introduce new ideas when the opportunity exists or in the face of challenging circumstances
- Creativity in producing ideas and objects that are both novel or original and worthwhile or appropriate.

Interpersonal Tact

- The capability to understand interactions with others
- Being aware of how others see you and sensing how to interact with them effectively
- Consciousness of character and motives of others and how that affects interacting with them.

Domain Knowledge

- Possessing facts, beliefs, and logical assumptions in relevant areas
- Technical knowledge—specialized information associated with a particular function or system
- Tactical knowledge—understanding military tactics related to securing a designated objective through military means
- Joint knowledge—understanding joint organizations, their procedures, and their roles in national defense
- Cultural and geopolitical knowledge—understanding cultural, geographic, and political differences and sensitivities.

KNOW: Skills You Have Mastered—A Leader With Intellectual Capacity

Competence in soldiering skills—what you *Know*—is as important as good character in your growth as an Army leader. Without it, your command will lack substance. To ask subordinates to perform to standard, you must first master the standard yourself. You must master five types of Army leadership attributes and skills in your training:

- *Mental agility*—having flexibility of mind, a tendency to anticipate or adapt to uncertain or changing situations
- *Sound judgment*—having a capacity to assess situations or circumstances shrewdly and to draw feasible conclusions

Critical Thinking

Discuss the attributes of leadership SGT Hester demonstrated during the ambush in Iraq (see Page 3).

- *Innovation*—the ability to introduce something new for the first time when needed or an opportunity exists
- *Interpersonal tact*—interacting with others and accepting the character, reactions, and motives of oneself and others
- *Domain knowledge*—possessing facts, beliefs, and logical assumptions and an understanding of military tactics related to securing a designated objective through military means.

A natural part of an Army officer's career is the opportunity for advancement and promotion. As you advance in rank and responsibility, you will face many new challenges. Having an understanding of and competence in basic Army skills will give you the ability to tackle these new challenges with confidence.

Core Leader Competencies—What an Army Leader Does

DO: How You Carry out Your Decisions—Leads, Develops, and Achieves

As you have already seen, leadership takes place in action. What you *Do* is every bit as important as the *Be* and *Know* aspects of your Army leadership philosophy. While character and knowledge are necessary, by themselves they are not enough. Leaders cannot be effective until they apply what they know. What leaders *Do*, or leader actions, is directly related to the influence they have on others and on what is done.

While the process of influencing others may seem a little vague or intangible at first, the concept becomes concrete when coupled with *operating actions*. Operating actions are those you take to achieve the short-term goal of accomplishing a mission, such as holding a briefing or conducting a drill. While all direct leaders perform operating actions, the type and scope of such actions become more complex as your rank and level of responsibility change. Moreover, it is a natural part of humans' competitive drive to want to get better and better at what they do. Leaders—in seeking to build morale, unit **esprit de corps**, and performance—strive to improve the Soldiers, facilities, equipment, training, and resources under their command. Nothing speaks more clearly to your subordinates about your commitment to excellence and improvement than your ongoing assessment of the unit's performance and your leading the way toward improvement. Your investment of time, effort, and interest in your subordinates' improved performance will pay dividends in building trust and *esprit de corps*.

esprit de corps

a shared sense of comradeship and devotion to the cause among members of a group, team, or unit

TABLE 1.3	The Core Leadership Competencies
Leads	Leading is all about influencing others. Leaders and commanders set goals and establish a vision, and then must motivate or influence others to pursue the goals. Leaders influence others in one of two ways. Either the leader and followers communicate directly, or the leader provides an example through everyday actions. The key to effective communication is to come to a common or shared understanding.
Develops	Developing the organization involves three competencies: creating a positive environment in which the organization can flourish, preparing oneself, and developing other leaders. The environment is shaped by leaders taking actions to foster working together, encouraging initiative and personal acknowledgment of responsibility, setting and maintaining realistic expectations, and demonstrating care for people—a leader's No. 1 resource.
Achieves	Achieving is the third competency. Ultimately, leaders exist to accomplish those endeavors that the Army has prescribed for them. Getting results, accomplishing the mission, and fulfilling goals and objectives are all ways to say that leaders exist at the discretion of the organization to achieve something of value. Leaders get results through the influence they provide in direction and priorities. They develop and execute plans and must consistently accomplish goals to a high ethical standard.

Levels of Army Leadership

Army leadership positions divide into three levels—*direct*, *organizational*, and *strategic*. The leadership level involves a number of factors, including:

- Span of control
- Headquarters level
- Extent of the influence of the leader holding the position
- Size of the unit or organization
- Type of operations the unit conducts

Figure 1.2 Army Leadership Levels

- Number of people assigned
- The unit's long-term mission or how far in advance it develops plans.

Direct Leadership

Direct leadership is face-to-face, first-line leadership. Subordinates of direct leaders see them all the time at the team, squad, section, platoon, company, battery, squadron, and battalion levels. The direct leader may command anywhere from a handful to several hundred people. Direct leaders influence their subordinates one-on-one, but may still guide the organization through subordinate officers and noncommissioned officers (NCOs). Direct leaders quickly see what works, what doesn't work, and how to address problems.

Organizational Leadership

Organizational leaders command several hundred to several thousand people. Their command is indirect, generally through more levels of subordinates. This "chain of command" sometimes makes it difficult for them to see results. Organizational leaders usually employ staffs of subordinate officers to help manage their organizations' resources. Organizational leaders are responsible for establishing policy and the organization's working climate. Their skills are the same as those of direct leaders, but they cope with more complexity, more people, greater uncertainty, and a greater number of unintended consequences. They have little face-to-face contact with the rank-and-file Soldier and command at the brigade through corps levels. Typically, their focus is on planning and missions in the next two to 10 years.

Strategic Leadership

Strategic leaders include military and Department of the Army (DA) civilian leaders from the major command level through the Department of Defense leadership. Strategic leaders are responsible for large organizations and influence several thousand to hundreds of thousands of people. They establish force size and structure, allocate resources, communicate strategic vision, and prepare their commands for their future roles. Strategic leaders consider the total environment in which the Army functions. They may take into account such things as congressional hearings, Army budgetary constraints, new-systems acquisition, civilian programs, research, development, and interservice cooperation.

Leadership Versus Management

The Art of Delegating Downward

The challenge of command is to empower your subordinate leaders. Give them a task, delegate the necessary authority, and then let them do the work. Check on them frequently enough to keep track of what is going on, but don't get in their way. Your mastery of this skill will improve through practice.

As you can see, leadership operates through a wide range of levels, organization sizes, and conditions. Depending on the course of your career as an officer, your path might lead to almost any of these levels and assignments if you are willing to work hard to develop your character, competence, and behavior. You should prepare to embrace the opportunity for promotion when it arises. This path will also take you on an exciting journey through Army life that will almost always provide fulfilling work. One aspect of your job to which you should pay particular attention is the tendency toward the "management mindset." Granted, much of your work as an Army officer will be managerial: putting people and resources to work in the most efficient ways. And managers and good leaders have much in common as both focus on results.

But as Table 1.4 shows, managers and good leaders differ in how they approach their jobs. For example, managers administer, while leaders innovate. And while leaders, like managers, must also keep the organization running smoothly, as a leader you must constantly ponder the next steps, come up with better ways to accomplish the goal, and creatively engage your subordinates to produce more or better results.

TABLE 1.4	Management vs. Leadership
Managers	**Leaders**
Administer	Innovate
Maintain	Develop
Control	Inspire
Short-term view	Long-term view
Imitate	Originate
Ask how/when	Ask what/why
Accept status quo	Challenge status quo

In short, leaders continually "push the envelope," searching for ways to change and improve their commands.

Effective leaders build trust and understanding by encouraging their subordinates to seize the initiative and act. They give their Soldiers room to work. This does not mean allowing them to repeat mistakes—your job is to help your subordinates succeed through empowering and coaching. By providing purpose, direction, and motivation for them to operate in support of the mission, you train them to operate independently. A pure management mindset is never able to *let go and lead*.

The Cadet Command Leadership Development Program

The Cadet Command Leadership Development Program is a process designed to develop leadership skills, including those skills you have just reviewed, within a variety of training and educational environments. It is administered on campus by the professor of military science and during summer training by TAC (Train, Advise, Counsel) officers. As you progress through the ROTC program, you will see a variety of different LDP (Leadership Development Program) assessment tools that focus on the seven Army Values and the 16 leadership dimensions. The Blue Card, the Cadet Evaluation Report, the Officer Evaluation Report, and the Developmental Support Form all share common traits—each drawing on the Army leadership model, which is designed to assist you in maximizing your potential.

You achieve excellence when your Soldiers habitually show discipline and commitment to Army Values. Individuals and organizations pursue excellence to improve. The Army cherishes leaders of character who are good role models, consistently set the example, and accomplish the mission while improving their units. The Cadet Command Leadership Development Program is a preview of the Officer Evaluation System, an ongoing performance assessment of regular Army officers, and gives you a foretaste of how others will help you improve your leadership skills.

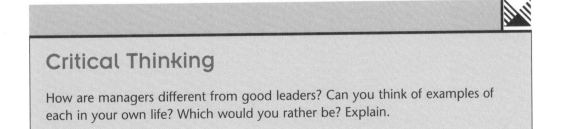

Critical Thinking

How are managers different from good leaders? Can you think of examples of each in your own life? Which would you rather be? Explain.

Just as the diamond requires three properties for its formation—carbon, heat, and pressure—successful leaders require the interaction of three properties—character, knowledge, and application. Like carbon to the diamond, character is the basic quality of the leader. But as carbon alone does not create a diamond, neither can character alone create a leader. The diamond needs heat. Man needs knowledge, study, and preparation. The third property, pressure—acting in conjunction with carbon and heat—forms the diamond. Similarly, one's character, attended by knowledge, blooms through application to produce a leader.

GEN Edward C. Meyer

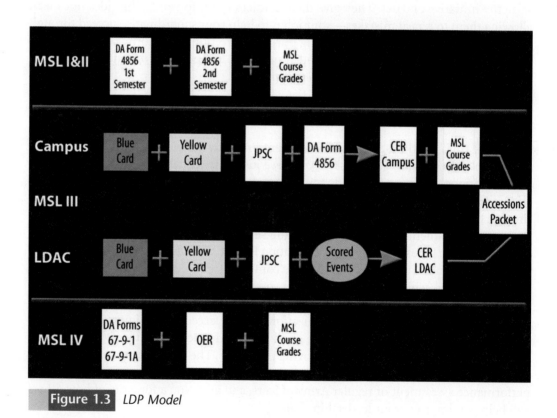

Figure 1.3 *LDP Model*

Cadet Evaluation Report	Type of Report
For use of this form see CC Reg 145-3; staff proponent is USACC DOLD	**CAMPUS**

PART I - ADMINISTRATIVE DATA

a. NAME (LAST, FIRST, MIDDLE INITIAL)		b. SSN	c. SEX	d. REGION	e. REGT/CO/PLT
f. SCHOOL	g. SCHOOL CODE	h. APFT	i. DATE	j. ESTP (Y/N)	k. HEIGHT	l. WEIGHT

PART II - AUTHENTICATION
(Rated cadet's signature verifies cadet has seen completed part I-VI and the administrative data is correct)
(Rater & Sr. Rater's signatures verify that the cadet has been counseled)

a. NAME OF RATER (LAST, FIRST, MI)	b. SSN	c. RANK	d. POSITION	e. SIGNATURE	f. DATE
g. NAME OF SENIOR RATER (LAST, FIRST, MI)	h. SSN	i. RANK	j. POSITION	k. SIGNATURE	l. DATE

m. RATER'S TELEPHONE NUMBER	n. SENIOR RATER'S TELEPHONE NUMBER
o. PERIOD COVERED FROM: TO:	p. SIGNATURE OF RATED CADET	q. DATE

PART III - LEADERSHIP POSITIONS
List the evaluated leadership positions from the JPSC (Minimum of 5)

PART IV - PERFORMANCE DATA

NOT USED

PART V - PERFORMANCE EVALUATION - PROFESSIONALISM (Primary Assessor/PLT TAC)
CHARACTER Disposition of the leader: combination of values, attributes, and skills affecting leader actions

a. Values - Indicate "S" or "N" for each OBSERVED value   "N" Ratings must be justified by observation in Part VI below

	S	N		S	N
1. LOYALTY (LO): Bears true faith and allegiance to the Constitution, Army, Units and soldier			5. HONOR (HO): Adheres to ARMY'S CODE OF VALUES		
2. DUTY (DU): Fulfills professional, legal and moral obligations			6. INTEGRITY (IT): Exhibits high personal moral standards		
3. RESPECT (RE): Promotes dignity, consideration, fairness and EO			7. PERSONAL COURAGE (PC): Manifests physical and moral courage		
4. SELFLESS SERVICES (SS): Places Army priorities before self					

b. LEADERSHIP ATTRIBUTES/SKILLS/ACTIONS: Place an "X" in the appropriate rating block for dimension within Attributes, Skills, and Actions.
"E" and "N" must be justified by observations in Part VI.

ATTRIBUTES Fundamental qualities and characteristics	1. MENTAL (ME) Posses desire, will, initiative, and discipline	E	S	N	2. PHYSICAL (PH) Maintains appropriate level of physical fitness and military bearing	E	S	N	3. EMOTIONAL (EM) Display self control; calm under pressure	E	S	N
SKILLS Skill development is a part of self-development; prerequisite to action	4. CONCEPTUAL (CN) Demonstrates sound judgment, critical /creative thinking, moral reasoning	E	S	N	5. INTERPERSONAL (IP) Shows skill with people coaching, teaching, counseling, motivating, and empowering	E	S	N	6. TECHNICAL (TE) Possess the necessary expertise to accomplish all tasks and functions	E	S	N
	7. TACTICAL (TA) Demonstrates proficiency in inquired professional knowledge, judgment, and warfighting	E	S	N								
INFLUENCING Method of reaching goals while operating/improving	8. COMMUNICATING (CO) Display good oral, writing, and listening skills for individuals/groups	E	S	N	9. DECISION MAKING (DM) Employs sound judgment, logical reasoning, and uses resources wisely	E	S	N	10. MOTIVATING (MO) Inspires, motivates, and guides other toward mission accomplishment	E	S	N
OPERATING Short-term mission accomplishment	11. PLANNING/ PREPARING (PL) Develops detailed executable plans that are feasible, acceptable, and executable	E	S	N	12. EXECUTING (EX) Shows tactical proficiency, meets mission standards, and takes care of people resources	E	S	N	13. ASSESSING (AS) Uses after action and evaluation tools to facilitate consistent improvement	E	S	N
IMPROVING Long-term improvement in the Army; its people and organizations	14. DEVELOPING (DE) Invests adequate time and effort to develop individual subordinates	E	S	N	15. BUILDING (BD) Spends time and resources improving individuals, teams, groups, and units; fosters ethical climate	E	S	N	16. LEARNING (LR) Seeks self-improvement and organizational growth; envisioning, adapting, and leading changes	E	S	N

ROTC CDT CMD FORM 67-9

Figure 1.4a *Sample Cadet Evaluation Report*

NAME	SSN	PERIOD COVERED FROM	TO

PART VI - PERFORMANCE AND POTENTIAL EVALUATION (PLT TAC/Primary Assessor)

a. EVALUATE THE RATED CADET'S PERFORMANCE DURING THE RATING PERIOD AND HIS/HER LEADERSHIP POTENTIAL FOR COMMISSIONING

☐ E-OUTSTANDING PERFORMANCE MUST COMMISSION   ☐ S-SATISFACTORY PERFORMANCE COMMISSION   ☐ N-NEEDS IMPROVEMENT BEFORE COMMISSIONING

b. COMMENT ON SPECIFIC ASPECT OF THE PERFORMANCE AND POTENTIAL FOR COMMISSIONING

c. IDENTIFY ANY UNIQUE PROFESSIONAL SKILLS OR AREAS OF EXPERTISE OF VALUE TO THE ARMY THAT THIS CADET POSSESSES WHICH MAY ASSIST IN DETERMINING BRANCH AND COMPONENT SELECTION

PART VI - SENIOR RATER (PMS)

a. EVALUATE THE RATED CADET LEADER POTENTIAL FOR COMMISSIONING

☐ BEST QUALIFIED   ☐ FULLY QUALIFIED   ☐ QUALIFIED

b. PERFORMANCE COMPARE WITH CADETS IN THE SAME UNIT (Campus Only)

☐ BEST QUALIFIED

☐ FULLY QUALIFIED

☐ QUALIFIED

☐ OTHER

   I RANK THIS CADET
   _____ OF _____

c. COMMENT ON PERFORMANCE/POTENTIAL

ROTC CDT CMD FORM 67-9

Figure 1.4b *continued*

CONCLUSION

Excellence in leadership does not mean perfection. Rather, an excellent leader allows people room to learn from their mistakes as well as savor their successes. Your subordinates will learn to trust that, when they fail—as they will—you will coach them to do better. As you reflect on the Army leader attributes and core leader competencies, developing the skills your position requires, you will become a leader of character and competence. This is the heart of true leadership— influencing people by providing purpose, direction, and motivation while operating to accomplish the mission and improving the organization.

You have learned that effective leadership—particularly in field operations—is your primary and most important challenge as an Army officer. You practice values that lead to excellence and develop a team that can prevail in defense of the United States. The Army expects you, as one of its leaders, to Be, Know, and Do to the very best of your ability. This model is the keystone for high morale and outstanding performance throughout the entire organization.

Learning Assessment

1. What are the leader attributes and core leader competencies of *Be, Know, Do* in Army leadership?
2. What are the three levels of Army leadership?
3. Explain the difference between leadership and management attributes.
4. Explain how *Be, Know, Do* applies to your daily activities on campus and in ROTC.
5. What are the key components of the Cadet Command Leadership Development Program at the MSL I and II levels?

Key Words

leadership
command
Be, Know, Do
esprit de corps

References

CCR-145-3, *Reserve Officers Training Corps Precommissioning Training and Leadership Development.* 1 September 2005.

Field Manual 6-22, *Army Leadership: Competent, Confident, and Agile.* 12 October 2006.

Wood, S. (17 June 2005). Female Soldier Receives Silver Star in Iraq. *American Forces Press Service.* Retrieved 12 July 2005 from http://www4.army.mil/ocpa/soldierstories

Section

2

ARMY LEADERSHIP— CHARACTER

Key Points

1 Seven Core Army Values

2 Empathy

3 Warrior Ethos

4 Character Development

> God grant that men of principle shall be our principal men.
>
> Thomas Jefferson

Introduction

The old wisdom is that an army runs on its stomach. But the physical well-being and ultimate success of an army in the field depends far more on the character of its leaders. Quality leadership grows out of sound values and attributes. Such leadership instills trust, confidence, and loyalty in your subordinates—and produces results. The essential **values** and attributes of **character** discussed here will be the moral compass on your journey to becoming a respected, effective leader.

Our values are never tested more strenuously than during times of crisis. Those who can keep a level head and act with character, particularly in the face of grave danger, testify to the importance of the Army Values and leader attributes. Consider how one Army leader in Vietnam reacted with integrity and heroism in a combat situation.

values

the central ideas that form the foundation of your character and guide your decision making and behavior

character

who you are, defined by your values, beliefs, and behavior

Incident at My Lai

On March 16, 1968, Warrant Officer (WO1) Hugh C. Thompson, Jr., and his two-man crew were on a reconnaissance mission over the village of My Lai, Republic of Vietnam. WO1 Thompson watched in horror as he saw an American Soldier shoot an injured Vietnamese child. Minutes later, when he observed American Soldiers advancing on a number of civilians in a ditch, WO1 Thompson landed his helicopter and questioned a young officer about what was happening on the ground. Told that the ground action was none of his business, WO1 Thompson took off and continued to circle the area. When it became apparent that the American Soldiers were now firing on civilians, WO1 Thompson landed his helicopter between the Soldiers and a group of 10 villagers who were headed for a homemade bomb shelter. He ordered his gunner to train his weapon on the approaching American Soldiers and to fire if necessary. Then he personally coaxed the civilians out of the shelter and airlifted them to safety. WO1 Thompson's radio reports of what was happening were instrumental in bringing about the cease-fire order that saved the lives of more civilians. His willingness to place himself in physical danger in order to do the morally right thing is a sterling example of personal courage.

Critical Thinking

How did WO1 Thompson exhibit character at My Lai? What was at stake for Thompson? Can you infer anything about the difference between the character of Thompson and that of the young officer he questioned?

Seven Core Army Values

You enter the Army with your personal values developed in childhood and nurtured over many years of personal experience. By taking an oath to serve the nation and the institution, you also agree to live and act by a new set of values—Army Values. Army Values consist of the principles, standards, and qualities considered essential for successful Army leaders. They are fundamental to helping you make the right decision in any situation.

Army Values firmly bind all Army members into a fellowship dedicated to serving the nation and the Army. They apply to everyone, in every situation, anywhere in the Army. The trust Soldiers have for each other, and the trust the American people have in you, all depend on how well you embody the Army Values.

The Army recognizes seven values that must be developed in all Army individuals. The first letters form the acronym "LDRSHIP":

- Loyalty
- Duty
- Respect
- Selfless service
- Honor
- Integrity
- Personal courage.

Loyalty

Bear true faith and allegiance to the US Constitution, the Army, your unit, and other Soldiers.

All Soldiers and government civilians swear a sacred oath to support and defend the Constitution of the United States. The Constitution established the legal basis for the existence of our Army. As a logical consequence, you have an obligation to be faithful to the Army and its people.

> Loyalty is the big thing, the greatest battle asset of all. But no man ever wins the loyalty of troops by preaching loyalty. It is given him by them as he proves his possession of the other virtues.
>
> BG S. L. A. Marshall
>
> *Men Against Fire (1947)*

> There is a great deal of talk about loyalty from the bottom to the top. Loyalty from the top down is even more necessary and much less prevalent.
>
> GEN George S. Patton
>
> *War As I Knew It (1947)*

Loyalty is a two-way commitment between leaders and subordinates. The loyalty of subordinates is a gift given when a leader deserves it. Leaders earn subordinates' loyalty by training them well, treating them fairly, and living the Army Values. Leaders who are loyal to their subordinates never let Soldiers be misused or abused. Subordinates who believe in their leaders will stand with them no matter how difficult the situation.

Few examples better illustrate loyalty to country, the Army, its people, and self better than that of World War II GEN Jonathan Wainwright.

Loyal in War and in Captivity

The Japanese invaded the Philippines in December 1941. In March 1942, GEN Douglas MacArthur left his Philippine command and evacuated to Australia. Although GEN MacArthur intended to stay in command from Australia, GEN Jonathan Wainwright, a tall, thin and loyal general officer assumed full command from the Malinta Tunnel on Corregidor, while MG Edward King replaced Wainwright as commander of the American Forces and Filipino Scouts defending Bataan. Soon, the Japanese grip on the islands tightened and the Philippine defenders at Bataan were surrounded and without any support other than artillery fire from Corregidor. Disease, exhaustion, and malnutrition ultimately accomplished what thousands of Japanese soldiers had not done for 90 days— Bataan was lost. When Bataan fell to the Japanese, more than 12,000 Filipino Scouts and 17,000 Americans became prisoners. On the initial march to Camp O'Donnell, the Japanese beheaded many who became too weak to continue the trip. Other prisoners were used for bayonet practice or pushed to their deaths from cliffs.

The situation at Corregidor was no better. Soldiers were weary, wounded, malnourished, and diseased. GEN Wainwright directed the defenses with the limited resources available. Wainwright made frequent visits to the front to check on his men and to inspire them personally. He never feared coming under direct fire from enemy soldiers. A tenacious warrior, he was used to seeing men next to him die and had often personally returned fire on the enemy.

GEN Wainwright was a unique kind of frontline commander—a fighting general who earned the loyalty of his troops by sharing their hardships. GEN Wainwright and his steadfast troops at Corregidor were the last organized resistance on Luzon. After holding the Japanese against impossible odds for a full six months, Wainwright had exhausted all possibilities—no outside help could be expected.

On 6 May 1942, GEN Wainwright notified his command of his intent to surrender and sent a message to the President of the United States to explain the painful decision. He was proud of his country and his men and he had been forthright and loyal to both. His Soldiers had come to love, admire, and willingly obey the fighting general. President Roosevelt reassured GEN Wainwright of the Nation's loyalty and in one of his last messages to him wrote: "You and your devoted followers have become the living symbol of our war aims and the guarantee of victory."

Following the surrender, the Japanese shipped the defenders of Corregidor across the bay to Manila where they were paraded in disgrace. To humiliate him personally, the Japanese forced GEN Wainwright to march through his defeated Soldiers. Despite their wounds, their illness, their broken spirit, and shattered bodies, Wainwright's Soldiers once again demonstrated their loyalty and respect for their leader. As he passed among their ranks, the men struggled to their feet and saluted.

During his more than three years of captivity as the highest-ranking and oldest American prisoner of war in World War II, GEN Wainwright kept faith and loyalty with his fellow prisoners and suffered many deprivations, humiliation, abuse, and torture. Despite his steadfast posture in captivity, GEN Wainwright feared the moment of his return to America, expecting to be considered a coward and a traitor for his surrender at Corregidor. Americans at home had not forgotten and remained loyal to the fighting general and his courageous troops. To honor him and his men, GEN Wainwright was placed behind GEN of the Army MacArthur, together with British GEN Percival, during the signing of Japan's official surrender on board the battleship USS Missouri, on 2 September 1945.

GEN Jonathan Wainwright subsequently returned home not to shame but to a hero's welcome. During a surprise ceremony on 10 September 1945, President Truman awarded Jonathan Wainwright the Medal of Honor.

Duty

Fulfill your obligations.

You must always work not just to meet the minimum standard, but to do your very best. Your duty is to commit to excellence in all aspects of your professional responsibility.

Part of fulfilling duty is to exercise initiative—anticipating what needs to be done before someone tells you what to do. You must exercise initiative when you fulfill the purpose, not merely the letter, of the tasks assigned you and the orders you have received. The task is not complete until you achieve your intended outcome.

> I go anywhere in the world they tell me to go, any time they tell me to, to fight anybody they want me to fight. I move my family anywhere they tell me to move, on a day's notice, and live in whatever quarters they assign me. I work whenever they tell me to work.... And I like it.
>
> James H. Webb
>
> *Former US Marine and Secretary of the Navy (1987-1988), United States Senator (2007-)*

Conscientiousness is the internalization of duty. Conscientiousness means having a high sense of responsibility for your personal contributions to the Army, demonstrated through dedicated effort, organization, thoroughness, reliability, and practicality. Your own conscientiousness consistently alerts you to do what is right—even when you are tired or demoralized.

In rare cases, your sense of duty also has to detect and prevent an illegal order. Duty requires refusal to obey it. Leaders have no choice but to do what is ethically and legally right.

Respect

Treat people as they should be treated.

Respect for the individual is the basis for the rule of law—the very essence of what the nation stands for. Respect means you must treat others as they should be treated—with dignity and respect.

Over the course of history, America has become more culturally diverse, requiring Army leaders to deal with people from a wider range of ethnic, racial, and religious backgrounds. You must prevent misunderstandings arising from cultural differences. Actively seek to learn about people whose culture is different. Be sensitive to other cultures. This will help you in mentoring, coaching, and counseling subordinates. See things from their perspective, and appreciate what is important to them.

Army leaders should consistently foster a climate in which everyone is treated with dignity and respect, regardless of race, gender, creed, or religious belief. Fostering a balanced and dignified work climate begins with your personal example. How you live the Army Values shows subordinates how they should behave. Teaching values is one of your most important responsibilities. It helps create a common understanding of the Army Values and standards.

The discipline which makes the Soldiers of a free country reliable in battle is not to be gained by harsh or tyrannical treatment. On the contrary, such treatment is far more likely to destroy than to make an army. It is possible to impart instruction and to give commands in such manner and such a tone of voice to inspire in the Soldier no feeling but an intense desire to obey, while the opposite manner and tone of voice cannot fail to excite strong resentment and a desire to disobey. The one mode or the other of dealing with subordinates springs from a corresponding spirit in the breast of the commander. He who feels the respect which is due to others cannot fail to inspire in them regard for himself, while he who feels, and hence manifests, disrespect toward others, especially his inferiors, cannot fail to inspire hatred against himself.

MG John M. Schofield

Address to the United States Corps of Cadets, 11 August 1879

> ... [A]sk not what your country can do for you; ask what you can do for your country.
>
> John F. Kennedy
>
> *Inaugural speech as 35th President of the United States (1961)*

Selfless Service

Put the welfare of the nation, the Army, and subordinates before your own.

The military is often referred to as "the Service." As an Army leader you serve the United States of America. Selfless service means doing what is right for the nation, the Army, the organization, and subordinates. While the needs of the Army and the nation should come first, selfless service does not imply neglect of your family or yourself. To the contrary, such neglect of these important elements weakens you and can cause the Army more harm than good.

A strong but harnessed ego, high self-esteem, and a healthy ambition can be compatible with selfless service, as long as you treat your people fairly and give them the credit they deserve. You know that the Army cannot function except as a team. For a team to excel, everyone, including you, must give up self-interest for the good of the whole.

On 11 September 2001, after the attack on the Pentagon, the selfless team effort between military personnel and civilian workers did not come as a surprise. Civilians and Soldiers struggled side-by-side to save each other's lives, while together they ensured that critical operations around the world continued without loss of command and control.

Honor

Live up to all the Army Values.

Honor provides a moral compass for character and personal conduct in the Army. It means that you live by words and actions consistent with high ideals.

Honor is the glue that holds the Army Values together. Honor requires that you always demonstrate an understanding of what is right. Military ceremonies recognizing your achievements and that of your unit demonstrate and reinforce the importance the Army places on honor.

You must demonstrate an understanding of what is right and take pride in that reputation by living up to the Army Values. Living honorably, in line with the Army Values, sets an example for every member of the organization and contributes to the organization's positive climate and morale.

> War must be carried on systematically, and to do it you must have men of character activated by principles of honor.
>
> George Washington
>
> *Commander, Continental Army (1775-81), and President of the United States (1789-97)*

How you conduct yourself and meet obligations defines you as a person and leader. In turn, how the Army meets the nation's commitments defines the Army as an institution. Honor demands putting the Army Values above self-interest and above career and personal comfort. It requires putting the Army Values above self-preservation. Honor gives the strength of will to live according to the Army Values, especially in the face of personal danger. It is not coincidence that our military's highest award is the Medal of Honor. Its recipients clearly went beyond what is expected and beyond the call of duty.

Honor, Courage, and Selfless Service in Korea

On 14 June 1952 SGT David B. Bleak, a medical aidman in Medical Company, 223rd Infantry Regiment, 40th Infantry Division volunteered to accompany a combat patrol tasked to capture enemy forces for interrogation. While moving up the rugged slope of Hill 499, near Minari-gol, Korea, the patrol came under intense automatic weapons and small arms fire several times, suffering several casualties. An enemy group fired at SGT Bleak from a nearby trench while he tended the wounded.

Determined to protect the wounded, the brave aidman faced the enemy. He entered the trench and killed two enemy soldiers with his bare hands and a third with his trench knife. While exiting, SGT Bleak detected a concussion grenade as it fell in front of a comrade. Bleak quickly shifted to shield the man from the blast.

Disregarding his own injury, he carried the most severely wounded comrade down a hillside. Attacked by two enemy soldiers with bayonets, Bleak lowered the wounded man and put both adversaries out of action by slamming their heads together. He then carried the wounded American Soldier to safety.

SGT Bleak's courageous actions saved fellow Soldiers' lives and preserved the patrol's combat effectiveness. For his actions, President Dwight D. Eisenhower awarded him the Medal of Honor on 27 October 1953.

Integrity

Do what's right—legally and morally.

As a leader of integrity you must act consistently according to clear principles, not just what works now. The Army relies on leaders of integrity who possess high moral standards

> No nation can safely trust its martial honor to leaders who do not maintain the universal code which distinguishes between those things that are right and those things that are wrong.
>
> GEN Douglas MacArthur
>
> *Patriot Hearts (2000)*

and who are honest in word and deed. You must be honest to others by not presenting yourself or your actions as anything other than what they are, remaining committed to the truth.

Here is how you stand for the truth: If a mission cannot be accomplished, your integrity requires you to inform the chain of command. If your unit's operational readiness rate is truly 70 percent, despite the senior commander's required standard of 90 percent, you will not instruct subordinates to adjust numbers. It is your duty to report the truth and develop solutions to meet the standard with honor and integrity. Identifying the underlying maintenance issues and raising the quality bar could ultimately save Soldiers' lives.

If you inadvertently pass on bad information, you should correct it as soon as you discover the error. Do the right thing not because it is convenient or because you have no other choice. Choose the path of truth because your character permits nothing less.

You should always be able to separate right from wrong in every situation. Just as important, you should do what is right, even at personal cost. As an Army leader, you cannot hide what you do, so you must carefully decide how to act. Army leaders are always on display. To instill the Army Values in others, you must demonstrate them personally.

You must resolve conflicts between personal and Army Values, so you can become a morally complete Army leader. If you have doubts, consult a mentor whose values and judgment you respect.

Personal Courage

Face fear, danger, or adversity (physical and moral).

As Army Air Corps World War I fighter ace CPT Eddie Rickenbacker put it, personal courage is not the absence of fear. It is the ability to put fear aside and do what is necessary. Personal courage takes two forms: physical and moral. You must be able to demonstrate both.

Physical courage requires overcoming fears of bodily harm and doing your duty. It triggers bravery that allows you to take risks in combat in spite of the fear of wounds or even death. One lieutenant serving during World War II displayed such courage despite serving in a time when he and his fellow African-American Soldiers were not fully recognized for their actions.

Courage and Inspiration for Soldiers Then and Now

Of all the Medals of Honor awarded during World War II, none went to an African-American. In 1993, the Army contracted Shaw University in Raleigh, North Carolina, to research racial disparities in the selection of Medal of Honor recipients. As a result, the Army ultimately decided to recommend seven Soldiers for the award.

Fifty-two years after they earned them, the men were awarded the medals along with the nation's silent apology for ignoring the Soldiers in the once-

> Courage is doing what you're afraid to do. There can be no courage unless you're scared.
>
> CPT Eddie Rickenbacker
>
> *US Army Air Corps, World War I*

segregated Army. The only Soldier still alive to receive his award was Vernon J. Baker, an exceptionally courageous and inspirational leader.

On 5 and 6 April 1945, 2LT Baker of the 370th Infantry Regiment demonstrated leadership by example near Viareggio, Italy, during his company's attack against strongly entrenched German positions in mountainous terrain.

When his company was stopped by fire from several machine gun emplacements, 2LT Baker crawled to one position and destroyed it, killing three German soldiers. He then attacked an enemy observation post and killed two occupants. With the aid of one of his men, 2LT Baker continued the advance and destroyed two more machine gun nests, killing or wounding the soldiers occupying these positions. After consolidating his position, 2LT Baker finally covered the evacuation of the wounded personnel of his unit by occupying an exposed position and drawing the enemy's fire.

On the night following his heroic combat performance, 2LT Baker again volunteered to lead a battalion advance toward his division's objective through enemy mine fields and heavy fire. Two-thirds of his company was wounded or dead and there were no reinforcements in sight. His commander ordered a withdrawal. Baker, in tears protested, "Captain, we can't withdraw. We must stay here and fight it out."

2LT Baker stands as an inspiration to the many African-American Soldiers who served with him and since that time. He stood courageously against the enemy and stood proudly to represent his fallen comrades when he received his Medal of Honor.

Long after he saw combat in Italy, Vernon J. Baker still thought of his black comrades who died around him as they awaited reinforcements that never came. In a CNN interview, he summed up his feelings with the following modest words: "This day will vindicate those men and make things right."

Moral courage is the willingness to stand firm on values, principles, and convictions. It enables you to stand up for what you believe is right, regardless of the consequences.

The concept of professional courage does not always mean being as tough as nails, either. It also suggests a willingness to listen to the Soldiers' problems, to go to bat for them in a tough situation and it means knowing just how far they can go. It also means being willing to tell the boss when he is wrong.

William Connelly
Sergeant Major of the Army (1979-1983)

Critical Thinking

Discuss whether character may be especially essential in the face of an enemy who exhibits none. What examples from history or current events can you cite to illustrate this concept?

When you take full responsibility for your decisions and actions, even when things go wrong, you display moral courage.

GEN Dwight D. Eisenhower was a leader of great moral courage during his service as the Supreme Commander of Allied Forces Europe during World War II. He displayed this moral courage in a handwritten note he prepared for public release, in case the Normandy landings failed.

> *Our landings in the Cherbourg-Havre area have failed to gain a satisfactory foothold and I have withdrawn the troops. My decision to attack at this time and place was based upon the best information available. The troops, the air, and the Navy did all that bravery and devotion to duty could do. If any blame or fault attaches to the attempt it is mine alone—June 5 [1944].*

Moral courage also expresses itself as candor. Candor means being frank, honest, and sincere with others. It requires steering clear of bias, prejudice, or malice, even when it is uncomfortable or may seem better to keep quiet.

Trust relationships between you and your subordinates rely on candor. Without it, subordinates will not know if they have met the standard and you will not know what is going on in their organization.

Empathy

empathy

the ability to see something from another person's point of view

When planning and deciding an operation, try to envision the impact on Soldiers and other subordinates. The ability to see something from another person's point of view, to identify with and enter into another person's feelings and emotions, enables you to better care for everyone under your command.

As a competent and empathetic leader, you take care of Soldiers by giving them the training, equipment, and all the support they need to keep them alive in combat and accomplish the mission. During wartime and difficult operations, you share the hardships with your people to gauge if their plans and decisions are realistic. As a competent and empathetic leader, you also recognize the need to provide Soldiers with reasonable comforts and rest periods to maintain good morale and mission effectiveness. When a unit or organization suffers injuries or death, you can help ease the trauma and suffering in the organization to restore full readiness as quickly as possible.

Empathy also includes nourishing a close relationship between the Army and Army families. To build a strong and ready force, you must promote self-sufficient and healthy families. Empathy for families includes allowing Soldiers recovery time from difficult missions, protecting leave periods, permitting critical appointments, as well as supporting events that allow information exchange and family team-building.

The requirement for leader empathy extends beyond Soldiers and their families. Within the larger operational environment, leader empathy may be helpful when dealing with local populations and prisoners of war. Providing the local population within an area of operations with the necessities of life often turns an initially hostile disposition into one of cooperation.

The Warrior Ethos

GEN Eric Shinseki, former Army Chief of Staff, described the need for a common Warrior Ethos with emphasis on the uniformed members of the Army team:

> *Every organization has an internal culture and ethos. A true warrior ethos must underpin the Army's enduring traditions and values…. Soldiers imbued with an ethically grounded warrior ethos clearly symbolize the Army's unwavering commitment to the nation we serve. The Army has always embraced this ethos, but the demands of Transformation will require a renewed effort to ensure that all Soldiers truly understand and embody this warrior ethos.*

The Warrior Ethos refers to the professional attitudes and beliefs that characterize the American Soldier. It echoes through the precepts of the Code of Conduct and reflects your selfless commitment to the nation, mission, unit, and fellow Soldiers. Discipline, commitment to the Army Values, and pride in the Army's heritage develop and sustain the Warrior Ethos. Lived by Soldiers and supported by dedicated Army civilians, a strong Warrior Ethos is the foundation for the winning spirit that permeates the institution.

The Warrior Ethos

the professional attitudes and beliefs that characterize the American Soldier

U.S Army Soldiers embrace the Warrior Ethos as defined in the Soldier's Creed (Figure 2.1).

The Warrior Ethos is more than persevering in war. It fuels the fire to fight through any demanding conditions—no matter the time or effort required. It is one thing to make a snap decision to risk your life for a brief period. It is quite another to sustain the will to win when the situation looks hopeless and shows no indication of getting better, when being away from home and family is already a profound hardship. The Soldier who jumps on a grenade to save comrades is courageous without question—that action requires great mental and physical courage. Pursuing victory over extended periods with multiple deployments requires deep moral courage, one that focuses on the mission. This is the Warrior Ethos.

I am an American Soldier.

I am a Warrior and a member of a team. I serve the people of the United States and live the Army Values.

Warrior Ethos

I will always place the mission first.

I will never accept defeat.

I will never quit.

I will never leave a fallen comrade.

I am disciplined, physically and mentally tough, trained and proficient in my Warrior tasks and drills.

I will always maintain my arms, my equipment, and myself.

I am an expert and I am a professional.

I stand ready to deploy, engage, and destroy the enemies of the United States in close combat.

I am a guardian of freedom and the American way of life.

I am an American Soldier.

Figure 2.1 The Soldier's Creed

> Wars may be fought with weapons, but they are won by men. It is the spirit of the men who follow and of the man who leads that gains the victory.
>
> GEN George S. Patton
>
> *Cavalry Journal (1933)*

The actions of all who have fought courageously in wars past exemplify the essence of the Army's Warrior Ethos. Developed through discipline, commitment to the Army Values, and knowledge of the Army's proud heritage, the Warrior Ethos makes clear that military service is much more than just another job. It is about your total commitment. It is your absolute faith in yourself and your comrades that makes the Army invariably persuasive in peace and invincible in war. The Warrior Ethos forges victory from the chaos of battle. It fortifies you and your people to overcome fear, hunger, deprivation, and fatigue.

The Warrior Ethos is a component of character. It shapes and guides what you do. It is linked tightly to the Army Values such as personal courage, loyalty to comrades, and dedication to duty. During the Korean War, one leader displayed these traits and surpassed traditional bounds of rank to lead his Soldiers.

Task Force Kingston

1LT Joseph Kingston, a boyish-looking platoon leader in K Company, 3d Battalion, 32d Infantry, was commanding the lead element for his battalion's move northward. The terrain was mountainous in that part of Korea, the weather bitterly cold—the temperature often below zero—and the cornered enemy still dangerous.

1LT Kingston inched his way forward, the battalion gradually adding elements to his force. Soon, he had antiaircraft jeeps mounted with quad .50 caliber machine guns, a tank, a squad (later a platoon) of engineers, and an artillery forward observer under his control. Some of the new attachments were commanded by lieutenants who outranked him, as did the tactical air controller—a captain. 1LT Kingston remained in command, and battalion headquarters began referring to his growing force as, "Task Force Kingston."

Bogged down in Yongsong-ni with casualties mounting, Task Force Kingston received reinforcements that brought its strength to nearly 300. 1LT Kingston's battalion commander wanted him to remain in command, even though he pushed forward several more officers who outranked 1LT Kingston. One of the attached units was a rifle company, commanded by a captain. Nonetheless, the cooperative command arrangement worked—because 1LT Kingston was a very competent leader.

Despite tough fighting, the force advanced. Hit while leading an assault on one enemy stronghold, Kingston managed to toss a grenade just as a North Korean soldier fired a shot that glanced off his helmet. The lieutenant's resilience and personal courage inspired every Soldier from the wide array of units under his control.

Task Force Kingston succeeded in battle because of a competent young leader who inspired his people by demonstrating many attributes common to the Warrior Ethos and the Army Values that the Army currently espouses.

The Warrior Ethos requires your unrelenting and consistent determination to do what is right and to do it with pride. Understanding what is right requires that you respect both comrades and all people involved in complex missions, such as stability and reconstruction operations.

You must continually affirm, develop, and sustain the Warrior Ethos. It connects American warriors of today with those whose sacrifices have sustained the country's very existence since America's founding. The Army's continuing drive to be the best, to triumph over all adversity, and to remain focused on mission accomplishment, does more than preserve the Army's institutional culture—it sustains the nation.

Character Development

You join the Army with your character preshaped by your background, beliefs, education, and experience. Your job would be simpler if you merely checked your team members' personal values against the Army Values and developed a simple plan to align them. Reality is much different. Becoming a person of character and a leader of character is a career-long process. It involves day-to-day experience, education, self-development, developmental counseling, coaching, and mentoring. While individuals are responsible for their own **character development**, you can develop as a leader of character only through continual study, reflection, experience, and feedback. You will hold yourself and your subordinates to the highest standards. The standards and values then spread throughout the team, unit, or organization and ultimately throughout the Army.

Doing the right thing is good. Doing the right thing for the right reason and with the right goal is better. You must possess the desire to act ethically in all situations. One of your primary responsibilities is to maintain an ethical climate that supports development of such character. When your unit's ethical climate nurtures ethical behavior, your people will, over time, think, feel, and act ethically. They will internalize the aspects of sound character.

character development

the development of character through continual study, reflection, experience, and feedback

CONCLUSION

True leaders are made, not born. And true authority derives first from self-control. Soldiers will take direction from officers who themselves appear self-directed. In learning and applying the seven core Army Values, learning empathy, practicing the Warrior Ethos, and working to develop your character, you will discover that success and respect are natural outcomes of your pursuit of excellence as an Army leader.

Learning Assessment

1. Name the seven core Army Values and give an example of how each forms part of the foundation of an effective leader's character. How would the lack of that particular value negatively affect a leader's performance?

2. What is empathy? Why is it so important to making good decisions?

3. Define the Warrior Ethos. How does it give courage to yourself and the people under you?

4. Why is character development important for an Army leader?

Key Words

values
character
empathy
The Warrior Ethos
character development

References

DA PAM 600-65, *Leadership Statements and Quotes*. 1 November 1985.

Field Manual 6-22, *Army Leadership: Competent, Confident, and Agile*. 12 October 2006.

Section

3

ARMY LEADERSHIP— PRESENCE

Key Points

1 Military Bearing

2 Physical Fitness

3 Confidence

4 Resilience

... [L]eadership is not a natural trait, something inherited like the color of eyes or hair. Actually, leadership is a skill that can be studied, learned, and perfected by practice.

The Noncom's Guide (1962)

Introduction

The Army invests a tremendous amount of time, energy, and resources in training you as a leader because you will help set and maintain standards of excellence in the future. A major part of your task will be to develop a sense of *presence* that will inspire people to trust and follow you. Presence is not something you are born with, such as the color of your eyes and hair. Presence is something you can learn. This chapter will show you what it takes.

Sometimes being a leader with presence requires making a hard or unpopular choice, as one sergeant discovered at a post in Vietnam.

Rusty Rifles

While serving in the Republic of Vietnam, SFC Jackson was transferred from platoon sergeant of one platoon to platoon leader of another platoon in the same company. SFC Jackson quickly sized up the existing standards in the platoon. He wasn't pleased. One problem was that his Soldiers were not keeping their weapons cleaned properly: Rifles were dirty and rusty. He put out the word: weapons would be cleaned to standard each day, each squad leader would inspect each day, and he would inspect a sample of the weapons each day. He gave this order three days before the platoon was to go to the division rest and recuperation (R&R) area on the South China Sea.

The next day SFC Jackson checked several weapons in each squad. Most weapons were still unacceptable. He called the squad leaders together and explained the policy and his reasons for implementing it. SFC Jackson checked again the following day and still found dirty and rusty weapons. He decided there were two causes for the problem. First, the squad leaders were not doing their jobs. Second, the squad leaders and troops were bucking him—testing him to see who would really make the rules in the platoon. He sensed that, because he was new, they resisted his leadership. He knew he had a serious discipline problem he had to handle correctly. He called the squad leaders together again. Once again, he explained his standards clearly. He then said, "Tomorrow we are due to go on R&R for three days and I'll be inspecting rifles. We won't go on R&R until each weapon in this platoon meets the standard."

The next morning SFC Jackson inspected and found that most weapons in each squad were still below standard. He called the squad leaders together. With a determined look and a firm voice, he told them he would hold a formal in-ranks inspection at 1300 hours, even though the platoon was scheduled to board helicopters for R&R then. If every weapon didn't meet the standard, he would conduct another in-ranks inspection for squad leaders and troops with substandard weapons. He would continue inspections until all weapons met the standard. At 1300 hours the platoon formed up, surly and angry with the new platoon leader, who was taking their hard-earned R&R time. The Soldiers could

Critical Thinking

In SFC Jackson's decision to enforce minimal basic weapons standards in his platoon, what was he attempting to emphasize over his Soldiers' comfort and convenience? Why was such a stand necessary, despite its unpopularity?

---

hardly believe it, but his message was starting to sink in. This leader meant what he said. This time all weapons met the standard.

The impression that you make on others contributes to your success in leading them. How others perceive you depends on your outward appearance, demeanor, actions, and words.

Followers need a way to size up their leaders. This means they need to see you where they are. Good leaders are willing to go everywhere, including where the conditions are the most severe. They illustrate through their presence that they care. There is no greater inspiration than leaders who routinely share in team hardships and dangers. Moving to where duties are performed will allow you to have firsthand knowledge of the real conditions your Soldiers and civilians face. Soldiers and civilians who see or hear from the boss appreciate knowing that their unit has an important part to play.

Presence is not just a matter of showing up. It requires projecting an image. You convey presence through actions, words, and the manner in which you carry yourself. You convey your reputation by the respect that others show you, how they refer to you, and how they respond to your guidance. Presence is a critical attribute that you need to understand. Your effectiveness is dramatically enhanced by understanding and developing the following areas:

- **Military bearing**: projecting a commanding presence, a professional image of authority
- **Physical fitness**: having sound health, strength, and endurance, which sustain emotional health and conceptual abilities under prolonged stress
- **Confidence**: projecting self-confidence and certainty in the unit's ability to succeed in whatever it does; being able to demonstrate composure and outward calm through steady control over emotion
- **Resilience**: showing a tendency to recover quickly from setbacks, shock, injuries, adversity, and stress while maintaining a mission and organizational focus.

Military Bearing

Pride in self starts with pride in appearance. As an Army leader, you are expected to look and act like a professional. You must know how to wear the appropriate uniform or civilian attire and do so with pride. Soldiers seen in public with their jackets unbuttoned and ties undone do not send a message of pride and professionalism. Instead, they let down their unit and fellow Soldiers in the eyes of the American people. Meeting prescribed height and weight standards is another integral part of the professional role. How leaders carry themselves when displaying military courtesy and appearance sends a clear signal: I am proud of my uniform, my unit, and my country.

military bearing

projecting a commanding presence, a professional image of authority

physical fitness

having sound health, strength, and endurance, which sustain emotional health and conceptual abilities under prolonged stress

confidence

projecting self-confidence and certainty in the unit's ability to succeed in whatever it does; able to demonstrate composure and outward calm through steady control over emotion

resilience

showing a tendency to recover quickly from setbacks, shock, injuries, adversity, and stress while maintaining a mission and organizational focus

> ## Our quality soldiers should look as good as they are.
>
> Julius W. Gates
>
> *Sergeant Major of the Army (1987-1991)*

Skillful use of professional bearing—fitness, courtesy, and proper military appearance—can also aid in overcoming difficult situations. A professional presents a decent appearance because it commands respect. Professionals must be competent as well. They look good because they are good.

Physical Fitness

Unit readiness begins with physically fit Soldiers and leaders because combat drains people physically, mentally, and emotionally. Physical fitness, while crucial for success in battle, is important for all members of the Army team, not just Soldiers. Physically fit people feel more competent and confident, handle stress better, work longer and harder, and recover faster. These attributes provide valuable payoffs in any environment.

The physical demands of leadership, prolonged deployments, and continuous operations can erode more than your body. Physical fitness and adequate rest support mental functioning and emotional stability, both essential for sound leadership. You must be prepared for deprivation. It is difficult to maintain a high level of fitness during fast-paced, demanding operations. If you are not physically fit before deployment, your mental and emotional fitness will suffer as well. Combat operations in difficult terrain, extreme climates, and high altitude require extensive physical preconditioning. Once you are in the area of operations, you must make every effort to sustain physical readiness.

Preparedness for operational missions must be a primary focus of the unit's physical fitness program. Fitness programs that merely emphasize top scores on the Army Physical Fitness Test do not prepare Soldiers for the strenuous demands of actual combat. As a forward-looking leader, you develop a balanced physical fitness program that enables Soldiers to execute the unit's mission-essential task list. (FM 7-0 discusses the integration of Soldier, leader, and collective training based on the mission-essential task list.)

Ultimately, the physical fitness requirements for Army leaders have a significant impact on your personal performance and health. Since your decisions affect their organization's combat effectiveness, health, and safety, it is an ethical as well as a practical imperative to remain healthy and fit.

> ## ... I am obliged to sweat them tonight, sir, so that I can save their blood tomorrow.
>
> LTG Thomas J. "Stonewall" Jackson
>
> *Confederate Civil War General (1861-1863)*

Confidence

Confidence is the faith that leaders place in their abilities to act properly in any situation, even under stress and with little information. Leaders who know their own capabilities and believe in themselves are confident. Self-confidence grows from professional competence. But too much confidence can be as detrimental as too little confidence. Both extremes impede learning and adaptability. Bluster—loudmouthed bragging or self-promotion—is not confidence. Truly confident leaders do not need to advertise their gifts because their actions prove their abilities.

Confidence is important for leaders and teams. Your confidence is contagious and quickly permeates the entire organization, especially in dire situations. In combat, you can help Soldiers control doubt while reducing team anxiety. Combined with strong will and self-discipline, confidence spurs you to do what you must in circumstances in which it would be easier to do nothing.

Resilience

Resilient leaders can recover quickly from setbacks, shock, injuries, adversity, and stress while maintaining their mission and organizational focus. Their resilience rests on will, the inner drive that compels them to keep going, even when exhausted, hungry, afraid, cold, and wet. Resilience helps leaders and their organizations to carry difficult missions to their conclusion.

Your resilience and will to succeed are not sufficient to carry the day during adversity. Your competence and knowledge will guide you to pursue courses of action that lead to success and victory in battle. Your premier task is to instill resilience and a winning spirit in subordinates. That begins with tough and realistic training.

Resilience is essential when accomplishing your mission. No matter what the working conditions are, a strong personal attitude helps prevail over any adverse external conditions. You will experience situations when it would seem easier to quit rather than finish the task. During those times, you need an inner source of energy to press on to mission completion. When things go badly, you must draw on inner reserves to persevere.

The following story of an intrepid Army helicopter pilot in action illustrates how he showed resilience and discipline when faced with the most difficult combat conditions.

MAJ Bruce Crandall at Landing Zone X-Ray

MAJ Bruce P. Crandall distinguished himself by extraordinary heroism as a Flight Commander in the Republic of Vietnam, while serving with Company A, 229th Assault Helicopter Battalion, 1st Cavalry Division (Airmobile). On 14 November 1965, his flight of 16 helicopters was lifting troops for a search and destroy mission from Plei Me, Vietnam, to Landing Zone X-Ray in the Ia Drang Valley. On the fourth troop lift, the airlift began to take enemy fire, and by the time the aircraft had refueled and returned for the next troop lift, the enemy had Landing Zone X-Ray targeted.

As MAJ Crandall and the first eight helicopters landed to discharge troops on his fifth troop lift, his unarmed helicopter came under such intense enemy fire that the ground commander ordered the second flight of eight aircraft to abort their mission. As MAJ Crandall flew back to Plei Me, his base of operations, he determined that the ground commander of the besieged infantry battalion desperately needed more ammunition.

MAJ Crandall then decided to adjust his base of operations to Artillery Firebase Falcon in order to shorten the flight distance to deliver ammunition and evacuate wounded soldiers. While medical evacuation was not his mission, he immediately sought volunteers and with complete disregard for his own personal safety, led the two aircraft to Landing Zone X-Ray. Despite the fact that the landing zone was still under relentless enemy fire, MAJ Crandall landed and proceeded to supervise the loading of seriously wounded soldiers aboard his aircraft. MAJ Crandall's voluntary decision to land under the most extreme fire instilled in the other pilots the will and spirit to continue to land their own aircraft, and in the ground forces the realization that they would be resupplied and that friendly wounded would be promptly evacuated. This greatly enhanced morale and the will to fight at a critical time.

After his first medical evacuation, MAJ Crandall continued to fly into and out of the landing zone throughout the day and into the evening. That day he completed a total of 22 flights, most under intense enemy fire, retiring from the battlefield only after all possible service had been rendered to the infantry battalion. His actions provided critical resupply of ammunition and evacuation of the wounded. MAJ Crandall's daring acts of bravery and courage in the face of an overwhelming and determined enemy are in keeping with the highest traditions of the military service and reflect great credit upon himself, his unit, and the United States Army.

On 26 February 2008, President George W. Bush awarded MAJ Crandall the Medal of Honor.

CONCLUSION

To be an effective Army leader, you need a commanding presence. Through conscientious efforts to improve and maintain your military bearing, physical fitness, confidence, and resilience, you will attain that sense of presence. Others will become aware of it and be influenced by it. And you will become a leader the Army and the nation will be proud of.

Learning Assessment

1. What are the four main elements of Army leadership presence?
2. Why does pride in your appearance help you to lead others?
3. Physical fitness and mental fitness go hand in hand. Explain why.
4. How are bragging and self-promotion different from real confidence?
5. Why is resilience an important leadership trait in a combat situation?

Key Words

military bearing
physical fitness
confidence
resilience

References

Field Manual 6-22, *Army Leadership: Competent, Confident, and Agile*. 12 October 2006.

Medal of Honor: Major Bruce P. Crandall. (n.d.). Retrieved 17 July 2008 from http://www.army.mil/medalofhonor/crandall/

Section
4

ARMY LEADERSHIP— LEADER INTELLIGENCE

Key Points

1 Leader Intelligence

2 Mental Agility

3 Sound Judgment

4 Innovation

5 Interpersonal Tact

6 Domain Knowledge

> Never tell people how to do things. Tell them what to do, and they will surprise you with their ingenuity.
>
> GEN George S. Patton

Introduction

The best training in the world can't make you an effective, respected leader if you are not intelligent about your leadership. An intelligent Army leader is one who is mentally agile, sound in judgment, innovative, tactful, and knowledgeable. This section will help you understand what that means for you, your unit, and the Army.

Intelligent action will get you through many difficult situations, as SGT Alvin York discovered in France during a lopsided fight against a German infantry battalion in World War I.

SGT York

Alvin York performed an exploit of almost unbelievable heroism in the morning hours of 8 October 1918 in France's Argonne Forest. He was now a corporal (CPL), having won his stripes during combat in the Lorraine. That morning CPL York's battalion was moving across a valley to seize a German-held rail point when a German infantry battalion, hidden on a wooded ridge overlooking the valley, opened up with machine gun fire. The American battalion dived for cover, and the attack stalled. CPL York's platoon, already reduced to 16 men, was sent to flank the enemy machine guns.

As the platoon advanced through the woods to the rear of the German outfit, it surprised a group of about 25 German soldiers. The shocked enemy offered only token resistance, but then more hidden machine guns swept the clearing with fire. The Germans dropped safely to the ground, but nine Americans, including the platoon leader and the other two corporals, fell dead or wounded. CPL York was the only unwounded leader remaining.

CPL York found his platoon trapped and under fire within 25 yards of the enemy's machine gun pits. Nonetheless, he didn't panic. Instead, he began firing into the nearest enemy position, aware that the Germans would have to expose themselves to get an aimed shot at him. An expert marksman, CPL York was able to hit every enemy soldier who popped his head over the parapet.

After he had shot more than a dozen enemy [troops], six German soldiers charged him with fixed bayonets. As the Germans ran toward him, CPL York once again drew on the instincts of a Tennessee hunter and shot the last man first (so the ones in front wouldn't see the ones he shot fall), then the fifth, and so on.

After he had shot all the assaulting Germans, CPL York again turned his attention to the machine gun pits. In between shots, he called for the Germans to give up. It may have initially seemed ludicrous for a lone Soldier in the open to call on a well-entrenched enemy to surrender, but their situation looked desperate to the German battalion commander, who had seen over 20 of his Soldiers killed by this one American. The commander advanced and offered to surrender if CPL York would stop shooting.

CPL York now faced a daunting task. His platoon, now numbering seven unwounded Soldiers, was isolated behind enemy lines with several dozen prisoners. However, when one American said their predicament was hopeless, CPL York told him to be quiet and began organizing the prisoners for a movement. CPL York moved his unit and prisoners toward American lines, encountering other German positions and forcing their surrender. By the time the platoon reached the edge of the valley they had left just a few hours before, the hill was clear of German machine guns. The fire on the Americans in the valley was substantially reduced and their advance began again.

CPL York returned to American lines, having taken a total of 132 prisoners and putting 35 machine guns out of action. He left the prisoners and headed back to his own outfit. Intelligence officers questioned the prisoners and learned from their testimony the incredible story of how a fighting battalion was destroyed by one determined Soldier armed only with a rifle and pistol. Alvin C. York was promoted to sergeant and awarded the Medal of Honor for this action. His character, physical courage, technical competence, and leadership enabled him to destroy the morale and effectiveness of an entire enemy infantry battalion.

Leader Intelligence

Your intelligence draws on your mental tendencies and resources, shaping your conceptual abilities. These conceptual abilities enable you to exercise sound judgment about your duties and responsibilities even before you implement your concepts and plans. They help you think creatively and reason analytically, critically, ethically, and with cultural sensitivity. Conceptual abilities enable you to consider unintended as well as intended consequences.

Like a chess player trying to anticipate an opponent's moves three or four turns in advance (action-reaction-counteraction), you must always think through what you expect to occur as a result of a decision. Some decisions may set off a chain of events, so you must attempt to anticipate the second- and third-order effects of your actions, no matter at which level you are leading.

The conceptual components affecting the Army leader's intelligence include:

* Mental agility
* Judgment
* Innovation
* Interpersonal tact
* Domain knowledge.

Critical Thinking

How much of SGT York's heroism was gut instinct and how much was leader intelligence? Which leadership skills did York rely on most?

Mental Agility

Mental agility is a flexibility of mind, a tendency to anticipate or adapt to uncertain or changing situations. Agility assists you in thinking through second- and third-order effects when current decisions or actions don't produce the desired effects. It helps you to break from habitual thought patterns. It also helps you improvise when faced with conceptual impasses, as well as quickly apply multiple perspectives when considering new approaches or solutions.

Your mental agility is important because great military leaders adapt to fight the enemy, not the plan. When you are agile, you stay ahead of changing environments and overcome incomplete planning to preempt problems. In the operational sense, agility also means an ability to develop units that adapt to changing situations. Such units can change their behavior from full-scale maneuver war to stability operations in urban areas.

Mental agility is the ability to reason critically while keeping your mind open to multiple possibilities. You reason until you reach the most sensible solution. Critical thinking is a thought process that aims to find truth in situations where direct observation is insufficient, impossible, or impractical. It allows you to think through and solve problems and is central to your decision making. Critical thinking is the key to understanding changing situations, finding causes, arriving at justifiable conclusions, making good judgments, and learning from experience.

Critical thinking implies examining a problem in depth, from multiple points of view, and not settling for the first answer that comes to mind. You need this ability because many of the choices you will face will require more than one solution. The first and most important step in finding an appropriate solution is to isolate the main problem. Sometimes determining the real problem presents you with a huge hurdle; at other times, you have to sort through distracting multiple problems to get to the real issue.

Your mental agility in quickly isolating a problem and identifying solutions allows you to take the initiative and adjust to change. Agility and initiative do not appear magically. You must instill them within all your subordinates by creating a climate that encourages team participation. Identifying honest mistakes in training, for example, makes subordinates more likely to develop their own initiative.

Modern Army training and education focus on improving leader agility and small-unit initiative. Combat deployments in Grenada, Panama, Kosovo, Somalia, Afghanistan, and Iraq have emphasized the demands on mental agility and tactical initiative down to the level of the individual Soldier. Contemporary Operating Environments call for more-agile junior officers and noncommissioned officers—men and women able to effectively lead small and versatile units across the spectrum of conflicts.

mental agility

a flexibility of mind, a tendency to anticipate or adapt to uncertain or changing situations

> It is not genius which reveals to me suddenly and secretly what I should do in circumstances unexpected by others; it is thought and meditation.
>
> Napoleon Bonaparte
>
> *French general (1789-1804) and Emperor of France (1804-1814)*

> Judgment comes from experience and experience comes from bad judgments.
>
> General of the Army Omar N. Bradley
>
> *Address at the US Army War College (1971)*

Sound Judgment

Sound judgment goes hand in hand with agility. Judgment requires being able to assess situations or circumstances and draw conclusions. Good judgment enables you to form sound opinions and make sensible decisions and reliable guesses. Good judgment on a consistent basis is important for successful Army leaders, and much of it comes from experience.

Leaders acquire experience through trial and error and by watching the experiences of others. Learning from others can occur through mentoring and coaching by superiors, peers, and even some subordinates. Another method of expanding experience is self-development by reading biographies and autobiographies of notable men and women. You can learn from their successes and failures.

Often, leaders must juggle facts, questionable data, and gut-level feelings to arrive at a quality decision. Good judgment helps to make the best decision for the situation at hand. It is a key attribute of the art of command and the transformation of knowledge into understanding and quality execution. FM 6-0 discusses how leaders convert data and information into knowledge and understanding.

Good judgment contributes to an ability to determine possible courses of action and decide what action to take. Before choosing the course of action, you must consider the consequences and think methodically. Some sources that aid judgment are senior leaders' intents, the desired outcome, rules, laws, regulations, experience, and values. Good judgment includes the ability to size up subordinates, peers, and the enemy for strengths and weaknesses, and to create appropriate solutions and action. Like agility, it is a critical part of problem solving and decision making.

Innovation

Innovation is the ability to introduce something for the first time. Being innovative means producing ideas that are original and worthwhile.

Sometimes a new problem presents itself or an old problem requires a new solution. You should seize such opportunities to think creatively and innovate. The key concept for creative thinking is to develop ways to challenge subordinates with new ideas. It also involves devising new ways for Soldiers and civilians to accomplish tasks and missions. Creative thinking includes using adaptive approaches (drawing from previous similar circumstances) or innovative approaches (coming up with a completely new idea).

You can and must think creatively to adapt to new environments. A unit deployed for stability operations may find itself isolated on a small, secure compound with limited athletic facilities and without much room to run. In this case you would devise reliable ways to maintain your Soldiers' physical fitness. Innovative solutions might include weight training, games, stationary runs, aerobics, treadmills, and other fitness drills.

As an innovative leader, you prevent complacency by finding new ways to challenge subordinates with forward-looking approaches and ideas. To be an innovator, you must learn to rely on intuition, experience, knowledge, and input from subordinates. You must also reinforce team building by making everybody responsible for the innovation process.

Interpersonal Tact

Interacting effectively with others means being able to see things through their eyes. It requires accepting the character, reactions, and motives of others as being just as valid as yours. **Interpersonal tact** combines these skills, along with recognizing diversity and displaying self-control, balance, and stability in all situations.

Recognizing Diversity

Soldiers, civilians, and contractors come from vastly different backgrounds and are shaped by schooling, race, gender, religion, as well as a host of other influences. People should avoid snap conclusions based on stereotypes. It is better to understand individuals by acknowledging their differences, qualifications, contributions, and potential.

Those who join the Army agree to accept the Army's culture. This initial bond holds everyone together. You can strengthen the team effort by creating an environment where subordinates know they are valued for their talents, contributions, and differences. Your job is not to make everyone the same; it is to take advantage of the different capabilities and talents brought to the team. The biggest challenge is to put each member in the right place to build the best possible team.

Keep an open mind about cultural diversity. It is important because you never know how the talents of certain individuals or groups will contribute to mission accomplishment. During World War II, US Marines from the Navajo nation formed a group of radio-communications specialists called the Navajo Code Talkers. The code talkers used their native language—a unique talent—to handle command radio traffic. Using the Navajo code significantly contributed to successful ground operations because the best Japanese code breakers could not decipher their messages.

Self-Control

Good leaders control their emotions. Instead of hysterics or showing no emotion at all, leaders should display the right amount of sensitivity and passion to tap into subordinates' emotions. Maintaining self-control inspires calm confidence in the team. Self-control encourages feedback from subordinates that can help in understanding what is really happening. Self-control in combat is especially important for Army leaders. If you lose your self-control, you cannot expect those who follow you to maintain theirs.

> **interpersonal tact**
>
> *the ability to accept the character, reactions, and motives of others as valid, as well as to recognize diversity and display self-control, balance, and stability in all situations*

... [A]n officer or noncommissioned officer who loses his temper and flies into a tantrum has failed to obtain his first triumph in discipline.

Noncommissioned Officer's Manual (1917)

The Lieutenant's Temper

Captain William C. Louisell [the new company commander] was a West Pointer and a former tactics instructor at the military academy....

One day I was in the orderly room on the phone, shouting at a fellow lieutenant at the top of my lungs, when Louisell walked in. He took me aside and chewed me out for my behavior. Shortly afterward, I received my efficiency report. To the layman, it might not seem disastrous. Louisell had said of me, "He has a quick temper which he makes a mature effort to control." But in the code of efficiency report writing, I had taken a hit. These words marked the only negative comment on my performance since the first day I had put on a uniform in ROTC. Louisell called me in, sat me down, and raised the matter of the blowup on the phone. "Don't ever show your temper like that to me or anyone else," he warned. It was demeaning to everybody. I still have a hot temper. I still explode occasionally. And whenever I do, I hear Bill Louisell's warning voice.

GEN Colin Powell

An Army leader's self-control, balance, and stability greatly influence his or her ability to interact with others. People are human beings with hopes, fears, concerns, and dreams. Your understanding that motivation and endurance are sparked by emotional energy gives you a powerful leadership tool. Giving others constructive feedback will help mobilize your team's emotional energies to accomplish difficult missions during tough times.

Self-control, balance, and stability also assist making the right ethical choices. An ethical leader successfully applies ethical principles to decision making and retains self-control. Leaders cannot be at the mercy of emotion. It is critical for leaders to remain calm under pressure and expend energy on things they can positively influence and not worry about things they cannot affect.

Emotionally mature and competent leaders are also aware of their own strengths and weaknesses. They spend their energy on self-improvement, while immature leaders usually waste their energy denying that there is anything wrong or analyzing the shortcomings of others. Mature, less defensive leaders benefit from feedback in ways that immature people cannot.

... [A]nyone can get angry—that is easy ... but to [get angry with] the right person, to the right extent, at the right time, for the right reason, and in the right way is no longer something easy that anyone can do.

Aristotle

Greek philosopher and tutor to Alexander the Great

Balance

If you are an emotionally balanced leader, you are able to display the right emotion for a given situation and can read others' emotional state. You draw on your experience and provide your subordinates the proper perspective on unfolding events. You have a range of attitudes, from relaxed to intense, with which to approach diverse situations. You know how to choose the one appropriate for the circumstances. Balanced leaders know how to convey that things are urgent without throwing the entire organization into chaos. They are able to encourage their people to continue the mission, even in the toughest of moments.

Stability

Effective leaders are steady, levelheaded when under pressure and fatigued, and calm in the face of danger. These characteristics stabilize their subordinates, who are always looking to their leader's example. Therefore, you should:

- model the emotions for subordinates to display
- not give in to the temptation to do what personally feels good
- remember that if you're under great stress, it might feel better to vent—but will that help the organization?
- keep in mind that if subordinates are to be calm and rational under pressure, their leaders must display the same stability.

BG Thomas J. Jackson's actions during the Civil War's First Battle of Bull Run (Manassas) serve as a vivid example of how one leader's self-control under fire can stabilize an uncertain situation and ultimately turn the tide in battle.

He Stood Like a Stone Wall

At a crucial juncture in the First Battle of Bull Run, the Confederate line was being beaten back from Matthews Hill by Union forces. Confederate BG Thomas J. Jackson and his 2,000-man brigade of Virginians, hearing the sounds of battle to the left of their position, pressed on to the action. Despite a painful shrapnel wound, General Jackson calmly placed his men in a defensive position on Henry Hill and assured them that all was well.

As men of the broken regiments flowed past, one of their officers, BG Barnard E. Bee exclaimed to Jackson, "General, they are driving us!"

Calmly looking toward the direction of the enemy, BG Jackson replied, "Sir, we will give them the bayonet."

Impressed by BG Jackson's confidence, stability, and self-control, BG Bee rode off towards what was left of the officers and men of his brigade. As he rode into the throng, he gestured with his sword toward Henry Hill and shouted, "Look, men! There is Jackson standing like a stone wall! Let us determine to die here, and we will conquer! Follow me!"

Bee would later be mortally wounded, but the Confederate line stabilized. The nickname he gave to BG Jackson would live on in American history.

Domain Knowledge

Domain knowledge requires possessing facts, beliefs, and logical assumptions in many areas. There are four types of domain knowledge:

- *Tactical knowledge,* or an understanding of military tactics related to securing a designated objective through military means
- *Technical knowledge,* or the specialized information associated with a particular function or system
- *Joint knowledge,* or an understanding of joint organizations, their procedures, and their roles in national defense
- *Cultural and geopolitical knowledge,* or awareness of cultural, geographic, and political differences and sensitivities.

Tactical Knowledge

Tactics is the art and science of employing available means to win battles and engagements. The science of tactics includes capabilities, techniques, and procedures that can be codified. The art includes the creative and flexible array of means to accomplish assigned missions, decision making when facing an intelligent enemy, and the effects of combat on Soldiers.

Fieldcraft

Fieldcraft describes the skills Soldiers require to sustain themselves in the field. Proficiency in fieldcraft reduces the likelihood of casualties. Understanding and excelling at fieldcraft sets conditions for mission success. You must make sure your Soldiers take care of themselves, and you must provide them with the means to do so.

You gain proficiency in fieldcraft through formal training, study, and practice. Although easily learned, fieldcraft skills are often neglected during training exercises. That is why during peacetime exercises, you must strictly enforce tactical discipline and make sure your Soldiers practice fieldcraft to keep them from becoming casualties in wartime. The Army's Combat Training Centers set the right example on how to conduct realistic training in an environment that enforces tactical and fieldcraft discipline. During Combat Training Center rotations, skilled observers and controllers assess appropriate training casualties and make recommendations to reinforce the appropriate fieldcraft standards.

Tactical Proficiency

While practicing tactical abilities is generally challenging, you should try to reproduce actual operational conditions during battle-focused training Unfortunately, you can't always

> The commander must decide how he will fight the battle before it begins. He must then decide how he will use the military effort at his disposal to force the battle to swing the way he wishes it to go; he must make the enemy dance to his tune from the beginning, and never vice versa.
>
> Field Marshal Viscount Montgomery
>
> *Memoirs (1958)*

take your entire unit to the field for full-scale maneuvers. You must therefore learn to achieve maximum readiness by training parts of a scenario or a unit on the ground, while exercising larger echelons with simulations. Despite distractions and limitations, train for war as realistically as possible.

A well-trained unit is one that is ready to respond at a moment's notice, as this lieutenant proved in Iraq.

1AD Lieutenant Earns Silver Star

November 23, 2004—Like many Soldiers honored as heroes, 1st Lt. Christopher Dean of V Corps' 1st Armored Division says he was just doing his job the day he earned a Silver Star for leading the rescue of a patrol ambushed in Baghdad.

"People don't say, 'I'm going to try to win a Silver Star today.' We go out and we're put in an extraordinary position, and the right people recognize what we are doing," said Dean. "I wouldn't say I was in the right place at the right time, but I guess I was fortunate to be in the wrong place at the right time."

Dean, a platoon leader in the division's Company C, 2nd Battalion 37th Armor, based in Friedberg, Germany, was helping to hand authority for the division mission over to the incoming 1st Cavalry Division at that "right time"—April 4. More important, the lieutenant's assignment that day was to serve as Quick Reaction Force tank platoon leader, with oversight for the "wrong place"—Sadr City, arguably the most violent section of Baghdad.

A patrol from 1st Cavalry was ambushed in the city. Dean rolled out immediately with four tanks under his charge. Traveling at top speed, they headed to the grid coordinates given by the besieged patrol. As soon as they arrived, the QRF was hit by a barrage of gunfire.

"We had rounds coming in from everywhere," said Dean. "It sounded like Rice Krispies popping." One of his Soldiers was killed.

Dean then led a seven-tank attack back into the engagement area to find the ambushed patrol. The .50-caliber machine gun was taken out by enemy fire, leaving him atop the vehicle with only his M4 rifle. He was hit by shrapnel from a rocket-propelled grenade blast.

Reaching the ambushed patrol, the QRF dismounted to help get the patrol out. Under heavy enemy fire they pulled out the dead and wounded and put them inside the tanks, then used one of Dean's tanks to push two damaged vehicles out of the area.

Dean's team rescued 19 Soldiers from the ambush.

Technical Knowledge

Knowing Your Equipment

Technical knowledge relates to equipment, weapons, and systems—everything from a gun sight to the computer that tracks personnel actions. Since you are closer to your equipment than organizational and strategic leaders, you have a greater need to know how it works and how to use it. You serve as the expert called upon to solve problems with equipment. You must be able to figure out how to make it work better, how to apply it, how to fix it, and even how to modify it. If you do not know the specifics, you must know who does know how to solve issues with it. Subordinates expect their first-line leaders to know the equipment and be experts in all the applicable technical skills. As a platoon leader, you are one of the Army's technical experts and teachers.

Operating Equipment

Know how to operate your organization's equipment, and ensure your people do as well. You can often set an example with a hands-on approach. When new equipment arrives, learn how to use it and train your subordinates to do the same. Once individuals are trained, then teams, and in turn, whole units train together. Army leaders know understanding equipment strengths and weaknesses is critical to success in combat.

Employing Equipment

Direct-, organizational-, and strategic-level leaders need to know what functional value the equipment has for their operations and how to employ the equipment in their units and organizations. You have a responsibility to keep alert to the effect that fielding the equipment will have on your organization. You must ensure that your organization has all necessary resources to properly field, train, maintain, operate, inventory, and turn in equipment.

Joint Knowledge

Joint warfare is team warfare. The 1986 Goldwater-Nichols legislation mandated a higher level of cooperation among America's military services, based on experiences drawn from previous deployments. Since then, Army leaders from the most junior field leader to the generals serving at the strategic level have embraced the importance of joint warfare. Leaders acquire joint knowledge through formal training in the Joint Professional Military Education program and assignments in joint organizations and staffs. All the services— the Army, Air Force, Navy, and Marines—bring their own strengths and limitations to the battlefield. Only close cooperation among them all can ensure swift mission accomplishment in the complex operational environments our militaries face.

Cultural and Geopolitical Knowledge

Culture consists of shared beliefs, values, and assumptions among a group of people about what is important. Army leaders are mindful of cultural factors in three contexts:

- *Team members:* They are sensitive to their different backgrounds in order to best leverage their talents
- *Countries:* They are aware of the culture of the nations in which their organization operates

> If you can wear Arab kit when with the tribes you will acquire their trust and intimacy to a degree impossible in uniform.
>
> T. E. Lawrence
>
> *Twenty-Seven Articles (1917)*

- *Partners:* They consider and evaluate the possible implications of partners' customs, traditions, doctrinal principles, and operational methods when working with forces of another nation.

Understanding the culture of adversaries and of the country in which your organization is operating is just as important as understanding the culture of your own country and organization. Contemporary Operating Environments, which place smaller units into more culturally complex situations with continuous media coverage, require even greater cultural and geopolitical awareness on your part. Be aware of current events—particularly those in areas where the United States has national interests. Before deploying, ensure that your Soldiers and platoon are properly prepared to deal with the population of particular areas—either as partners, neutrals, or adversaries. The more everyone knows about them, including their language, the better off the unit will be.

Understanding other cultures applies to full spectrum operations, not only stability and reconstruction operations. For example, you may employ different tactics against an adversary who considers surrender a dishonor worse than death, than against those for whom surrender remains an honorable option. Likewise, if your organization is operating as part of a multinational team, how well you understand partners' capabilities and limitations will affect how well your team accomplishes its mission.

Cultural understanding is crucial to the success of multinational operations. Take the time to learn your partners' customs and traditions as well as their operational procedures and doctrine. To be able to operate successfully in a multinational setting, you must be aware of any differences in doctrinal terminology and the interpretation of orders and instructions. Learn how and why others think and act as they do. In multinational forces, effective leaders often create a "third culture" by adopting practices from several cultures to create a common operating basis.

Working in a multicultural environment requires you to keep plans and orders as simple as possible to prevent misunderstandings and unnecessary losses. If possible, you and your Soldiers should learn some of the language in which those around you operate. Dedicated liaison teams and linguists provide a cultural bridge between partners to mitigate some differences, but they cannot eliminate all of them.

Cultural awareness played a major role in the peaceful capture of Najaf during Operation Iraqi Freedom in April 2003.

No Slack Soldiers Take a Knee

The Soldiers of LTC Christopher Hughes' 2nd Battalion, 327th Infantry were tired following several weeks of battling insurgents on their journey to Najaf. It was early April 2003 and elements from the 101st Airborne Division were taking part in a bigger effort to secure the holy city on the road to Baghdad.

The 2-327th had served in Vietnam, and one of their finest had been killed just days before rotating to the states. In his honor, and based on his favorite saying "cut the enemy no slack," the battalion now called themselves "No Slack."

Their leader, LTC Hughes, was no stranger to Muslim customs, learning all he could while investigating the bombing of the USS Cole and serving on a joint antiterrorism task force. Still, he took the opportunity to learn more about the Shiite people and the grand Ali Mosque in the city where he and his Soldiers were headed. Earlier that month, on the 54-hour drive out of Kuwait, Hughes had listened while his Iraqi-American translator explained the importance of the Ayatollah Ali Sistani, the years he spent imprisoned under Saddam Hussein, and how Shiites considered the gold-domed Mosque as a most holy site.

When Hughes and his Soldiers approached the mosque to ask Sistani to issue a fatwa (religious decree) allowing the Americans to go on to Baghdad without resistance, they met an angry crowd.

Hundreds of people protected the entrance to the mosque, concerned that the Americans had come to destroy it. They chanted "In city yes—in city OK. Mosque no!" Hughes had to act quickly to dispel their fears. At first, he pointed his weapon to the ground. No one noticed.

Next, he commanded his troops to take a knee. Some gave him a questioning glance, but still obeyed without hesitation. They trusted their leader. Many Iraqis in the crowd joined them; LTC Hughes went a step further. He told his Soldiers to smile. The Iraqis smiled back. The anger in the crowd was defused. A universal language of goodwill spread, and Hughes was able to have his Soldiers get up and walk away. As he turned to leave, Hughes put his right hand on his chest in a traditional Islamic gesture, "Peace be with you," he said, "Have a nice day." The fatwa was issued, Baghdad was taken, and unnecessary conflict was avoided.

Understanding the mixture of cultures, and with an adaptability that makes the American Soldier unique, these combat-hardened warriors allowed diplomacy and respect for others to rule the day.

CONCLUSION

To be an intelligent Army officer you need to be mentally agile, sound in judgment, innovative, tactful, and knowledgeable in many areas. Being physically ready for combat is difficult enough. To be mentally ready can be even more challenging. But the nation expects Army leaders to be up to the challenge, and the Army works hard to help them succeed. Your ROTC training is geared to help you meet that challenge.

Learning Assessment

1. What is mental agility and why is it an important trait for an Army officer?
2. List four ways in which you can expand your experience and add to your ability to exercise good judgment.
3. How can innovation be used to challenge complacent subordinates?
4. Define the four basic elements of interpersonal tact.
5. What are the four basic elements of domain knowledge, and how can this knowledge help you in your leadership capacity?

Key Words

mental agility
sound judgment
innovation
interpersonal tact
domain knowledge

References

Field Manual 6-22, *Army Leadership: Competent, Confident, and Agile.* 12 October 2006.

Powell, C. (with Persico, J.). (1995). *My American Journey.* New York: Random House, Inc.

US Army. (23 November 2004). 1st AD Lieutenant Earns Silver Star. *Soldier Stories.* Retrieved 24 August 2005 from http://www4.army.mil/ocpa/soldierstories/story.php?story_id_key=6591

Section 5

ARMY CORE LEADER COMPETENCIES

Key Points

1 Leading

2 Developing

3 Achieving

Army leaders in this century need to be pentathletes, multi-skilled leaders who can thrive in uncertain and complex operating environments ... innovative and adaptive leaders who are expert in the art and science of the profession of arms.

Dr. Francis J. Harvey
Secretary of the Army

Speech for US Army Command and General Staff College graduation (2005)

Introduction

Leaders provide purpose, direction, and motivation. Army leaders work hard to lead people, to develop themselves, their subordinates, and organizations, and to accomplish their missions across the spectrum of conflicts.

But continuously building and refining your values and attributes, as well as acquiring more professional knowledge, is only part of becoming a competent leader. Leadership succeeds when you act and apply the core leader competencies. As you move from direct leadership positions to the organizational and strategic leader levels, those competencies will take on different nuances and complexities.

GEN Matthew B. Ridgway exemplified the qualities of a true Army leader in two wars.

Achieving Success and Leadership Excellence

GEN Matthew B. Ridgway successfully led the 82d Airborne Division and XVIII Airborne Corps during World War II. He later commanded the Eighth (U.S.) Army during the Korean War. GEN Ridgway exemplified the qualities of the competent and multiskilled Army leader. His knowledge of American Soldiers, other services, allies, foreign cultures, and the overall strategic situation led him to certain expectations.

Those expectations gave him a baseline from which to assess his command once he arrived in theater. He continually visited units throughout the Eighth Army area, talked with Soldiers and their commanders, assessed command climate, and took action to mold attitudes with clear intent, supreme confidence, and unyielding tactical discipline.

GEN Ridgway constantly sought to develop and mentor subordinate commanders and their staffs by sharing his thoughts and expectations of combat leadership. He frequently visited the frontlines to feel the pulse of the fighting forces, shared their hardships, and demanded they be taken care of. He took care of his troops by pushing the logistic systems to provide creature comforts as well as war supplies. He eliminated the skepticism of purpose, gave Soldiers cause to fight, and helped them gain confidence by winning small victories. GEN Ridgway led by example. His actions during four months in command of the Eighth Army prior to his appointment as United Nations Supreme Commander bring to life the leader's competencies. He left a legacy that leaders can operate within the spheres of all levels of leadership to accomplish their mission consistently and ethically.

Figure 5.1 shows the Army Leadership Requirements Model. You will refer to this model a great deal during your ROTC studies. On the left are the attributes you've been studying in Sections 2 through 4—*character, presence,* and *leader intelligence* or intellect. On the right are the core leader competencies you'll read about in this section—*leading, developing,* and *achieving.*

Leading

The *leading* category includes four leader competencies. Two focus on who you are leading and with what degree of authority and influence: *leads others* and *extends influence beyond the chain of command.* The other competencies address two ways by which you convey influence: *leads by example* and *communicates.*

Leads others involves influencing Soldiers or Army civilians in your unit or organization. This competency has a number of components, including setting clear direction, enforcing standards, and balancing the care of followers against mission requirements.

Extends influence beyond the chain of command requires the ability to operate in an environment, including both higher and lower command structures, and using your influence outside the traditional chain of command. This includes connecting with joint, allied, and multinational partners; local nationals; and civilian-led governmental or nongovernmental agencies. In this area, you must often operate without designated authority or while others do not recognize your authority.

Leads by example is essential to leading effectively over the course of time. Whether you intend to or not, you provide an example that others consider and use in what

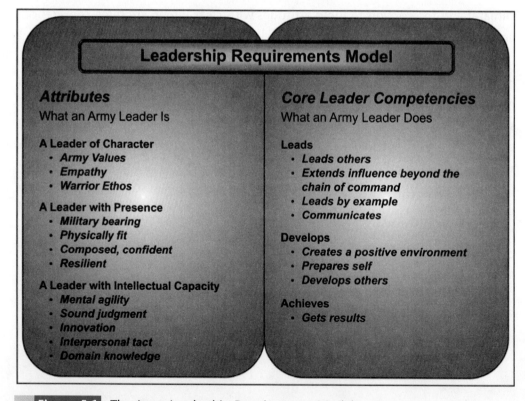

Figure 5.1 The Army Leadership Requirements Model

they do. This competency reminds you to serve as a role model. Your actions should be grounded in the Army Values and imbued with the Warrior Ethos.

Communicates ensures that you gain a clear understanding of what needs to be done, and why, within your organization. This competency deals with maintaining a clear focus on the team's efforts to achieve goals and tasks to accomplish missions. It helps build consensus and is a critical tool for successful operations in diverse multinational settings. You refine your communicating abilities by developing advanced oral, written, and listening skills.

Leads Others

All the Army's core leader competencies, especially *leading others,* involve influence. You can draw on a variety of techniques to influence others. These range from obtaining **compliance** to building a **commitment** to achieve. Resistance is the opposite of compliance and commitment. There are many techniques for influencing others to comply or commit, and you can use one or more of them to fit to the specifics of any situation.

Compliance-focused influence is based primarily on your authority. Giving a direct order to a follower is one approach to obtaining compliance during a task. Compliance is appropriate for short-term, immediate requirements and for situations where little risk can be tolerated. Compliance techniques are also appropriate for use with others who are relatively unfamiliar with their tasks or unwilling or unable to commit fully to the request. If something needs to be done with little time for delay, and there is no need for a subordinate to understand why the request is made, then compliance is an acceptable approach. Compliance-focused influence is not particularly effective when your greatest aim is to create initiative and high esteem within your team.

Commitment-focused influence generally produces longer-lasting and broader effects. Whereas compliance changes only a follower's behavior, commitment reaches deeper—changing attitudes and beliefs, as well as behavior. For example, when you build responsibility among followers, they will likely demonstrate more initiative, personal involvement, and creativity. Commitment grows from an individual's desire to gain a sense of control and develop self-worth by contributing to the organization. Depending on the objective of the influence, leaders can strengthen commitment by reinforcing followers' identification with the nation (loyalty), the Army (professionalism), the unit or organization (selfless service), the leadership in a unit (respect), and to the job (duty).

Influence Techniques

You can use several specific techniques for influence that fall along the continuum between compliance and commitment. The 10 techniques described below seek different degrees of compliance or commitment ranging from pressure at the compliance end to building relations at the commitment end.

- You *apply pressure* when you use explicit demands to achieve compliance, such as establishing deadlines for completing tasks, imposing negative consequences for failure to complete. Indirect pressure includes persistent reminders of the request and frequent checking.
- *Legitimate requests* occur when you refer to your source of authority to establish the basis for a request.
- *Exchange* is an influence technique that involves making an offer to provide some desired item or action in trade for compliance with a request. The exchange technique requires you to control certain resources or rewards that those you are influencing value.

compliance

the act of conforming to a specific requirement or demand

commitment

willing dedication or allegiance to a cause or organization

- *Personal appeals* occur when you ask the follower to comply with a request based on friendship or loyalty. This might often be useful in a difficult situation when mutual trust is the key to success.
- *Collaboration* occurs when you provide assistance or resources to carry out a directive or request. You make the choice more attractive by being prepared to step in and resolve any problems.
- *Rational persuasion* requires you to provide evidence, logical arguments, or explanations showing how a request is relevant to the goal. This is often the first approach to gaining compliance or commitment from followers.
- *Apprising* happens when you explain why a request will benefit followers, such as giving them greater satisfaction in their work or saving them time. In contrast to the exchange technique, the benefits are out of your control.
- *Inspiration* occurs when you fire up enthusiasm for a request by arousing strong emotions to build conviction. By appropriately stressing the results of stronger commitment, you can inspire followers to surpass minimal standards and reach elite performance status.
- *Participation* occurs when you ask a follower to help plan how to address a problem or meet an objective. Active participation leads to an increased sense of worth and recognition. It provides value to the effort and builds the follower's commitment to execute.
- *Relationship building* is a technique in which you build positive rapport and a relationship of mutual trust, making followers more willing to support requests. Examples include showing personal interest in a follower's well-being, offering praise, and understanding a follower's perspective.

Putting Influence Techniques to Work

To succeed and create true commitment, others should perceive your influencing techniques as authentic and sincere. Positive influence comes when you do what is right for the Army, the mission, the team, and each individual Soldier. Negative influence—real and perceived—happens when you focus primarily on personal gain and lack self-awareness. Even honorable intentions, if wrongly perceived by followers as self-serving, will yield mere compliance. False perception may trigger unintended side effects such as resentment toward you and deterioration of unit cohesion.

When influencing followers, you should consider that:

- the objectives for the use of influence should be in line with the Army Values, ethics, the Uniform Code of Military Justice, the Warrior Ethos, and the Civilian Creed
- various influence techniques can be used to obtain compliance and commitment
- compliance-seeking influence focuses on meeting and accounting for specific task demands

> The American Soldier ... demands professional competence in his leaders. In battle, he wants to know that the job is going to be done right, with no unnecessary casualties.
>
> Omar N. Bradley
> General of the Army (1950-1953)

- commitment-encouraging influence emphasizes empowerment and long-lasting trust.

Extends Influence Beyond the Chain of Command

While Army leaders traditionally exert influence within their unit and its established chain of command, as a multiskilled leader you must also be able to extend influence to others beyond your chain of command. *Extending influence* is the second leader competency. In today's politically and culturally charged operational environments, even direct leaders may work closely with joint, interagency, and multinational forces, the media, local civilians, political leaders, police forces, and nongovernmental agencies. Extending influence requires that you be especially aware of the differences in how influence works.

When extending influence beyond the traditional chain, you often have to influence without authority designated or implied by rank or position. You may find yourself in situations where you must build informal teams to accomplish organizational tasks.

A unique aspect of extending influence is that those who are targets of your influence outside the chain may not even recognize or willingly accept your authority as an Army leader. The key element of extending influence and building teams is for you to create a common vision among prospective team members.

Leading without authority requires adapting to your environment and the cultural sensitivities of the given situation. You must have cultural knowledge to understand different social customs and belief systems and to address issues in those contexts. When conducting peace operations, for example, you must understand that interaction with locals and their leaders can have dramatic impacts on the overall theater strategy. The manner in which your unit conducts house-to-house searches for insurgents can influence the local population's acceptance of authority, or become a recruiting incentive for the insurgency.

Extending influence includes competency in:

- building trust outside lines of military command authority
- understanding the sphere, means, and limits of influence
- negotiating, building consensus, and conflict resolution.

Building Trust Outside Lines of Authority

Forming effective, cohesive teams is often the first challenge when you work outside a traditional command structure. These teams usually have to be formed from disparate groups who are unfamiliar with military and Army customs and culture. Without some measure of trust, nothing will work well. To establish trust, you will have to identify areas of common interests and goals. Trust between two people or two groups is based largely on being able to anticipate what others understand and how they will respond in various situations. Keeping others informed also builds trust. Cementing and sustaining trust depends on following through on commitments.

Building alliances is similar to building teams. The difference is that in alliances the groups maintain greater independence. Trust is a common ingredient in effective alliances. Alliances are groomed over time by establishing contact with others, growing friendships, and identifying common interests.

Understanding Sphere, Means, and Limits of Influence

When you operate with an established command structure and common procedures, everyone's roles and responsibilities are readily apparent. When you lead outside an established organization, your ability to assess the parties involved becomes another part of the operation. Identifying who is who, what role they have, over whom they have authority or influence, and how they are likely to respond to your influence, are all important considerations.

The key to influence outside the chain of command is to learn about the people and organizations. By understanding their interests and desires, you will know what influence techniques are most likely to work.

Negotiating, Building Consensus, and Resolving Conflict

While operating outside the chain of command, you often have to resolve conflicts between Army interests and local populations or others. Conflict resolution identifies differences and similarities among the stances of the various groups. You analyze differences to understand what is behind them. You can make proposals for reinterpreting the differences or negotiating compromise to reach common understanding or shared goals. Trust, understanding, and knowing the right influence technique for the situation are the determining factors in negotiating, consensus building, and conflict resolution.

Leads by Example

Displaying Character

As an Army leader you set an example whether you know it or not. A leader of sound character exhibits good character at all times. Modeling the attributes of good character defines you to the people with whom you interact. As a leader of character you do not have to worry about being seen at the wrong moment doing the wrong thing.

When you live by the Army Values and the Warrior Ethos you display character and lead by example. This means putting the organization and your subordinates above personal self-interest, career, and comfort. For the Army leader, it requires putting the lives of others above a personal desire for self-preservation.

Leading With Confidence in Adverse Conditions

When you project confidence you are an inspiration to followers. Soldiers will follow leaders who are comfortable with their own abilities; they will question the leader who shows doubt.

Displaying confidence and composure when things are not going well can be a challenge for anyone. However, it is important when your task is to lead others through a grave situation. As you have read, confidence is a key component of leader presence. A leader who shows hesitation in the face of setbacks can trigger a chain reaction among others. On the other hand, a leader who is overconfident in difficult situations may lack the proper degree of care or concern.

Leading with confidence requires a heightened self-awareness and ability to master emotions. Developing the ability to remain confident, no matter what the situation, involves:

- having prior opportunities to experience reactions to severe situations
- maintaining a positive outlook when a situation becomes confusing or changes
- remaining decisive after mistakes have been discovered
- encouraging others when they show signs of weakness.

Displaying Moral Courage

Projecting confidence in combat and other situations requires physical and moral courage. While physical courage allows infantrymen to defend their ground, even when the enemy has broken the line of defense and ammunition runs critically short, moral courage empowers leaders to stand firm on values, principles, and convictions in the same situation. As a leader with moral courage, you take full responsibility for your decisions and actions. Morally courageous leaders are willing to critically look inside themselves, consider new ideas, and change what caused failure.

Moral courage is fundamental to living the Army Values of integrity and honor.

Demonstrating Competence

It does not take long for followers to become suspicious of a leader who acts confident but does not have the competence to back it up. Having the appropriate levels of domain knowledge is vital for you, in turn, to display confidence through your attitudes, actions, and words.

Leading by example demands that you stay aware of how your guidance and plans are executed. You cannot remain in safe, dry headquarters, designing complex plans without examining what your Soldiers and civilians are experiencing. You must have courage to get out to where the action is, whether the battlefield or the shop floor. You must connect with your followers by sharing hardships and communicating openly to clearly see and feel what goes on from a subordinate's perspective.

True warrior leaders lead from the front and share the experiences of their Soldiers. Seeing and feeling the plan transform into action empowers you to better assess the situation and influence the execution by your immediate presence. If you stay at a safe distance from the front, you risk destroying your Soldiers' trust and confidence.

GEN George Patton made it clear that leading from the front and making plans with a clear understanding of the front-line situation were keys to success. In his General Orders to the 3rd Army of 6 March 1944, he stipulated:

> The Commanding General or his Chief of Staff (never both at once) and one member of each of the General Staff sections, the Signal, Medical, Ordnance, Engineer, and Quartermaster sections, should visit the front daily. To save duplication, the Chief of Staff will designate the sector each is to visit.

> The function of these Staff officers is to observe, not to meddle. In addition to their own specialty, they must observe and report anything of military importance. … Remember, too, that your primary mission as a leader is to see with your own eyes and be seen by your troops while engaged in personal reconnaissance.

Communicates

Competent leadership that gets results depends on good communication. Although communication is usually viewed as a process of providing information, communication as a competency involves more than the simple transmission of information. Communication needs to achieve a new understanding. It must create new or better awareness. Communicating critical information in a clear fashion is important to reaching a shared understanding of issues and solutions. It is conveying thoughts, presenting recommendations, bridging cultural sensitivities, and reaching consensus. You cannot lead, supervise, build teams, counsel, coach, or mentor without the ability to communicate clearly.

Developing

Good leaders strive to leave an organization better than they found it and expect other leaders throughout the Army to do the same. You can create a positive organizational climate, prepare yourself to do well in your own duties, and help others to perform well. As a good leader you should look ahead and prepare talented Soldiers and civilians to assume positions with greater leadership responsibility in their own organizations and in future assignments. You should also work on your own development to prepare for new challenges.

The Army leader who develops people and the organization with a long-term perspective possesses the following three competencies:

- Creates a positive environment
- Seeks self-improvement

● Invests adequate time and effort to developing individual subordinates and building effective teams.

Creates a Positive Environment

climate

the environment of units and organizations, primarily shaped by organizational and direct leaders

culture

the environment of the Army as an institution and of major elements or communities within it

Climate and **culture** describe the environment in which you lead. Climate refers to the environment of units and organizations, primarily those shaped by organizational and direct leaders. Culture refers to the environment of the Army as an institution and of major elements or communities within it.

You take care of people and maximize their performance by influencing your organization's climate. Climate is how members feel about the organization and comes from shared perceptions and attitudes about the unit's daily functioning. These things have a great impact on their motivation and the trust they feel for their team and their leaders. Climate is generally a short-term experience, depending on a network of the personalities in a small organization. The organization's climate changes as people come and go. When a Soldier says, "My last platoon sergeant was pretty good, but this new one is great," the Soldier is pinpointing one of the many elements that affect an organization's climate.

Culture is a longer lasting and more complex set of shared expectations than climate. While climate is a reflection about how people think and feel about their organization right now, culture consists of the shared attitudes, values, goals, and practices that characterize the larger institution over time. It is deeply rooted in long-held beliefs, customs, and practices. You must establish a climate consistent with the culture of the Army as an enduring institution. You must also use the culture to let your people know they are part of something bigger than just themselves, that they have responsibilities not only to the people around them but also to those who have gone before and those who will come after.

Seeks Self-Improvement

To prepare for increasingly demanding operational environments, Army leaders must invest more time in self-study and self-development than before. Besides becoming multiskilled, Army leaders have to balance the demands of diplomat and warrior. Acquiring these capabilities to succeed across the spectrum of conflicts is challenging, but critical. In no other profession is the cost of being unprepared as unforgiving, often resulting in mission failure and unnecessary casualties.

Be Prepared for Expected and Unexpected Challenges

You know that in the physical arena, you must maintain high levels of fitness and health, not only to earn continuously the respect of subordinates, peers, and superiors, but also to withstand the stresses of leading and maintaining your ability to think clearly. While physical self-development is important, you must also exploit every available opportunity to sharpen your intellectual capacity and knowledge in relevant domains. The conceptual components affecting the Army leader's intelligence include agility, judgment, innovation, interpersonal tact, and domain knowledge. A developed intellect helps you think creatively and reason analytically, critically, ethically, and with cultural sensitivity.

When faced with diverse operational settings, you can draw on intellectual capacity, critical thinking abilities, and applicable domain knowledge. You create these capabilities by frequently studying doctrine, tactics, techniques, and procedures. You put the information into context with personal experiences, military history, and geopolitical awareness. Take the time to learn languages, customs, belief systems, motivational factors, and operational principles.

Self-development is continuous, and you must pursue it during both institutional and operational assignments. You prepare yourself for leadership positions through lifelong learning.

Self-awareness is a component of preparing yourself. It can help you become better adjusted and more effective. Self-awareness enables you to recognize your strengths and weaknesses across a range of environments and progressively leverage strengths to correct these weaknesses.

Every leader has the ability to be self-aware. Competent leaders understand the importance of self-awareness and work to develop it.

self-awareness

being aware of oneself, including one's traits, feelings, and behaviors

Develops Others

Leader development is a deliberate, continuous, sequential, and progressive process grounded in the Army Values. It grows Soldiers and civilians into competent and confident leaders capable of directing teams and organizations to execute decisive action. You develop as a leader through your lifelong synthesis of the knowledge, skills, and experiences that you gain through institutional training and education, organizational training, operational experience, and self-development. And you train Soldiers now to develop leaders for the future.

Assessing Developmental Needs

The first step in developing others is to understand what areas are already strong and what areas should be stronger. If you know your subordinates well, you have an idea where to encourage them to develop. You can observe new subordinates under different task conditions to identify strengths and weaknesses and to see how quickly they pick up new information and skills.

To objectively assess subordinates, leaders do the following:

- Observe and record subordinates' performance in the core leader competencies
- Determine if the performances meet, exceed, or fall below expected standards
- Tell subordinates what they observed and provide an opportunity to comment
- Help subordinates develop an individual development plan (IDP) to improve performance.

Supporting Professional and Personal Growth

Preparing yourself and subordinates to lead aims at the goal of developing multiskilled leaders—leader pentathletes. The multiskilled leader has not only warfighting skills but also creativity and a degree of diplomacy combined with multicultural sensitivity. To achieve this balance, the Army creates positive learning environments at all levels to support its lifelong learning strategy.

It takes openness and imagination to create an effective organizational learning environment. Do not be afraid to make mistakes. Instead, stay positive and learn from those mistakes. You must remain confident in your own and your subordinates' ability to make learning the profession of arms a lifelong commitment.

Helping People Learn

It is your responsibility to help subordinates learn. Explain why a subject is important. Show how it will help them and the organization perform better and actively involve subordinates in the learning process. For instance, never try to teach someone how to drive a vehicle with classroom instruction alone. Ultimately, the person has to get behind the wheel. To keep things interesting, keep lectures to a minimum and maximize hands-on training.

Counseling, Coaching, and Mentoring

Leaders have three principal ways of developing others:

- Counseling—reviewing a subordinate's demonstrated performance and potential, often in relation to a programmed performance evaluation

- Coaching—guiding another person's development in new or existing skills during the practice of those skills
- Mentoring—providing guidance and advice from the standpoint of greater experience.

counseling

the process of advising someone based on the counselor's superior experience or knowledge

Counseling is central to leader development. When you serve as a designated rater you prepare your subordinate to be a better Soldier. Good counseling focuses on the subordinate's performance and problems with an eye toward tomorrow's plans and solutions. Counseling cannot be an occasional event but should be part of a comprehensive program to develop subordinates.

Coaching refers to helping someone through a set of tasks. It relies primarily on teaching and guidance to bring out and enhance a subordinate's capabilities. A coach helps people understand their current level of performance and instructs them how to reach the next level of knowledge and skill.

coaching

the process of helping someone through a set of tasks

Coaching is a development technique that tends to be used for a skill and task-specific orientation. Coaches should possess considerable knowledge in the specific area in which they coach others.

An important aspect of coaching is identifying and planning for short- and long-term goals. The coach and the person being coached discuss strengths, weaknesses, and courses of action to sustain or improve. Coaches focus goals, clarify the self-awareness of the person they are coaching, uncover their potential, eliminate developmental barriers, develop action plans and commitment, and then follow up to see how the person is progressing.

Future battlefield environments will place pressures on developing leaders at a rapid pace. To help these leaders acquire the requisite abilities, the Army relies on a leader development system that compresses and accelerates development of professional expertise, maturity, and conceptual and team-building skills. **Mentoring** is a developmental tool that can effectively support many of these learning objectives. It is a combat multiplier because it boosts positive leadership behaviors on a voluntary basis.

mentoring

the process whereby a person of greater experience helps a person of lesser experience to develop— the relationship is characterized by mutual trust and respect

Contrary to common belief, mentoring relationships are not confined to the superior-subordinate relationship. They may also be found between peers and notably between senior NCOs and junior officers. This relationship can occur across many levels of rank. In many circumstances, this relationship extends past the point where one or the other has left the chain of command.

Supportive mentoring occurs when a mentor does not outrank the person being mentored, but has more extensive knowledge and experience. Early in your career, you may be paired with a senior experienced NCO. The relationship that frequently comes from this experience can be instrumental in your development. Often, officers recognize that the noncommissioned officer in their first or second assignment was a critical mentor with a major impact on their development.

> The cohesion that matters on the battlefield is that which is developed at the company, platoon, and squad levels....
>
> GEN Edward C. Meyer
> Chief of Staff, Army (1979-1983)

Understanding GIs

My first platoon sergeant was Robert D. Edwards, from deepest Alabama.... The troops feared Edwards, and with reason. Once, I had to explain to him why he could not keep a Soldier who had gone AWOL chained to the barracks radiator. Edwards found my reasons puzzling and went off muttering about the decline of discipline. While he was feared, he was, at the same time, respected and revered by the men. They understood Edwards. He was in their corner. No matter how primitive his methods, he had one concern—the welfare of the platoon and the men in it. If they soldiered right, he looked out for them. I came to understand GIs during my tour at Gelnhausen [in Germany]. I learned what made them tick, lessons that stuck for thirty-five years. American Soldiers love to win. They want to be part of a successful team. They respect a leader who holds them to a high standard and pushes them to the limit, as long as they see a worthwhile objective. American Soldiers will gripe constantly about being driven to higher performance. They will swear they would rather serve somewhere easier. But at the end of the day, they always ask: "How'd we do?" And I learned what it meant when Soldiers brought you problems.... The day Soldiers stop bringing you their problems is the day you have stopped leading them. They have either lost confidence in you or concluded you do not care. Either case is a failure of leadership.

GEN Colin Powell

Achieving

Achieving focuses on accomplishing the mission. It begins in the short term by setting objectives. In the long term, achieving gets results in pursuit of those objectives.

Getting results means getting the job done on time and to standard. The successful Army leader in this area has the following competencies:

- Provides direction, guidance, and clear priorities that involve guiding teams in what needs to be done and how
- Develops and executes plans for accomplishing missions and tasks, anticipating how to carry out what needs to be done, managing the resources used to get it done, and conducting the necessary actions
- Accomplishes missions consistently and ethically, using monitoring to identify strengths and correct weaknesses in organizational, group, and individual performance.

Provides Direction, Guidance, and Priorities

Always provide guidance from both near-term and long-term perspectives. A near-term focus is based on critical actions that must be accomplished immediately. A long-term focus prepares others to handle future tasks competently.

Make feedback an embedded, natural part of the work. You should provide feedback on a regular basis. Making feedback part of the normal performance of work is a technique leaders use to guide how duties are accomplished.

Often the most challenging part of your job as leader is to identify and clarify conflicts in your followers' roles and responsibilities. Good communication techniques with back briefs are useful for identifying conflicts. Role differences may arise during execution, and you should resolve them as they occur.

Develops and Executes Plans

In daily peacetime or combat training and operations, your primary responsibility is to help the organization function effectively. Your unit must accomplish its mission despite any surrounding chaos. This all begins with a well-thought-out plan and thorough preparation.

Planning

Use planning to ensure that an approach for reaching goals will be practical. Planning reduces confusion, builds subordinates' confidence in themselves and their organization, and allows the flexibility to adjust to changing situations. Good planning boosts shared understanding and ensures that a mission is accomplished with a minimum of wasted effort and fewer casualties in combat.

Preparing

Preparation complements planning. Preparation includes detailed coordination with other organizations involved or affected by the operation or project. In the case of nontactical requirements, preparation may include ensuring the necessary facilities (for example, hospitals, labs, maintenance shops) and other resources (for example, firefighters, police, and other first responders) are available to support the mission.

A rehearsal is a critical element of preparation. It allows everyone involved in a mission to develop a mental picture of responsibilities and what should happen. It helps the team synchronize operations at times and places critical to successful mission accomplishment. Rehearsing key combat actions allows subordinates to see how things are supposed to work and builds confidence in the plan.

Executing

Successful execution of a plan is based on all the work that has gone before. Executing for success requires situational understanding, supervising task completion, assessing progress, and implementing required execution or adjustment decisions.

Executing in combat means putting a plan into action by applying combat power to accomplish the mission. It also means using situational understanding to assess progress and make execution and adjustment decisions. In combat, you strive to integrate and synchronize all elements of the joint and combined arms team as well as nonmilitary assets. The goal is to assign specific tasks or objectives to the most capable organization and empower its leaders to execute and exercise initiative within the given intent.

Accomplishes Missions

Achieving consistent results hinges on doing all the right things that come under other leadership competencies—having a clear vision, taking care of people, setting the right example, building up the organization, encouraging leader growth, and so on. You can achieve consistent performance by using techniques to:

- monitor collective performance
- reinforce good performance
- implement systems to improve performance.

Monitoring Performance

It is critical for you to be able to assess a situation accurately and reliably against desired outcomes, established values, and ethical standards. Assessment occurs continually during planning, preparation, and execution; it is not solely an after-the-fact evaluation. Accurate assessment requires instinct and intuition based on experience and learning. It also demands a feel for the reliability and validity of information and its sources. Periodic assessment is necessary to determine organizational weaknesses and prevent mishaps. Accurately determining causes is essential to training management, developing subordinate leadership, and initiating quality improvements.

There are many different ways to gather information for assessment purposes. These include asking team members questions to find out if information is getting to them, meeting people to inquire if tasks and objectives are appropriate, and checking for plan synchronization. Assessing can also involve researching and analyzing electronic databases. No matter which techniques you use, it is important that information be verified as accurate.

Reinforcing Good Performance

To accomplish missions consistently you must maintain your team's motivation. One of the best ways to do this is to recognize and reward good performance. If you recognize individual and team accomplishments, you will shape positive motivation and actions for the future. Recognizing individuals and teams in front of superiors and others gives those contributors an increased sense of worth. You encourage Soldiers and civilians to sustain and improve performance when they feel their contributions are valued. Don't overlook giving credit to subordinates. Sharing credit has enormous payoffs in terms of building trust and motivation for future actions.

Improving Organizational Performance

You must encourage a performance improvement mindset in your unit—one that allows for conformity but goes beyond merely meeting standards—to strive for increased efficiencies and effectiveness. Several actions are characteristic of performance improvement:

- Ask incisive questions about how tasks can be performed better
- Anticipate the need for change and action
- Analyze activities to determine how desired end states are achieved or affected
- Identify ways to improve unit or organizational procedures
- Consider how information and communication technologies can improve effectiveness
- Model critical and creative thinking and encourage it from others.

Too often, leaders unknowingly discourage ideas. As a result, subordinates become less inclined to approach leaders with new ideas for doing business. Encourage a climate of reflection about the organization and encourage ideas for improvement. The concept of lifelong learning applies equally to the collective organization as well as to the individual.

CONCLUSION

Competent Army leaders do the nation, the Army, the unit, and themselves proud. In leading others, their leadership extends beyond the chain of command. They lead by example, and they communicate well.

Army leaders develop leadership skills in others by creating a positive environment, seeking self-improvement, and providing support. Support includes fostering growth, helping people learn, and providing counseling, coaching, and mentoring.

Army leaders also support mission accomplishment by providing direction and guidance, developing and executing plans, and accomplishing those missions consistently and ethically.

At the end of the day or a career, you should be able to look back confidently and say that your efforts have helped create an Army of consistent excellence. Whether you command an invasion force of thousands or supervise a small unit, you should be able to say that you made a positive difference.

Learning Assessment

1. Define, and give examples of, the four leader competencies that are critical to the skill of leading well.

2. What are the three competencies for developing people and organizations with a long-term perspective?

3. What are the three competencies involved in achieving results that will lead to success in accomplishing missions?

Key Words

compliance
commitment
climate
culture
self-awareness
counseling
coaching
mentoring

References

Field Manual 6-22, *Army Leadership: Competent, Confident, and Agile.* 12 October 2006.

Powell, C. (with Persico, J.). (1995). *My American Journey.* New York: Random House, Inc.

TIME MANAGEMENT

Key Points

1 The Process for Effective Time Management

2 Barriers to Time Management

3 SMART Goals

4 The POWER Model

In the Army, we speak of resources in terms of the three M's—men, money, and materials. To these three, we must add *time*. However, there is a distinct difference between time and the three other resources. If we do not use our money or materials today, they are available tomorrow. To a lesser degree, this is also true of men. It is not at all true of time, for time is a highly perishable commodity. An hour lost today is lost forever!

GEN Bruce C. Clarke

Introduction

To succeed as a leader, you must competently manage your resources—people, materials, and information. But perhaps the most precious resource you must manage is time. You can't replace time once it's gone.

Time management can also be called "personal management," since *you* are the only thing you can control. The time-management skills you develop as a Cadet and student will set a pattern for you as a future Army officer. That's why you must cultivate a process for effectively managing time *today.*

As this section points out, you will encounter significant barriers to effective time management. But you can overcome those barriers by setting goals and using systematic techniques.

The Process for Effective Time Management

Time management is a system for getting things done as efficiently and productively as possible. As you assume leadership responsibilities in the Army, your time will become even more valuable and its management more complex. You will need to manage not just your own time, but also the time of those you lead. When you put an efficient time-management system into action, you become a more effective leader because your team members perceive the value you place on both your time and theirs. The respect you show for their time will support everyone's efforts to become more efficient as the unit works toward meeting task deadlines and completing the mission schedule.

But it all starts here in ROTC, where your college studies require significant time-management skills. Your success at cultivating good time-management skills depends on your ability to set aside enough time for each of your classes, sports, and other activities. Doing this efficiently requires that you:

1. Recognize time wasters (black holes)
2. Set goals that will reduce patterns of wasted time
3. Adopt a system like the POWER model.

The POWER model, discussed later in this section, will move you toward your personal, professional, and career goals.

Barriers to Time Management

Have you ever heard of a black hole in astronomy? It's a point in space where a massive object pulls in all light near it. Nothing can escape.

Critical Thinking

Why do you think good time-management skills in an officer foster a productive work ethic among Soldiers in the officer's small Army unit? How does the value you place on time management translate into your team members wasting less time? Is there a trickle-down effect?

Your Calendar

Create your own semester calendar that includes all classes, key assignments, fitness workouts, sports events, extracurricular activities, social events, and any other important times for the coming semester. Use this calendar to determine how much time you still have open and to identify weeks (usually during midterms and finals) when you will need to plan and work ahead to avoid becoming overwhelmed.

Critical Thinking

Pick a goal you have set for yourself: Make enough money to buy a car; graduate with honors; land a summer internship at the state capital; improve your foreign language skills. Now turn it into a SMART goal using the model below. What did you learn about yourself and your goal?

In your schedule, "black holes" are spaces of time that eat into your productivity and prevent you from reaching your goals and the goals of others you work with. Black holes devour productive time and consume your efficiency.

The ability to identify black holes is the first and most important aspect of good time management. To do this, you should conduct an informal inventory of how you use your time. Consider a typical week and, within that week, a typical day. Most people are surprised at how much of their time is unfocused and unstructured—without a specific goal or purpose. Two causes of black holes are *procrastination*—putting things off—and *distracters*—things that take you away from your planned work or activities.

One way to fight procrastination is to realize that it will only make things worse. As George H. Lorimer, editor of the old *Saturday Evening Post,* once put it, "Putting off an easy thing makes it hard, and putting off a hard one makes it impossible." Distracters are often subtle. They might be talking on the phone with friends or relatives, losing track of time while Instant Messaging or playing video games, or helping other people on their projects. Or you may face an unexpected change in your work schedule. Learning to deal with distracters—saying no when necessary; turning off your cell phone, the IM, or the video game; negotiating your schedule with your supervisor; even finding a different spot to work or study away from distractions—builds the discipline that helps you stay on course.

Trying to overcome these two sources of black holes in your life goes a long way toward improving your use of available time. Additionally, the better you get at completing work on schedule, the better you'll get at scheduling time for recreation, hobbies, social activities, and other things you enjoy.

SMART Goals

Goal setting is a critical part of managing your time. If you don't know where you are going, how can you possibly calculate how long it will take you to get there?

TABLE 1.1	The **SMART** Model
Specific	make the goal concrete and clear
Measurable	decide how you will measure success in reaching the goal
Achievable	keep goals reasonable—milestones are helpful
Realistic	consider other factors that may affect the goal
Time-bound	make yourself accountable for a specific date

TABLE 1.2	The **POWER** Model
Prepare	set SMART goals
Organize	keep a calendar to know where you are, where you've been, and what's ahead
Work	work on establishing boundaries for your time—prioritize activities, avoid procrastinating, learn when to say no, and keep track of how long important tasks take
Evaluate	review how you're spending your time
Rethink	explore better and better ways of managing your time—identify what you need to change

The SMART model for goal setting, spelled out in Table 1.1, is a useful starting point for filling up black holes with useful activities—activities that get you where you want to go on your mission, in your career, and in your life.

The POWER Model

Once you have established your goals, you need to apply an effective time-management system to reach them. The POWER model outlined in the table above provides you with such a system. Practice techniques of good time management, such as completing tasks before moving to the next item or limiting distractions when doing exercise or homework. Some useful tools include a calendar, a weekly schedule, and a To-Do list. You can find sophisticated time-management aids at an office-supply store or perhaps your student bookstore. Your personal computer may also have useful time-management software.

In applying any time-management strategy, it's a good idea to keep in mind that you must be flexible. Since no one can foresee the future, you need to be willing to modify your plans to accommodate events and even a few surprises.

Tools for Productive Time Management:

1. Calendar
2. Weekly Schedule
3. To-Do List.

Time management is a system for getting things done as efficiently and productively as possible.

CONCLUSION

Successful leaders such as GEN Bruce Clarke recognize that using time more efficiently than the enemy is the first requirement for victory. They also realize that successful time management is a never-ending process.

As a Cadet and future Army leader, you must adopt time-management systems that allow you to envision how to achieve goals and objectives, plan to reach those goals, organize your time, and continue to improve.

It's time to take control of your time using the SMART technique and POWER model you've learned. Start today!

Learning Assessment

1. Trade one of your personal goals for this semester with a fellow Cadet in the class. How specific is his or her goal? Is it measurable? Achievable? Realistic? What is the timetable for achieving the goal? Brief your partner on your SMART observations about his or her goal.

2. Describe the POWER model for effective time management. List some of the barriers you might encounter and how you would plan to overcome them.

References

Clark, B. C. (1973). *Guidelines for the Leader and Commander*. Harrisburg, PA: Stackpole Books.

Ellis, D. (2003). *Becoming a Master Student* (10th Ed.). Boston: Houghton Mifflin Company.

Hughes, R. L., Ginnett, R. C., & Curphy, G. J. (1999). *Leadership: Enhancing the Lessons of Experience* (3rd Ed.). New York: Irwin/McGraw-Hill.

Section

2

HEALTH AND FITNESS

Key Points

1 Components of Fitness

2 Principles of Exercise

3 Frequency, Intensity, Time, Type (FITT)

4 Safety and Smart Training

5 Nutrition and Diet

> To every man there comes in his lifetime that special moment when he is figuratively tapped on the shoulder and asked to do a very special thing—unique to him and his talents. What a tragedy if that moment finds him unprepared or unqualified for that work.
>
> Sir Winston Churchill

Introduction

Have you ever noticed during sports competition that the individual or team that tires first often loses? It's the same for Soldiers. Your ability to cope with battlefield challenges depends greatly on your level of physical fitness. Physical fitness not only determines how well you perform in combat, but also enhances your overall quality of life, improves your productivity, and brings about positive physical and mental changes.

Your physical fitness benefits both the Army and you. The Army needs physically fit Soldiers, and when you are fit, you are more likely to lead an enjoyable, productive life.

As an officer, how important is your level of physical fitness? How does your fitness affect your unit's combat readiness?

You're probably tired of hearing how important it is to be in great shape as an officer, but it's a basic truth. You don't have to be the best at everything, but you definitely need to be one of the most physically fit Soldiers in your platoon. Morale improves when your Soldiers are constantly trying to beat you in a run or in an individual event like pull-ups or the rope climb. When that happened to me as a platoon leader that meant instant respect. My Soldiers all knew I could run or road march to the end with any of them. You can't motivate Soldiers in a road march if you are visibly in bad shape. It's a sad [sight] when a lieutenant can't lead his Soldiers physically. Ask yourself: How can you lead or motivate your Soldiers if you're not at the head of the formation? When it comes to the combat environment, physical fitness is crucial. If you allow your Soldiers to deploy in poor condition, you have failed them. Being physically fit out here [in Afghanistan] will help your Soldiers bear some of the rigors of a combat tour: less sleep, very random and increasingly changing rest patterns, extreme heat, heavy weights, and less than standard nutrition, to name a few. Staying in shape in a combat environment can be a tough task, because you may lack the time or facilities to exercise as you may have been able to in garrison. However, solid cardiovascular fitness will make a significant difference in higher elevations, and upper body and leg strength may prevent exhaustion from heavy gear in hot weather (3rd Brigade, 25th Infantry Division (L), 2005).

ILT Eliel Pimentel

Components of Fitness

Your physical fitness is your ability to perform physical work, training, and other activities throughout your daily work schedule. Physical fitness is multidimensional, and—based on your goals—some components will be more valuable than others.

Five key components define your physical fitness:

- *Cardiorespiratory (CR) endurance*—how efficiently your body delivers oxygen and nutrients for muscular activity and transports waste from the cells
- *Muscular strength*—the greatest amount of force your muscle or muscle group can exert in a single effort
- *Muscular endurance*—the ability of your muscle or muscle group to perform repeated movements for extended periods
- *Flexibility*—the ability to move your joints (elbow or knee, for example) or any group of joints through their entire normal range of motion
- *Body composition*—the amount of body fat you have in comparison with your total body mass.

Improving the first three of these components will improve your body composition by decreasing your body fat. Excessive body fat detracts from the other fitness measures, reduces your physical and mental performance, detracts from your appearance, and increases overall health risks. One measurement of body fat is as a percentage of your total weight. The Army's maximum allowable percentages of body fat, by age and gender, are listed in Figure 2.1.

Besides your physical fitness, you should also work to improve your *motor fitness*. Motor fitness—speed, agility, muscle power, eye-hand coordination, and eye-foot coordination—directly affect a Soldier's performance on the battlefield. Appropriate training will improve these elements up to each Soldier's individual potential.

The goal of the Army's fitness program is to improve physical and motor fitness through sound, progressive, mission-specific physical training at both the individual and unit levels.

Body Fat Standards				
Ages	17–20	21–27	28–39	40+
Males	20%	22%	24%	26%
Females	30%	32%	34%	36%

Figure 2.1 Body Fat Standards

Principles of Exercise

P-R-O-V-R-B-S

*the basic exercise principles—**P**rogression, **R**egularity, **O**verload, **V**ariety, **R**ecovery, **B**alance, and **S**pecificity*

Practicing the basic exercise principles is crucial for you to develop an effective fitness-training program. The principles of exercise apply to everyone at all levels of physical training, from the Olympic champion to the weekend golfer. They apply especially to fitness training for military personnel because having standard fitness principles across the organization saves time, energy, resources—and prevents injury.

You can easily remember the basic principles of exercise if you recall the **P-R-O-V-R-B-S** acronym:

P *Progression*—The intensity and duration of exercise must gradually increase to improve your fitness level. A good guideline for improvement is a 10 percent gain at specified intervals.

R *Regularity*—To achieve effective training you should schedule workouts in each of the first four fitness components at least three times a week. Regularity is also key in resting, sleeping, and following a good diet.

O *Overload*—The workload of each exercise session must exceed the normal demands placed on your body to bring about a training effect. You've often heard this expressed as "No pain, no gain." A fitness trainer, such as your ROTC instructor, can help you learn to tell the difference between pain that results from an optimum level of overload and pain that indicates potential injury.

V *Variety*—Changing activities reduces the boredom and increases your motivation to progress.

R *Recovery*—You should follow a hard day of training for a given component of fitness by an easier training or rest day for that component. This helps your body recover. Another way to promote recovery is to alternate the muscle groups you exercise every other day, especially when training for strength and muscle endurance.

B *Balance*—To be effective, a fitness program should address all the fitness components, since overemphasizing any one of them may detract from the others.

S *Specificity*—You must gear training toward specific goals. For example, Soldiers become better runners if their training emphasizes running drills and techniques. Although swimming is great exercise, it will not improve a two-mile-run time as much as a coordinated running program does.

Frequency, Intensity, Time, Type (FITT)

To succeed in any fitness-training program you undertake, you must track your frequency, intensity, time, and type of exercise (FITT). You can use the acronym **FITT** to remember these factors easily. While FITT is just one method of developing a proper long-term physical fitness regime, fitness experts agree that you need these factors to have an effective, safe daily workout program.

Frequency

Frequency is the number of workouts you perform each week. A basic guideline is three to five cardiovascular workouts, two to three strength workouts, two to five calisthenics workouts, and three to six flexibility workouts weekly.

Intensity

Intensity is how hard you work out. You can measure intensity by something called RPE (Rating of Perceived Exertion), which is a psychological scale and reflects how hard the workout feels to you.

The most commonly used indicator of your workout intensity is your heart rate. Ideally, you should stay within a productive heart-rate zone. You can use your age to find your Target Heart Rate (THR).

Finding Your THR

- Your maximum heart rate (MHR) is approximately 220 minus your age
- Your lowest target heart rate is equal to MHR × .60
- Your highest target heart rate is equal to MHR × .85.

FITT

the factors of a successful fitness-training program: frequency, intensity, time, and type

Rating of Perceived Exertion—Two RPE scales are in common use. The scales are either 6 to 20 or 0 to 10. Although the RPE scale of 6–20 does not measure heart rate, it theoretically correlates (for example: 6=60 heartbeats per minute, or bpm; 7 = 70bpm; 20 = 200bpm). Your RPE on the 6-20 scale should be between 12 and 16.

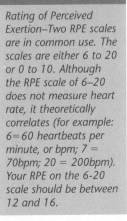

How Do You Take Your Pulse?

The first step is to find your pulse. If you are right-handed, use the pads of your index, middle, and ring fingers to find the pulse on your left wrist. Do the reverse if you are left-handed or wearing a watch on your left wrist. Move your fingers to just below the base of your thumb on your wrist and press down with your finger pads until you feel the throb of your pulse.

Time your pulse for 10 seconds with the first beat counted as zero rather than one. Then multiply this number by six to find the number of "heartbeats per minute (bpm)." When you measure your heartbeats per minute during a workout, you want the rate to be within your target heart zone.

Your THR zone is between the lowest and highest THR calculated above. As you begin your exercise routine, your heart rate should be on the lower end of your THR zone. Exercising above the zone increases your risk of injury and reduces your ability to perform optimally.

Easy Versus Hard

Exercise in moderation. Never exercise a particular muscle group hard (at a high intensity or for a long time) two days in a row. You should always follow a hard workout with a light day or a day off. For the best development, more is not always better.

Time

Like intensity, the *time* you spend exercising depends on the type of exercise you are doing. At least 20 to 30 continuous minutes of intense exercise will improve cardiorespiratory endurance. For muscular endurance and strength, exercise time equals the number of repetitions you do. For the average person, eight to 12 repetitions with enough resistance to cause muscle failure will improve both muscular endurance and strength. As you progress, you will make better strength gains by doing two or three sets of each resistance exercise.

Use flexibility exercises or stretches for varying times, depending on the objective of the session. While warming-up before a run, for example, hold each stretch for 10 to 15 seconds. To improve flexibility, stretch during your cool-down as well, holding each stretch for 30 to 60 seconds. If flexibility improvement is your goal, devote at least one session per week to developing that component.

Type

Type refers to the kind of exercise you perform. When choosing the type, consider the principle of specificity. Some people overemphasize cross training and you should avoid this pitfall. For example, to improve your level of CR fitness (the major fitness component in the two-mile run), do CR types of exercises. The basic rule is that to improve performance, you must practice the particular exercise, activity, or skill you want to improve. For example, to be good at push-ups, *you must do push-ups.* No other exercise will improve push-up performance as effectively.

Safety and Smart Training

Before you begin an exercise program, ask your physician to give you a checkup. Your doctor can advise you to avoid or participate in activities based on your current health and history. Be sure to stay within your limits. If you are injured while exercising, remember to **P-R-I-C-E** your recovery.

P-R-I-C-E

the procedures for early injury treatment: protect, rest, ice, compression, and elevation

P   *Protect*—Protect the injured area from further injury. You can wrap it lightly in an elastic bandage or wear a padded brace. Do not tightly or heavily tape up an injury, as good circulation is important to healing.

Critical Thinking

Describe a stressful physical event you have experienced (in training, sports, work, or school). How might improved physical fitness have helped you?

R *Rest*—Rest the injured area. Use a sling, cane, brace, or crutch as necessary to take your weight and decrease activity off the affected body part. Keep the joint or muscle as inactive as possible.

I *Ice*—Apply ice to the injured area for five to 15 minutes. Wrap several handfuls of crushed ice in a towel and hold it on and around the injured area. Many people instinctively try to soak an injury in warm water, and while this increases blood flow to the injury, it does not ease the inflammation and swelling.

C *Compression*—Wrap an elastic bandage around the ice to compress the injured area lightly—but not enough to cut off circulation to the injured area. After the cold compress, wrap the affected area lightly in an elastic bandage or use a flexible brace. Don't wrap any injury too tightly, as this will cut off good circulation to the injury.

E *Elevation*—Raise the affected area slightly to reduce swelling and inflammation.

In addition to P-R-I-C-E, you can talk to your doctor about using anti-inflammatory medication as needed, such as aspirin, acetaminophen, or ibuprofen. You should check to see if you have allergies to these drugs before use. *Under no circumstances* should you take them while drinking alcohol.

Smart Training

You live in your skin and know how your body feels and works best. That is why you should take responsibility for managing your own fitness-training program. Knowing your limits and capabilities is key to setting goals for physical fitness improvement.

Smart training means observing some well-recognized guidelines:

- *Progression*—As you have seen, increasing intensity and/or duration by 10 percent at regular intervals is a good idea.
- *Warm-up*—Always take a few minutes to warm up your muscles to reduce your chances of injury. Your warm-up should include some running in place or slow jogging, stretching, and calisthenics. It should last five to seven minutes and should occur just before the CR or muscular endurance and strength part of the workout.
- *Stretching*—Critical to improving your flexibility, stretching increases your overall fitness and reduces the chance of muscle injury. After exercising, you should cool down by walking and stretching until your heartbeat reaches 100 bpm and heavy sweating stops.
- *Mechanics*—Concentrate on your form when exercising. Maintain intensity levels, but don't let your form suffer. You will not improve by doing exercises or repetitions incorrectly—you only increase your chances of injury.
- *Healthy Diet*—You've heard that "You are what you eat." Food is your source of strength and energy. What you eat will dramatically affect your ability to maintain and improve your overall fitness.

Nutrition and Diet

Complete physical fitness is not just about exercise, but also includes good nutrition and a sensible diet. You maintain a healthy body weight and body fat percentage through sound diet and exercise to ensure the best health, fitness, and physical performance. All of these things are relevant to maintaining military readiness and achieving peak performance.

The Food Pyramid

Knowing the US Department of Agriculture (USDA) Guidelines and understanding the **Food Pyramid** to determine your daily requirements of carbohydrates, proteins, and fat will help you make healthy food choices and improve your physical fitness. A new version

Food Pyramid

an Agriculture Department nutrition tool to help you choose the foods and amounts right for you

of the pyramid debuted in 2005 and shows the types of foods and the proportions that most healthy people should eat.

In addition, USDA has an interactive website to help you track your diet. Visit *www.MyPyramid.gov*, where you can personalize your diet by age, gender, and general fitness level.

A healthy diet has the right kinds of foods in the right amounts. Look at the Food Pyramid in Figure 2.2. The person walking up the steps on the left represents the need for daily physical activity and different individuals' different nutrition needs. The different widths of the food group bands indicate the need for proportion—how much you should choose from each group.

The six color bands symbolize the food you need daily from each group for good health.

- Orange (grains): USDA recommends you eat at least three ounces of whole-grain bread, cereal, crackers, rice, or pasta every day. Half your grains should be whole. To make sure you're eating whole grains, look for the word "whole" before the grain name on the list of ingredients.
- Green (vegetables): You should vary vegetable servings, eating more dark green vegetables, orange vegetables, and dried beans and peas.
- Red (fruits): Eat a variety of fresh, frozen, canned, or dried fruit, but go easy on fruit juices, which may contain empty calories in the form of added sugars and sweeteners.
- Yellow (oils and fats): Most of your fats should come from fish, nuts, and vegetable oils. Limit your consumption of solid fats like butter, stick margarine, shortening, and lard. Instead, when possible, consume foods with omega fish oils, which help maintain your cardiovascular health.
- Blue (milk, an important source of calcium): Choose low-fat or fat-free milk. If you don't or can't drink milk, choose lactose-free products or other sources of calcium, such as hard cheese (cheddar, mozzarella, Swiss, or parmesan), cottage cheese, and low-fat or fat-free yogurt (including frozen yogurt).
- Purple (meat, beans, and eggs): You may notice that this band, like the yellow band for oils, is thinner than the others. This visually reminds you to "Go lean on protein." Choose low-fat or lean meats and poultry that are baked, broiled, or grilled

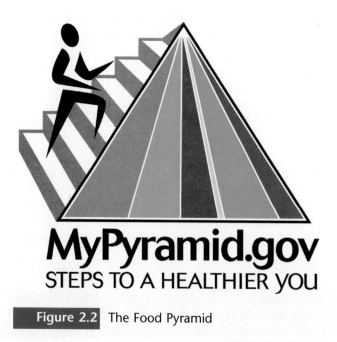

Figure 2.2 The Food Pyramid

rather than fried. Vary your choices, including more fish, beans, peas, nuts, and seeds. If meat typically covers most of your plate, take another look at the Food Pyramid.

Substances to Avoid

Proper health and fitness reflect a mature decision you make to set a good example for your unit. Moreover, it's a wise lifestyle choice that will help you live a longer, more productive life. As an officer in training, you should avoid substances that detract from your physical performance and even harm your health (drugs, tobacco, alcohol, etc.).

Alcohol

Many people in our society have traditionally believed that alcohol—wine, beer, or hard liquor—relaxes you, increases your self-confidence, and alters your perception of stress or fatigue. It's true that for most people, light consumption of alcoholic beverages can be a pleasant social diversion. But habitual, heavy drinking or binge drinking can cause severe dehydration, decreased performance, dependence, and harm to your metabolism.

The Army expects you to exercise your judgment and drink responsibly, which includes obeying all laws regarding driving and the legal drinking age, if you choose to drink at all. And never drink to "quench your thirst" before, during, or after a workout.

Tobacco

Cigarettes, cigars, and "smokeless" tobaccos contain a whole gamut of cancer-causing chemicals that provide no positive health effects. Some maintain that the "buzz" from tobacco leads to improved performance and reaction times, but no medical evidence supports this position. In the interest of good physical fitness, it is better if you don't smoke at all. If you do smoke, however, limit your intake and avoid smoking before, during, and after workouts. Smoking increases your heart rate and blood pressure.

Controlled Substances

Controlled substances are those strictly regulated by the government and may require medical prescription. You should use such substances only under medical supervision. Other drugs such as amphetamines, narcotics, steroids, and other so-called "performance enhancing drugs" are illegal and banned by the military. These drugs change performance by increasing central nervous system arousal. They increase your heart rate and blood pressure and they may cause dizziness, nausea, irritability, insomnia—even death. No one interested in good physical fitness consumes these substances; they can only detract from your performance in both the short and long term. The Army forbids their use.

You can find the Army's health-promotion and wellness website at www.hooah4health.com.

CONCLUSION

Health and fitness are integral parts of military life. They are critical for readiness and important to the well-being of the individual Soldier. Although not a cure-all, a properly planned fitness program yields many physical and mental benefits. Effective physical training can improve your body composition (decrease body fat and increase lean body weight), ability to work, mental alertness, self-confidence, and general well-being. Exercise also decreases metabolic and mental health risks, such as high blood pressure, coronary heart disease, stroke, anxiety, depression, and much more.

With assistance from your ROTC instructors, you now should be able to apply the Army's general physical fitness principles to create a self-directed physical training program that meets your needs and fulfills your personal and professional goals.

Learning Assessment

1. What are the components of physical fitness?
2. Describe the principles of physical fitness as expressed by the acronym P-R-O-V-R-B-S.
3. Explain the key factors of physical fitness training (FITT).
4. Explain how you can apply the USDA Food Pyramid to make improvements in your diet.

Key Words

P-R-O-V-R-B-S
FITT
P-R-I-C-E
Food Pyramid

References

3rd Brigade, 25 Infantry Division (L). May 2005. *Operation Enduring Freedom: Afghan Leader Book, April 2004–May 2005*. Retrieved 9 August 2005 from http://rotc.blackboard.com/courses/1/CCR/content/_488714_1/Operation_Enduring_Freedom_Leader_Book_Apr_04___May_05.pdf

AR 40-501, *Standards of Medical Fitness*. 14 December 2007.

AR 350-15, *Army Physical Fitness Program*. November 1989.

AR 600-9, *The Army Weight Control Program*. 27 November 2006.

DA PAM 350-18, *US Military Academy Cadet Army Orientation Training*. 28 May 1974.

Field Manual 7-1, *Battle Focused Training*. 15 September 2003.

Field Manual 21-18, *Foot Marches*. 1 June 1990.

Field Manual 21-20, *Physical Fitness Training*. Change 1. 1 October 1998.

INTRODUCTION TO STRESS MANAGEMENT

Key Points

1 Defining Stress

2 Causes of Stress

3 Symptoms of Distress

4 Managing Stress

5 Depression

6 Suicide

Remember that the mind and body are one and that psychological health is just as important as physical health to your overall well-being.

Health Tips from Army Medicine

Introduction

Stress is a fact of life, wherever you are and whatever you are doing. You cannot avoid stress, but you can learn to manage it so it doesn't manage you.

Changes in our lives—such as going to college, getting married, changing jobs, or illness—are frequent sources of stress. Keep in mind that changes that cause stress can also benefit you. Moving away from home to attend college, for example, creates personal-development opportunities—new challenges, friends, and living arrangements. That is why it's important to know yourself and carefully consider the causes of stress. Learning to do this takes time, and although you cannot avoid stress, the good news is that you can minimize the harmful effects of stress, such as depression or hypertension. The key is to develop an awareness of how you interpret, and react to, circumstances. This awareness will help you develop coping techniques for managing stress. For example, as an Army platoon leader, managing stress will require techniques that include an awareness of yourself and your Soldiers.

As you will see, the stress you encounter as a student differs in intensity from what you may experience in the Army, particularly while deployed or in combat. The principles and techniques you use to manage stress are similar, however, as reported by this second lieutenant after returning from the war in Afghanistan:

stress

physical and psychological responses to the pressures of daily life

How do you combat fatigue, stress, and fear in yourself? In your Soldiers?

In the past seven months (in Afghanistan) I have learned a lot about how I deal with combat fatigue and stress. I have found that finding a little time for myself each day or even each week allows me to regenerate and focus. Having a sense of humor and not taking things so personally have also helped reduce my stress levels. Keeping a notebook with me at all times and writing tasks, missions, or even just things to do has helped me keep my mind at ease, rather than thinking that I have forgotten to do something. Maintaining communication with my family and friends, whether through e-mail or phone conversations, also keeps me grounded . . . (3rd Brigade, 25th Infantry Division (L)).

2LT Gisela Mendonca

Defining Stress

Stress is the way human beings react both physically and mentally to changes, events, and situations in their lives. People experience stress in different ways and for different reasons. The reaction is based on your perception of an event or situation. If you view a situation negatively, you will likely feel *distressed*—overwhelmed, oppressed, or out of control. Distress is the more familiar form of stress. The other form, *eustress*, results from a "positive" view of an event or situation, which is why it is also called "good stress."

Eustress helps you rise to a challenge and can be an antidote to boredom because it engages focused energy. That energy can easily turn to *distress*, however, if something causes you to view the situation as unmanageable or out of control. Many people regard public speaking or airplane flights as very stressful—causing physical reactions such as an increased heart rate and a loss of appetite—while others look forward to the event. It's often a question of perception: A positive stressor for one person can be a negative stressor for another.

Causes of Stress

The most frequent reasons for "stressing out" fall into three main categories:

1. The unsettling effects of change
2. The feeling that an outside force is challenging or threatening you
3. The feeling that you have lost personal control.

Life events such as marriage, changing jobs, divorce, or the death of a relative or friend are the most common causes of stress. Although life-threatening events are less common, they can be the most physiologically and psychologically acute. They are usually associated with public service career fields in which people experience intense stress levels because of imminent danger and a high degree of uncertainty—police officer, fire and rescue worker, emergency relief worker, and the military.

You may not plan to enter a high-stress career, but as a college student, you may find that the demands of college life can create stressful situations. The National Institute of Mental Health (NIMH) notes some of the more common stressors for college students:

- Increased academic demands
- Being on your own in a new environment
- Changes in family relations
- Financial responsibilities
- Changes in your social life
- Exposure to new people, ideas, and temptations
- Awareness of your sexual identity and orientation
- Preparing for life after graduation.

Symptoms of Distress

Symptoms of stress fall into three general, but interrelated, categories—physical, mental, and emotional. Review this list carefully. If you find yourself frequently experiencing these symptoms, you are likely feeling *distressed*:

- Headaches
- Fatigue
- Gastrointestinal problems
- Hypertension (high blood pressure)
- Heart problems, such as palpitations
- Inability to focus/lack of concentration
- Sleep disturbances, whether it's sleeping too much or an inability to sleep
- Sweating palms/shaking hands
- Anxiety
- Sexual problems.

Even when you don't realize it, stress can cause or contribute to serious physical disorders. It increases hormones such as adrenaline and corticosterone, which affect your metabolism, immune reactions, and other stress responses. That can lead to increases in your heart rate, respiration, blood pressure, and physical demands on your internal organs.

Behavioral changes are also expressions of stress. They can include:

- Irritability
- Disruptive eating patterns (overeating or under eating)
- Harsh treatment of others
- Increased smoking or alcohol consumption

Stress management is key to academic success.

- Isolation
- Compulsive shopping.

A sustained high level of stress is no laughing matter. It can affect every area of your life—productivity in the workplace and classroom, increased health risks, and relationships, to name just a few.

Managing Stress

As noted in the Introduction, you can learn to manage stress. The first step is understanding yourself better—how you react in different situations, what causes you stress, and how you behave when you feel stressed. Once you've done that, take the following steps:

Set priorities. Use the time-management tips you learned in Section 1. Make a To-Do list. Decide what is really important to get done today, and what can wait. This helps you to know that you are working on your most immediate priorities, and you don't have the stress of trying to remember what you should be doing.

Practice facing stressful moments. Think about the event or situation you expect to face and rehearse your reactions. Find ways to practice dealing with the challenge. If you know that speaking in front of a group frightens you, practice doing it, perhaps with a trusted friend or fellow student. If the pressure of taking tests causes you to freeze up, buy some practice tests at the school bookstore or online and work with them when there are no time pressures.

Examine your expectations. Try to set realistic goals. It's good to push yourself to achieve, but make sure your expectations are realistic. Watch out for perfectionism. Be satisfied with doing the best you can. Nobody's perfect—not you, not your fellow Cadet, nobody. Allow people the liberty to make mistakes, and remember that mistakes can be a good teacher.

Live a healthy lifestyle. Get plenty of exercise. Eat healthy foods. Allow time for rest and relaxation. Find a relaxation technique that works for you—prayer, yoga, meditation, or breathing exercises. Look for the humor in life, and enjoy yourself.

Learn to accept change as a part of life. Nothing stays the same. Develop a support system of friends and relatives you can talk to when needed. Believe in yourself and your potential. Remember that many people from disadvantaged backgrounds have gone on to enjoy great success in life.

At the same time, avoid those activities that promise release from stress while actually adding to it. Drinking alcohol (despite what all those TV commercials imply), drinking caffeine, smoking, using narcotics (including marijuana), and overeating all add to the body's stress in addition to their other harmful effects.

Here are some other strategies for dealing with stress:

* Schedule time for vacation, breaks in your routine, hobbies, and fun activities.
* Try to arrange for uninterrupted time to accomplish tasks that need your concentration. Arrange some leisure time during which you can do things that you really enjoy.
* Avoid scheduling too many appointments, meetings, and classes back-to-back. Allow breaks to catch your breath. Take a few slow, deep breaths whenever you feel stressed. Breathe from the abdomen and, as you exhale, silently say to yourself, "I feel calm."
* Become an expert at managing your time. Read books, view videos, and attend seminars on time management. Once you cut down on time wasters, you'll find more time to recharge yourself.
* Learn to say "no." Setting limits can minimize stress. Spend time on *your* main responsibilities and priorities rather than allowing other people's priorities or needs to dictate how you spend your time.
* Exercise regularly to reduce muscle tension and promote a sense of well-being.
* Tap into your support network. Family, friends, and social groups can help when dealing with stressful events.

Depression

depression

a common mental illness that affects a person's body, mood, and thought—it causes people to lose pleasure from daily life, can complicate other medical conditions, and can even lead to suicide

Unfortunately, a person's inability to deal with stress can often lead to clinical **depression**. People with depression have similar symptoms to stress, except the symptoms are not temporary—they can last for weeks at a time. Because of the sustained symptoms, the effect on the body, mood, and behavior is often more serious than with temporary stress. Depression can have severe effects on your eating habits, your relationships, your ability to work and study, and how you think and feel. The illness is not unique to a particular group of people or area of the country. Millions of adult Americans, including many college students, suffer from clinical depression.

It's important to understand that clinical depression is a real, not an "imaginary" illness. It's not a passing mood or a sign of personal weakness. It demands treatment—and 80 percent of those treated begin to feel better in just a few weeks.

According to NIMH, the following symptoms are signs of major depression:

- Sadness, anxiety, or "empty" feelings
- Decreased energy, fatigue, being "slowed down"
- Loss of interest or pleasure in usual activities
- Sleep disturbances (insomnia, oversleeping, or waking much earlier than usual)
- Appetite and weight changes (either loss or gain)
- Feelings of hopelessness, guilt, and worthlessness
- Thoughts of death or suicide, or suicide attempts
- Difficulty concentrating, making decisions, or remembering
- Irritability or excessive crying
- Chronic aches and pains not explained by another physical condition.

It's normal to have some signs of depression some of the time. But the NIMH says that if someone has five or more symptoms for two weeks or longer, or suffers noticeable changes in normal functioning, that person should go to a mental health professional for evaluation. Depressed people often may not be thinking clearly and may therefore not seek help on their own. They frequently require encouragement from others—they "need help to get help."

Mental health professionals say depression among college students is a serious problem. A recent UCLA survey of college freshmen indicates that today's students are feeling more overwhelmed and stressed than students did 15 years ago. The National Mental Health Association reports that more than 30 percent of college freshmen report feeling overwhelmed a great deal of the time.

If you think you might be depressed, you should talk with a qualified health-care or mental-health professional. The resident adviser in your dorm, the student health center, your family health-care provider, or a clergy member can help steer you to treatment resources. Several effective treatments for depression are available, and—depending on the severity of the symptoms—can provide relief in just a few weeks. But individuals respond differently to treatment. If you don't start feeling better after a few weeks, talk to your treatment provider about other treatments, or seek a second opinion.

Suicide

As noted above, severe depression often manifests itself in thoughts about death or suicide, or in suicide attempts. Many people are understandably uncomfortable talking about suicide, but doing so can save lives. The NIMH reports that in 2000, suicide was the 11th leading cause of death for all Americans and the third leading cause of death for those aged 15 to 24. While women are three times as likely to attempt suicide as men, men are four times as likely as women to succeed.

There are many common myths about suicide:

- *If someone wants to die, nobody can stop that person.* False. Most people thinking about suicide don't want to die: They want help.
- *If I ask someone about suicide, I'll give that person the idea.* False. That you cared enough to ask may offer comfort to the person.
- *Suicide comes "out of the blue."* False. Usually, the person exhibits several warning signs.

Critical Thinking

What are some of the stressors you currently face? Develop an action plan to improve your stress management skills by either eliminating a cause of stress or reducing its effects on you. Incorporate at least three techniques described in this section of your textbook.

You should always take suicidal thoughts, impulses, or behavior seriously. If you are thinking or talking about hurting or killing yourself, or know someone who is, *seek help immediately*. The NIMH recommends you turn to your student health center; a family physician; a professor, coach, or adviser; a member of the clergy; a local suicide or emergency hotline (one number is 1-800-SUICIDE); or a hospital emergency room. If you have to, call 911.

Some of the warning signs of suicide include:

- Talking about suicide
- Statements about hopelessness, helplessness, or worthlessness
- Preoccupation with death
- Becoming suddenly happier or calmer
- Losing interest in things one cares about
- Setting one's affairs in order for no apparent reason—such as giving away prized possessions or making final arrangements regarding finances and property.

More on Stress

If you would like to do further research on stress, more information is available at these websites:

1. US Army HOOAH 4 Health:
   www.hooah4health.com/mind/combatstress/default.htm
2. If you enter "stress management" into web search engines such as Google, you will find numerous references from which you can choose.

CONCLUSION

Stress can have consequences far beyond temporary feelings of pressure. While you can't avoid stress, you can learn to manage it and develop skills to cope with the events or situations you find stressful. By learning to cope with stress, and by recognizing the symptoms of depression and the warning signs of suicide, you'll be better prepared to help not only yourself, but also friends, fellow students, and the Soldiers you will someday lead.

Learning Assessment

1. Define stress and list some of the symptoms.
2. Explain what causes stress and list some of the ways to deal with it.
3. What is the difference between stress and depression?
4. List some warning signs of suicide.

Key Words

stress
depression

References

3rd Brigade, 25 Infantry Division (L). May 2005. *Operation Enduring Freedom: Afghan Leader Book, April 2004–May 2005.* Retrieved 5 August 2005 from http://rotc.blackboard.com/courses/1/CCR/content/_488714_1/Operation_Enduring_Freedom_Leader_Book_Apr_04___May_05.pdf

Ayala, S. (October–November 2002). Stress. *Health Tips from Army Medicine.* Madigan Army Medical Center, Fort Lewis, WA. Retrieved 13 June 2008 from http://www.armymedicine.army.mil/hc/healthtips/08/stress.cfm

National Institute of Mental Health. (2003). In Harm's Way: Suicide in America. Retrieved 11 June 2008 from http://www.nimh.nih.gov/publicat/harmsway.cfm

National Institute of Mental Health. (2004). What do these students have in common? Retrieved 10 August 2005 from www.nimh.nih.gov/publicat/students.cfm

National Mental Health Association. (2005). Finding Hope and Help: College Student and Depression Pilot Initiative. Retrieved 11 August 2005 from http://www.nmha.org/camh/college/index.cfm

Pawelek, J., & Jeanise, S. (March 2004). Mental Health Myths. *Health Tips from Army Medicine.* Retrieved 13 June 2008 from http://www.armymedicine.army.mil/hc/healthtips/13/200403mhmyths.cfm

Vitt, A., & Calohan, J. (April–May 2002). Suicide Warning Signs. *Health Tips from Army Medicine.* Retrieved 13 June 2008 from http://www.armymedicine.army.mil/hc/healthtips/08/suicidewarning.cfm

Section

4

GOAL SETTING AND PERSONAL MISSION STATEMENT

Key Points

1 Defining a Vision

2 Writing a Personal Mission Statement

3 Writing SMART Goals to Support a Vision and Mission

If you do not know where you are going, every road will get you nowhere.

Henry Kissinger, former US Secretary of State

Introduction

Successful Army leaders such as George Washington, Dwight D. Eisenhower, and Colin Powell did not attain greatness by luck. They knew what they believed and where they wanted to go. They were men with solid values and defined goals, as well as a clear vision and sense of mission. Because of their resolve, when they were tested, they were ready to meet the challenges they faced.

As a college student and ROTC Cadet, you face many decisions in the next few years that will affect the course of your life. This section will discuss how you can develop a vision for your life based on your values, write a personal mission statement, and set concrete, attainable personal goals. GEN Colin Powell noted the value of vision when he wrote down his 13 "rules for command."

GEN Colin Powell's Rules for Command

1. It ain't as bad as you think. It will look better in the morning.
2. Get mad, then get over it.
3. Avoid having your ego so close to your position that when your position falls, your ego goes with it.
4. It can be done!
5. Be careful what you choose. You may get it.
6. Don't let adverse facts stand in the way of a good decision.
7. You can't make someone else's choices. You shouldn't let someone else make yours.
8. Check small things.
9. Share credit.
10. Remain calm. Be kind.
11. Have a vision. Be demanding.
12. Don't take counsel of your fears or nay sayers.
13. Perpetual optimism is a force multiplier.

GEN Colin Powell

Critical Thinking

Based on GEN Powell's rules, what do you think he values? How could guidelines like these help you at college?

Defining a Vision

vision

a vivid description of the future that focuses your efforts—your vision is a reference point to guide your decisions, planning, and actions for the future

Your **vision** is the guiding theme of your personal life and professional career. Your vision is a long-term picture that establishes your priorities for making short-term decisions. Your vision grows out of your values and, as a Cadet, from the core Army Values you've already studied in previous sections.

Some people ask: "Why have a vision? Why does it matter?" The answer is that vision provides direction for your life and context for your decisions. If you don't know where you are going—any road can take you there. To lead people—whether fellow Cadets, fellow students, Soldiers, or employees—you need to know where you want to go. Vision motivates people to perform to their potential and beyond. A vision reduces the likelihood of complacency, drifting, and mediocre performance.

Your strong vision also makes you a role model. When your subordinates see that you have a clearly defined vision in your life and career, they will imitate you. When you become a second lieutenant, your Soldiers will look to you and your vision to provide the framework and context not only for your command decisions but also for the orders you give and the work you ask them to perform.

Which Words Best Express Your Values?

Ambitious
Adaptable
Career-minded
Capable
Courageous
Family-focused
Flexible
Honest
Independent
Logical
Obedient
Responsible
Self-controlled
Health-focused
Environmentally
  conscious
Spiritually focused
Others?

Many people and organizations find it helpful to record their vision as a vision statement. This forces you to ask yourself some profound questions: What should your vision statement say? What do you want to be known for? What are the most important things in your life? What do you want to achieve? Think also about the model you will want to project to your fellow students, Cadets, and, when you become an officer, to your Soldiers. Your vision should include what matters most to you, so when you write your vision statement, you need to reflect on and clarify your values. Think about the words that best express who you want to be.

A vision statement is usually very concise—no more than a sentence or two. So you'll need to select only about five or six values or characteristics to go into your vision statement (see the marginal text for a partial list).

Of course, your priorities will shift as you get older, gain experience, and advance in your career. That's why you should think about your vision statement as a living document, something that can and will change with time. You are not carving your vision in stone. Plan to revisit your statement, reflect on your priorities, and make changes every year or two.

Here's an example of a possible vision statement: *"I am determined to be the best ROTC Cadet among my peers, the best student to my teachers, the best athlete to my coaches, and the best son (or daughter) to my parents that I can possibly be. I pledge to use my strengths to better my weaknesses in all areas of my life."*

Sounds like a promise, doesn't it? That's what a vision statement is: a commitment to your future, put into words to help guide your efforts. Can you draft your vision statement now?

Writing a Personal Mission Statement

mission

your purpose—personal and professional—which guides your planning and actions as you put your vision into practice

The next step is to develop your **mission** statement. A mission statement describes your fundamental purpose. It guides the planning and implementation of your vision. It's a description that encompasses your own personal objectives, long-term goals, and guiding philosophy—all of which touch your professional life, as well.

In a corporate environment, a mission statement is a description of what an organization wants to accomplish in business. Similarly, your own mission statement should embrace your personal and professional goals. And the best goals come from what *motivates* you.

Once you have reflected on your values and your motivations, you should be able to craft your mission statement without too much trouble. Remember, a mission statement should not be the Ten Commandments for the rest of your life. It should project perhaps three to five years into the future. Just as you will do with your vision, you should revisit your mission statement and adjust it as your life circumstances change—because they *will* change.

Here's an example of a possible mission statement that supports the vision statement on the previous page: *"During the next four years in college I want to achieve excellent grades (B+ or higher) in all my coursework. I will also seek experience in a leadership role in a club, team, or activity, and I will actively seek internships, networking opportunities, and other hands-on experience. In addition, I will volunteer in at least one community service organization on a regular basis. I will keep in close touch with my family as often as possible and help my parents with my younger siblings."*

Notice anything? The mission statement takes the aims of the vision statement and makes them more concrete. The tone of the mission statement is confident and determined. Do any of the aims expressed in this mission statement seem unreasonable or unreachable?

Now, you try it!

Writing SMART Goals to Support a Vision and Mission

To bring your vision to life and accomplish your personal mission, you need to do one more thing: set some definite **goals**. One way to think about these goals is to think of your vision and mission as your life *strategy* and your goals as those *tactics* that will help you work within and toward that strategy.

Think of goals as the dots you connect to create the picture described by your vision and mission. They are the *short-term milestones* that will keep you on track and help you achieve your greater mission.

But how can you write effective goals? One technique is to write SMART goals, which you read about in the section on time management. SMART goals have built-in features that help you attain them. They are specific, measurable, attainable, realistic, and time bound. Here's an example of how to write a SMART goal.

If your vision, is to be an excellent student and your mission in support of that is to attain excellent grades in all four years of college, how exactly do you get there? A SMART goal that implements those vision and mission statements might be to *get an A in math this semester by joining and regularly attending a study group by the third week of the term.* Notice how the goal sets a specific measurable benchmark and an attainable deadline. You can write goals for each of your classes and activities, if you find that helpful.

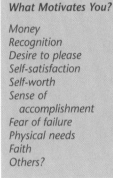

What Motivates You?

Money
Recognition
Desire to please
Self-satisfaction
Self-worth
Sense of accomplishment
Fear of failure
Physical needs
Faith
Others?

goals

things you set out to do or achieve—short or long term—to fulfill your mission and realize your vision

SMART Goals:

Specific
Measurable
Attainable
Realistic
Time bound

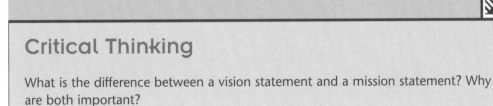

Critical Thinking

What is the difference between a vision statement and a mission statement? Why are both important?

The last step in this process is to prioritize your SMART goals. Put them in order of importance, time due or time required to complete, overall attainability, cost, geographic location, outside help required, or other organizing scheme. You should not randomly list your goals; otherwise, you'll waste time and effort. Whether you do the small stuff first and the challenging ones later—or vice versa—is up to you, but *organize* your time and effort.

> Leadership is not magnetic personality—that can just as well be a glib tongue. It is not "making friends and influencing people"—that is flattery. Leadership is lifting a person's vision to higher sights, the raising of a person's performance to a higher standard, the building of a personality beyond its normal limitations.
>
> Peter Drucker

CONCLUSION

Crafting a personal vision statement, mission statement, and SMART goals is a key step in developing your identity as an adult, a college student, an ROTC Cadet, and a future Army leader. Vision, mission, and goals will help bring out the best qualities of your personality and make you a desirable role model for your peers and your subordinates in the future.

You never know the limit of your potential until you reach it—and then step further. A clear vision, a specific mission, and definite goals are important tools that will help you reach and then exceed your expectations.

Learning Assessment

1. Define vision and describe a vision statement.
2. Describe a personal mission statement and its purpose.
3. Describe SMART goals and how they support a vision and mission.

Key Words

vision
mission
goals

References

Powell, C. (with Persico, J.). (1995). *My American Journey*. New York: Random House, Inc.

Department of the Army. (1984). *Quotes for the Military Writer*. (Cited in DA PAM 600-65, *Leadership Statements and Quotes*. 1 November 1985.) Retrieved 12 July 2005 from http://www.army.mil/usapa/epubs/pdf/p600_65.pdf

Section

5

INTRODUCTION TO EFFECTIVE ARMY COMMUNICATION

Key Points

1 **The Communication Process**

2 **Five Tips for Effective Communication**

3 **Four Tips for Effective Writing**

4 **Three Tips for Effective Speaking**

> … an order that *can* be misunderstood *will* be misunderstood.
>
> Field Marshal Helmuth von Moltke

Introduction

Your success as a military leader depends on your ability to think critically and creatively and to communicate your intention and decision to others. The ability to communicate clearly—to get your intent and ideas across so that others understand your message and act on it—is one of the primary qualities of leadership.

While you are a college student, your channels of communication include presentations and term papers. When you become an Army officer, these channels will expand to include training meetings, briefings, and operations orders. As you will see, the means to effective Army communication is to develop your speaking and writing skills so that you can deliver any message to any audience effectively. Keep in mind that communication also includes receiving messages from others through reading and listening.

Early in your Army career, much of your communication is *direct*. For example, coaching your Soldiers often requires communication that is one-on-one, immediate, and spoken. Later in your Army career, as your leadership responsibilities increase, you will inform subordinates and leaders through written orders, procedures, memos, and e-mail. This form of communication is *indirect*—it goes through other people or processes, is time-delayed, and written.

Your ability to communicate—to write, speak, and listen—affects your ability to inform, teach, coach, and motivate those around you. The good news is that you can develop these essential skills. This section will discuss the communication process and then provide you tips for effective writing and speaking.

It is difficult to overemphasize the importance of these skills. In military operations, as elsewhere, the inability to write and speak well can have tremendous costs. History is replete with examples of misunderstood messages. For example, many Civil War scholars believe that victory at Gettysburg may have depended on how a subordinate interpreted Confederate GEN Robert E. Lee's use of the word "practicable."

GEN Robert E. Lee

Day One at Gettysburg: Vague Orders Have Significant Consequences

[On the first day of the battle of Gettysburg, Pa., Confederate attacks drove Union troops through the town to the top of Cemetery Hill, a half-mile south.] The battle so far appeared to be another great Confederate victory.

But Lee could see that so long as the enemy held the high ground south of town, the battle was not over. He knew that the rest of the [Union] Army of the Potomac must be hurrying toward Gettysburg; his best chance to clinch the victory was to seize those hills and ridges before they arrived. So Lee gave [LTG Richard S.] Ewell discretionary orders to attack Cemetery Hill "if practicable." Had [LTG Thomas J. (Stonewall)] Jackson still lived, he undoubtedly would have found it practicable. But Ewell was not Jackson. Thinking the enemy position too strong, he did not attack—thereby creating one of the controversial "ifs" of Gettysburg that have echoed down the years.

James M. McPherson

The Communication Process

sender

the person who originates and sends a message

receiver

the person who receives the sender's message, or for whom the sender intends it

noise

whatever interferes with communication between the sender and receiver, from the wording used to audience distractions to bad handwriting

feedback

the receiver's response to the sender's message, which can indicate understanding, lack of understanding, misunderstanding, agreement, disagreement, desire for more information, and so on

As you will see, the Gettysburg vignette illustrates the parts of the communications process. Lee was the **sender**. He sent the message: Attack Cemetery Hill. Ewell, the **receiver**, read the words "if practicable," decided that Union artillery on the hill made an attack not "practicable," and did not attack.

The words "if practicable" made the message vague. (Who and what should define "if practicable"?) Obstacles to communication, such as this lack of clarity—along with other considerations, such as the demands of time, the ease of understanding the sender's speech, the ability to read the sender's handwriting, or the distractions in the area—make up what communications theorists call **noise**. Noise works against the clarity of communication.

Looking again at the vignette above, you find that Lee never checked with Ewell to see if he understood Lee's intent: "What do you intend to do?" Ewell never checked with Lee to clarify the message: "What do you mean by 'if practicable'?" The communication process included no **feedback**. Assume for a moment, as some historians do, that Lee intended that Ewell attack Cemetery Hill immediately and decisively. (These historians argue that Lee was used to issuing such vague orders to the aggressive Stonewall Jackson, who had died a few months earlier.) Throwing Billy Yank off the hilltop might well have allowed Lee to command the battlefield, perhaps even forcing the advancing Union armies to withdraw. That might have led to Lee's domination of southern Pennsylvania, choking off Washington from the North and ending the war on the Confederacy's terms.

If that *were* Lee's intent, the message failed. Ewell did not attack. The Union held onto the high ground and won the battle two days later—the beginning of the end for the Confederacy.

There's an important lesson in all this: *Effective communication occurs when the receiver's perceived idea matches the sender's intended idea.* The receiver understands what the sender *means*, not just what the sender says or writes. But how do you ensure that occurs?

Five Tips for Effective Communication

These five tips will help you eliminate noise and ensure that your receiver understands your message.

1. Focus your message

Every academic, business, or military message you will ever produce will fit into one of two categories:

- *Action-and-information messages* ask the receiver to do something: Schedule a make-up exam; prepare a marketing report; attack a hilltop.
- *Information-only messages* tell the receiver something: The primary cause of the American Civil War was states' rights; Estelle LaMonica is the new Vice President of Human Resources; Alpha Company has one vehicle down for battle damage.

You must focus—*clarify*—your message so your receiver is certain—*clear*—on what he or she is supposed to do or know. Too many action-and-information messages fail because the receiver mistakes them for information-only messages:

"I need a make-up exam," you send. "*You sure do*," *thinks the receiver.*

"If we knew the market better, we could increase our share." "*That's a good idea.*"

"The bad guys have a company-sized element on Hill 442." "*That's right. I saw the intelligence reports as well.*"

Decide *before you communicate* if your message is action-*and*-information or information-*only*. If you're communicating an action-and-information message, specify what your receiver must *do* and *know*. If you are communicating an information-*only* message, specify what your receiver needs to *know*.

2. Break through the noise

As the sender, as the one trying to communicate, you have the responsibility to communicate clearly—to break through the noise. Think in terms of your receiver. Use your receiver's terms of reference. If a military objective is to your front but to your receiver's flank, refer

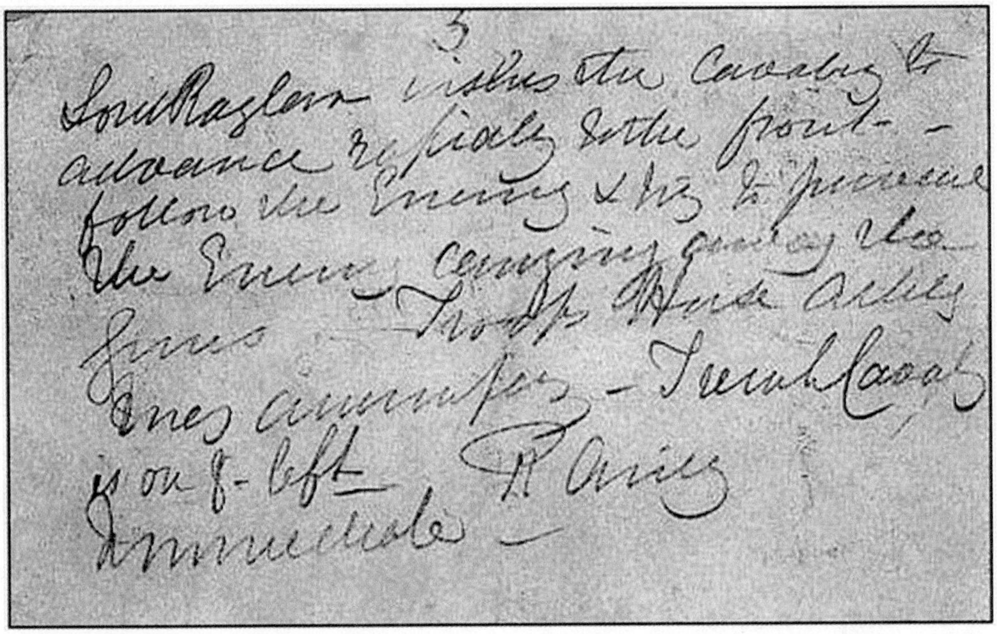

Figure 5.1 The Battle of Balaklava, 25 October 1854—Lord Raglan's reference to his front, rather than the cavalry's flank, sent the Light Brigade to its death: "Lord Raglan wishes the cavalry to advance rapidly to the front, follow the enemy and try to prevent the enemy carrying away the guns. Troop Horse Artillery may accompany. French cavalry is on your left. Immediate."

Critical Thinking

What action requests in the messages under "Focus Your Message" on page 103 were lost in transmission?

to the objective as to the flank. (This very mistake—*front* rather than *flank*—resulted in the deaths of 550 British cavalry troops at the Battle of Balaklava in the Crimean War.)

- *Use descriptive language.* Use visualization and analogies. Instead of saying, "The motor pool is big," say, "The motor pool is the size of a football field." Instead of saying, "I want you to snap that salute," say, "I want you to snap that salute as if you were saluting a Normandy veteran."
- *Ask for feedback.* It is not enough to ask, "Do you understand me?" The obvious answer is "Yes. Absolutely. Sure I do," *no matter what the understanding may be.* Lee's intent may have been "Take Cemetery Hill." Ewell's understanding may have been "Take Cemetery Hill only if I can do it without casualties." If Lee had asked, "Do you understand me?" Ewell's response—no matter the difference between intent and understanding—would have been "Yes. Absolutely. Sure I do." Craft your request for feedback so your receiver will have to demonstrate his or her understanding of the message. "What—specifically—do I want you to do?" "What—specifically— will you do now?" "How will you do it?"
- *Revise as you need to.* You may have to repeat your message several times before you communicate successfully. Use the feedback you get to adjust your message to the needs of your receiver.

3. Put your Bottom Line Up Front (BLUF)

Get to your point in the first 10 seconds of your message; put your Bottom Line Up Front (**BLUF**).

- Your point—your *bottom line*—in an action-and-information message is what you want your receiver to do: "Attack, seize, and hold Cemetery Hill."
- Your point—your bottom line—in an information-only message is what you want your receiver to know: "Alpha Company has one vehicle down for battle damage."
- Audiences—receivers—are impatient. "Get to the point," they say. "How does this affect me?" If you don't get to your point, if you don't explain how your message affects your receivers, they will tune out. They may be physically present during the rest of the message, but their minds are far away—thinking of food; thinking of home; thinking of other tasks and responsibilities they have to perform.

4. Use simple words

Great communicators use simple words.
Consider these examples:

"Carthage must be destroyed!" (Cato the Elder, an ancient Roman senator)
"The only thing we have to fear is fear itself." (Franklin D. Roosevelt)
"I have a dream." (Dr. Martin Luther King Jr.)
"Mr. Gorbachev, tear down this wall!" (Ronald Reagan)

BLUF

an acronym for Bottom Line Up Front, which reminds you to get to the point of your message within the first 10 seconds

Look closely at the examples. Notice the overwhelming use of single-syllable words. (Of the 24 words, only five are two-syllable words.) Notice the absence of any long "impressive" words. Given the choice between a simple word and a long word—and given there's no difference in the meaning of the two words—use the simple word. Your communication will be clearer.

5. Use concrete words

Concrete words draw pictures in your receiver's brain.
Consider the difference between these two phrases:

"An old car."
"A 1966 red Mustang convertible."

Which phrase draws a picture in your brain? You can visualize the Mustang far more easily, far more quickly, than you can visualize an old car. You can visualize "15 enemy soldiers with small arms and shoulder-fired antitank weapons" far more quickly, far more easily, than you can visualize "a bunch of bad guys."

Four Tips for Effective Writing

Writing takes special care. You can reread and study a written message, while a spoken message quickly vanishes into the air. As you saw above, an unclear written message can lead to disaster, especially if the receiver has no way to confirm his or her understanding of the message. These tips will help ensure your writing is as clear as possible.

1. Use the "Five Tips for Effective Communication"

The five tips—focus your message, break through the noise, put your Bottom Line Up Front, use simple words, and use concrete words—will make you a better writer. Because you don't have an audience in front of you and because you have no immediate feedback, clarity becomes critical. You must not only be sure the receiver understands you, but you must also remove the opportunity to misunderstand.

2. Use active voice, short sentences, and conversational language

Use active voice. *Active voice* describes a sentence in which the subject of the sentence performs the action of the sentence: "Sergeant Torres wrote the report." "Sergeant Torres" is the subject of the sentence; he is what the sentence is about. He does the action of the sentence: He writes the report.

Passive voice—the less-effective counterpart of active voice—describes a sentence in which the subject of the sentence receives the action: "The report was written by Sergeant Torres." Now the subject is "The report"; it receives the action; it "was written."

Active voice has three advantages over passive voice:

1. *It's more concise.* "Sergeant Torres wrote the report" has five words. "The report was written by Sergeant Torres" has seven. Active voice will *almost always* be more concise than passive voice.

2. *It's more direct.* It demands accountability. You cannot write in active voice unless you identify the doer of the action. Consider the ethical implications of "No action was taken." Who didn't take action? Why didn't they take action? And why didn't the writer name whoever didn't take action?

3. *It's more conversational.* It's more natural. You grow up speaking in active voice. When you were little, you may have said, "I want to be a soldier." You certainly didn't say, "To be a soldier is wanted by me."

A classic and valuable writing guide is The Elements of Style, *by William Strunk Jr. and E. B. White. The Fourth Edition is available online and in many bookstores. You can also find useful information and tips at Purdue University's Online Writing Lab (OWL), www.english.purdue.edu.*

active voice

in the active voice, the doer of the action is the subject of the verb

passive voice

in the passive voice, the subject of the verb receives the action— avoid this weak construction

> ## A document that looks hard to read is hard to read.
>
> Diane Brewster-Norman, communications-skills expert

Use short sentences. Short sentences are easier to read. They are easier to keep grammatically correct, and they are easier to punctuate. Keep your sentences to an average of 12 to 15 words per sentence.

Use conversational language. Use the language you use every day. As you are writing, ask yourself, "How would I say this?" In conversational language, you would never say "Upon completion of the above-entitled actions, forward the documents to the undersigned." You would probably say, "When you are done with this, return the papers to me." There is, however, a caution. Conversational written language does not exactly match the spoken language. It doesn't include the "ums" and "uhs." It doesn't include the half-sentences people start, then change.

3. Use lots of white space

White space lets your reader breathe. Keep your paragraphs to no more than about six lines long. Use headings and lists. Open up your document.

Examine this textbook section. Notice the short paragraphs, the headings, and the lists. It should look easy to read. The writers wrote it that way. Make your documents easy to read.

4. Use correct grammar, spelling, and punctuation

Using incorrect grammar, spelling, and punctuation presents two problems.

It can be confusing. What happens when you read, "We saw a motor pool walking through the battalion area"? You are not sure what the writer intended: Motor pools don't generally walk, let alone through battalion areas. Try "Walking through the battalion area, we saw a motor pool."

It affects your credibility. Readers assume that if you cannot take care of the little things, you cannot take care of the big things. If you cannot write a simple sentence, they wonder, how can you lead troops? The assumption may not be fair (GEN Ulysses S. Grant was a horrible speller), but it's real and has hampered many officers' careers.

A complete discussion of grammar, spelling, and punctuation is beyond the scope of this lesson, but here are three ways to improve your language ability.

Read professionally written and published material. The subject doesn't matter—as long as it is professionally written and published. Read good books. See the written word on the page. Get used to the standards of written English. As you become familiar with the standards, you will see your mistakes more easily.

Make writing skills a part of your professional development plan. Learn about grammar, spelling, and punctuation. Learn the principles. Learn the forms. Learn the expectations. Then coach your Soldiers.

Get someone to review your work. All too often, you will be too close to your document to see your errors. Your spell-checker won't catch errors that are spelled correctly.

Critical Thinking

Assuming that Lee wanted Ewell to take Cemetery Hill, how might the commander have written his order to make it clearer to Ewell what he intended? If Lee wanted Ewell to be cautious, how might he have written it?

Three Tips for Effective Speaking

Public speaking and briefing also require a mastery of the language, but involve different skills than writing. These tips will help.

1. Use the "Five Tips for Effective Communication"

The five tips—focus your message, break through the noise, put your Bottom Line Up Front, use simple words, and use concrete words—will make you a better speaker. Consider that the four examples you read in "Use simple words" (from Cato, Roosevelt, King, and Reagan) were all originally spoken.

2. Mark the parts of your presentation

Look at the page in front of you. Besides the words, you'll see headings, paragraphs, and lists. These mark the parts of the reading. As you move from one paragraph to another, you expect the ideas to transition or flow from one to the next. The page layout reinforces the ideas in the reading. The spoken word provides no such markers, however. There's no white space, no indents, no bolded lists. So you provide the markers.

Use pauses to indicate changes in ideas. When you've finished with an idea, pause for a few seconds. Count the seconds in your head. *One. Two. Three. Four. Five.* Then pick up the conversation. The silence—the pause—represents the white space on a page. You're moving to another point.

Use movement to indicate changes in ideas. If you're standing on your audience's left front while you're explaining your first point, move to your audience's right front to explain your second point.

"That concludes my first point." (Stop. Step. Step. Step.) "My second point . . . ." The physical movement represents the movement from your first point to your second.

Use gestures to indicate the parts of your presentation. You've worked very carefully to structure your presentation. Use your gestures as body language to complement that structure. "The first part of the five-paragraph field order . . . ." (Hold up your thumb or index finger.) " . . . is 'situation.' "

3. Listen actively

Speaking has certain advantages over writing. When you speak, you have your audience members in front of you. You get immediate feedback from them. You can observe their body language and determine how your message is going over.

Positive signs include audience members leaning forward, listening to what you say. They nod their heads in agreement. They make eye contact with you. They look at your slides.

Negative signs include closed body language: Audience members lean back in their chairs and fold their arms across their chests. They glance at their watches. (Some may check to see if their watches are still running.) They look around the room. The negative signs mean you need to change your approach or your delivery. Perhaps the best way is to pause and ask your audience for direct feedback: "I get the impression you're not comfortable with this discussion. What are your concerns?" Better to address the issues than ignore them.

CONCLUSION

Think of the great communicators of the last century: Franklin Roosevelt, Winston Churchill, Margaret Thatcher, Martin Luther King Jr., and Ronald Reagan. Would these men and women have *led* as well as they did if they didn't *communicate* as well as they did? You will soon lead young men and women. You cannot lead unless you can communicate.

Learning Assessment

1. How many parties does it take for communication to take place? Who are they?
2. Explain what BLUF means and why it is important.
3. How do you know if someone has understood you?
4. What are three reasons it is generally better to use active rather than passive voice?
5. Describe the five tips for effective communication.

Key Words

sender
receiver
noise
feedback
BLUF
active voice
passive voice

References

Department of the Army. PAM 600–67, *Effective Writing for Army Leaders*. 2 June 1986.

McPherson, J. M. (1988). *Battle Cry of Freedom*. New York: Ballantine Books.

ST 22-2, *Writing and Speaking Skills for Leaders at the Organizational Level*. (August 1991). Retrieved 8 July 2008 from www.au.af.mil/au/awc/awcgate/comm-skills/st22-2/st-1.doc

INTRODUCTION TO THE WARRIOR ETHOS

Key Points

1 The Warrior Ethos Defined

2 The Soldier's Creed

3 The Four Tenets of the Warrior Ethos

Every organization has an internal culture and ethos. A true Warrior Ethos must underpin the Army's enduring traditions and values. It must drive a personal commitment to excellence and ethical mission accomplishment to make our Soldiers different from all others in the world. This ethos must be a fundamental characteristic of the U.S. Army as Soldiers imbued with an ethically grounded Warrior Ethos who clearly symbolize the Army's unwavering commitment to the nation we serve. The Army has always embraced this ethos but the demands of Transformation will require a renewed effort to ensure all Soldiers truly understand and embody this Warrior Ethos.

GEN Eric K. Shinseki

Introduction

Every Soldier must know the Soldier's Creed and live the Warrior Ethos. As a Cadet and future officer, you must embody high professional standards and reflect American values. The Warrior Ethos demands a commitment on the part of all Soldiers to stand prepared and confident to accomplish their assigned tasks and face all challenges, including enemy resistance—anytime, anywhere.

This is not a simple or easy task. *First*, you must understand how the building blocks of the Warrior Ethos (see Figure 1.1) form a set of professional beliefs and attitudes that shape the American Soldier. *Second*, you must establish an unwavering personal commitment to excellence and ethical mission accomplishment, a commitment that cannot vary, no matter what the circumstances. *Finally*, as a leader, you must be the example for your Soldiers of what it means to live the Warrior Ethos, through your own conduct.

This section defines the Warrior Ethos, covers its four tenets as based on a commitment to selfless service to the nation and the Army Values, and demonstrates how the Soldier's Creed ties its concepts together.

The following vignette epitomizes the power of the Warrior Ethos in the Contemporary Operating Environment, a commitment to the welfare of others so strong that it sets a timeless example of sacrifice for one's fellow Soldiers.

MSG Gordon and SFC Shughart in Somalia

During a raid in Mogadishu in October 1993, MSG Gary Gordon and SFC Randall Shughart, leader and member of a sniper team, respectively, with Task Force Ranger in Somalia, were providing precision and suppressive fires from helicopters above two helicopter crash sites. Learning that no ground forces were available to rescue one of the downed aircrews and aware that a growing number

Figure 1.1 The Building Blocks of the Warrior Ethos

of enemy were closing in on the site, MSG Gordon and SFC Shughart volunteered to be inserted to protect their critically wounded comrades.

Their initial request was turned down because of the dangerous situation. They asked a second time; permission was denied. Only after their third request were they inserted.

MSG Gordon and SFC Shughart were inserted one hundred meters south of the downed chopper. Armed only with their personal weapons, the two NCOs fought their way to the downed fliers through intense small arms fire, a maze of shanties and shacks, and the enemy converging on the site. After MSG Gordon and SFC Shughart pulled the wounded from the wreckage, they established a perimeter, put themselves in the most dangerous position, and fought off a series of attacks. The two NCOs continued to protect their comrades until they had depleted their ammunition and were themselves fatally wounded. Their actions saved the life of an Army pilot.

No one will ever know what was running through the minds of MSG Gordon and SFC Shughart as they left the comparative safety of their helicopter to go to the aid of the downed aircrew. The two NCOs knew there was no ground rescue force available, and they certainly knew there was no going back to their helicopter. They may have suspected that things would turn out as they did; nonetheless, they did what they believed to be the right thing. They acted based on Army Values, which they had clearly made their own: *loyalty* to their fellow Soldiers; the *duty* to stand by them, regardless of the circumstances; the *personal courage* to act, even in the face of great danger; *selfless service*, the willingness to give their all. MSG Gary I. Gordon and SFC Randall D. Shughart lived Army Values to the end; they were posthumously awarded Medals of Honor.

The Warrior Ethos Defined

ethos

the disposition, character, or fundamental values peculiar to a specific person, people, culture, or movement

Warrior Ethos

the professional attitudes and beliefs that characterize the American Soldier—the Warrior Ethos is the foundation for the American Soldier's total commitment to victory in peace and war

Ethos is defined as the disposition, character, or fundamental values peculiar to a specific person, people, culture, or movement. The **Warrior Ethos**, the professional attitudes and beliefs that characterize the American Soldier, is a reflection of our nation's enduring values by the profession charged with protecting those values. The Warrior Ethos is the foundation for the American Soldier's total commitment to victory in peace and war.

At the core of every Soldier is the willingness and desire to serve the nation—both its people and its enduring values. Hence, the foundation for the pyramid representing the Warrior Ethos is a commitment to serve the nation. Soldiers who live the Warrior Ethos put the mission first, refuse to accept defeat, never quit, and never leave a fallen comrade. They have absolute faith in themselves and their team because they have common beliefs and values.

The seven Army Values of Loyalty, Duty, Respect, Selfless Service, Honor, Integrity, and Personal Courage (LDRSHIP) form the second level of this pyramid of the Warrior Ethos. Army Values are universal; they enable you to see what is right or wrong in any situation. When you encounter a situation that requires you to make a decision, you should apply the Army Values. If any one term is not applied, the decision will be flawed. As you can see, Army Values and the Warrior Ethos are integral parts of a unified system of beliefs—as with the Soldiers who follow them, they depend on each other. The Soldier's **Creed** ties this system together.

creed

a statement of beliefs, or a statement of a belief and a system of principles or opinions

The Soldier's Creed

The Soldier's Creed, first committed to memory and then increasingly applied to all your tasks—whether routine and safe, or urgent and dangerous—puts the Warrior Ethos into the practical context of the Basis of Army Leadership: Be, Know, and Do. The intent of the Soldier's Creed is to link your commitment to selfless service to the goal of every other American Soldier—*victory with honor*.

The Soldier's Creed unifies the Army's culture by expressing fundamental human beliefs from a warrior's perspective. It helps Soldiers understand that, no matter what their personal or professional backgrounds may be, all Soldiers are warriors and members of a team with difficult and dangerous tasks to perform. To develop into an effective leader of Soldiers, you must begin now to live by the seven Army Values, the Warrior Ethos and the Soldier's Creed.

The Soldier's Creed

I am an American Soldier. I am a warrior and a member of a team. I serve the people of the United States and live the Army Values. I will always place the mission first. I will never accept defeat. I will never quit. I will never leave a fallen comrade. I am disciplined, physically and mentally tough, trained and proficient in my warrior tasks and drills. I always maintain my arms, my equipment, and myself. I am an expert and I am a professional. I stand ready to deploy, engage, and destroy the enemies of the United States of America in close combat. I am a guardian of freedom and the American way of life. I am an American Soldier.

The Four Tenets of the Warrior Ethos

- Always place the mission first
- Never accept defeat
- Never quit
- Never leave a fallen comrade.

While all citizens hold beliefs and values that bring our nation together, Soldiers must take *action* to protect the nation. The four tenets of the Warrior Ethos provide the *motivation* for that action, motivation built on a comradeship that the Warrior Ethos creates. Because of that comradeship, Soldiers fight for each other, as well as for their nation and for their beliefs. Time and again you see that Soldiers would rather die than let their buddies down. It will be your job as a leader to ensure that your unit has the final ingredients necessary for victory. You must train and lead your Soldiers to become a competent, confident, flexible, and adaptable team—a team imbued with the Warrior Ethos.

Just such a team rescued more than 500 American and Allied prisoners of war from the Japanese at the end of World War II.

Great Raid on Cabanatuan Depicts Warrior Ethos

WASHINGTON (Army News Service, Aug. 10, 2005)—It was one of the most daring and successful Special Operations missions of World War II, full of drama, suspense and heroism—just the sort of thing that would make an exciting movie.

The 1945 raid by the U.S. Army's 6th Ranger Battalion to rescue Americans held at the Japanese POW camp near Cabanatuan in the Philippines is the subject of [the movie] "The Great Raid. . ."

The same raid was depicted in the opening scenes of an earlier movie, the 1945 "Back to Bataan," starring John Wayne and Anthony Quinn.

Regardless of how accurately either movie depicts the raid and those who lived through it, the real-life story is one worthy of study. It is noteworthy as an example of a well-planned and expertly conducted small-unit mission.

It may be even more valuable, however, as a reminder that the Warrior Ethos and Soldier's Creed that American Soldiers live by today are neither new nor exclusive to the men and women on the front lines in Iraq, Afghanistan, and elsewhere around the world.

Great Soldiers of the past lived and fought by those values. There are few better examples of this than what was done by the men of the 6th Ranger Battalion answering the call to duty in late January 1945.

'I will always place the mission first'

The more than 500 Americans inside the barbed wire of the Cabanatuan POW camp in early 1945 were survivors from America's darkest days, the fall of the Philippines in 1942. They were the lucky ones—if "lucky" means staying alive to be continually starved and mistreated by their captors.

Somehow these Soldiers, Marines, Sailors and Airmen, as well as American civilians and some allies, had survived the valiant but doomed battles of Bataan and Corregidor. Somehow many of them had survived the Bataan Death March, which followed Bataan's surrender on April 9, 1942 (Corregidor surrendered on May 6).

'I will never quit'

Somehow they had survived almost three years of starvation, mistreatment, minimal medical care and executions for various offenses proscribed by their guards. Somehow, they had missed the fate of thousands of their comrades who had died when American planes and submarines attacked and sank Japanese ships transporting them from the Philippines. The ships bore no indication of the human cargo they were carrying, so they were routinely attacked by the U.S. Navy and Army Air Force in the campaign to cut the enemy's supply lines.

As U.S. forces returned to the Philippines on Oct. 20, 1944, with the landing at Leyte, followed on Jan. 9, 1945, by landing on Luzon, the question became whether the POWs would be liberated before time ran out for them. It wasn't only a matter of malnutrition and disease catching up to the prisoners or their being moved farther away from the advancing American forces; it was whether they would be murdered before they could be freed.

This was a very real possibility. About 150 American prisoners at a POW camp on the Philippine island of Palawan had been killed by their guards on Dec. 14, 1944. A survivor of this massacre had reached friendly forces and what had happened was known to U.S. Army intelligence by the time of the Luzon invasion. [The possibility of] a similar fate for any captive Americans on Luzon could not be overlooked.

Rescuers: 'I will never accept defeat'

The U.S. Army was determined those who had upheld America's honor in the opening days of the war would not suffer [such] a fate.

To that end, the commanding general of Sixth U.S. Army, Lt. Gen. Walter Krueger, called on the commander of a unique unit under his command, the 6th Ranger Battalion, the only Ranger battalion in the Pacific theater (During World War II, the Army had six Ranger battalions. The 1st through the 5th fought in either the Mediterranean or European theaters; the 6th fought in the Philippines.)

Lt. Col. Henry A. Mucci, a 1936 graduate of West Point, commanded the 6th Ranger Battalion. He had taken command of it in April 1944 in New Guinea when it was the 98th Field Artillery Battalion and led it through its re-designation and transformation into the 6th Ranger Battalion, putting its members through a demanding training program and weeding out those who couldn't or wouldn't measure up to Ranger standards.

By January 1945, his men were all volunteers and ready for a mission. The 6th Rangers landed on three islands in Leyte Gulf Oct. 17, and performed some commando-type missions. Now they were called upon to raid the Cabanatuan POW camp. Specifically, Mucci was to infiltrate about 30 miles behind enemy lines, reach the camp, overcome the guard force, liberate the prisoners and return them safely to friendly lines before the Japanese could react.

The ground to be covered was open and great care would have to be taken to avoid being spotted enroute to the camp. In addition to overcoming the camp's guard force, there were numerous other enemy forces in the area. Because of its proximity to major roadways, the camp often played host to Japanese units in transit. Due to American aircraft, the Japanese made troop movements at night.

A Japanese battalion regularly bivouacked about a mile from the camp and a division-sized unit was believed to be around Cabanatuan City, three to four miles from the camp. These Japanese units had tanks and tanks were also known to be included in the nocturnal movements around the camp.

To accomplish the mission, which he would personally lead, Mucci chose one company of the 6th Rangers, Company C, commanded by Capt. Robert W. Prince. Company C would be reinforced by the 2nd Platoon of Company F, led by 1st Lt. John F. Murphy. The Ranger force would also include four combat photographers from the 832nd Signal Service Battalion and two teams of Sixth Army's elite recon unit, the Alamo Scouts. Counting a few additions from elsewhere in the battalion, the Ranger force consisted of about 120 men.

The Rangers would receive invaluable support from several hundred Filipino guerrillas under the commands of Captains Eduardo Joson and Juan Pajota. The guerrillas would provide intelligence, carry out security along the route to and from the camp, and interface with the civilian population for needed support for the Rangers and the liberated prisoners. The guerrillas would also play a critical role during the assault on the camp.

'I will never leave a fallen comrade'

When Mucci briefed them on the mission, the Rangers immediately knew just how important it was and how difficult it was going to be to pull it off. Each was given the opportunity to stay back. None took it.

It was clear to all of them that they were the only hope to bring out the survivors of Bataan and Corregidor before the Japanese killed them. Mucci ordered them to take an oath to die fighting before letting any harm come to those they were to rescue.

The Raid

The Rangers moved out early on Jan. 28 and soon linked up with guerillas commanded by Joson. By dark, the combined Ranger-guerilla force was inside enemy territory.

At the village of Balincarin, the Rangers were provided the latest intelligence from the Alamo Scouts, who had started their recon duties a day earlier. They were also joined there by Pajota's guerilla force. Working with Pajota, Prince coordinated for the guerillas to provide security, collect enough carabao carts to transport liberated POWs too weak to walk back and prepare enough food for several hundred men.

Mucci delayed the raid for a day in order to gather additional intelligence and to allow a large force of Japanese transiting the area to move away from the camp. The delay also allowed the Rangers to gather detailed information on the camp and its defenders.

The plan for the night-time assault on the compound gave the two guerilla forces the vital mission of stopping any enemy reaction forces coming from nearby Cabanatuan City and Cabu. A Ranger bazooka section would be attached to the guerillas to deal with expected Japanese tanks. The other Rangers would hit the camp from two sides, with Murphy's 2nd Platoon of Company F assaulting the rear entrance and Prince's Company C storming through the front gate of the camp. To distract the guards while the Rangers positioned themselves for the assault, a P-61 night fighter would fly overhead just prior to the attack.

The Rangers and guerillas moved into position at twilight on Jan. 30. The force attacking the front of the camp had to crawl a mile across open ground to reach their jump-off position. The overflight by the night flyer worked as planned, drawing the attention of both guards and prisoners to the sky.

At 7:45 p.m., Murphy on the rear side of the compound fired the first shot, the signal for the attack to commence. The Rangers hit the Japanese soldiers with overwhelming ferocity, using every weapon they had. They concentrated initially on the guard towers, pillboxes and all Japanese in the open. When all enemy positions had been neutralized, the Rangers stormed into the compound and continued to eliminate enemy soldiers and interior defensive positions.

Meanwhile the guerillas at the blocking positions had their own battle to fight. Pajota's men opened fire on the Japanese battalion in the bivouac next to Cabu Creek. Guerilla machine gunners stopped the Japanese counterattacks at the Cabu Creek bridge while the Ranger bazooka teams knocked out two tanks and a truck.

The other roadblock under Joson was not attacked, thanks to attacks by P-61 night fighters on a Japanese convoy headed toward Joson's position.

In less than 15 minutes, all serious resistance inside the POW compound had been eliminated, though a final trio of mortar rounds wounded six men and mortally wounded the battalion surgeon, one of only two Rangers to die in the attack. A total of seven were injured.

Within half an hour from the opening shot by Murphy, Prince had completed two searches of the camp and had determined all the prisoners had been found and removed from the camp. Although no prisoners were killed during the fighting, one weakened man suffered a fatal heart attack while leaving the camp.

One British POW who hid in the latrines during the raid wasn't found by the Rangers, but he was picked up the next day by Filipino guerrillas.

The Rangers and liberated prisoners made their withdrawal while Pajota continued to stop all Japanese attempts to pursue. By the time Pajota's men disengaged, they had essentially destroyed an enemy battalion while suffering no fatalities or serious wounds themselves.

Filipino citizens provided food and water to the liberated prisoners on the route back. Additional carabao carts arrived to transport former prisoners too weak to walk. The guerillas continued to provide all-around security.

About 12 hours after the assault on the camp, radio contact was made with Sixth Army. Trucks were requested to meet the force. A couple of hours later, the Rangers and prisoners returned to friendly lines and shortly thereafter, the heroes of Bataan and Corregidor were undergoing medical examination at the 92nd Evacuation Hospital.

The mission, which rescued 511 American and Allied POWs and killed or wounded some 520 Japanese at the cost of two Rangers killed, was completed.

The Cabanatuan raid rescuers and rescued may not have been able to recite the Warrior Ethos of today's Army, but they lived it.

Randy Pullen

Critical Thinking

How can you, as a Cadet, begin to live the Warrior Ethos in your ROTC activities and your daily life on campus?

CONCLUSION

The Warrior Ethos is your commitment to overcome all obstacles. It reflects a selfless dedication to the nation, mission, unit, and your fellow Soldiers. You will develop and maintain this attitude through discipline, rigorous training, learning and embodying Army Values, and recognizing that as a Cadet you represent the future of the Army's proud heritage.

Learning Assessment

1. Recite the Soldier's Creed from memory.
2. List the four building blocks of the Warrior Ethos.
3. Identify the four tenets of the Warrior Ethos.
4. List the seven Army Values.

Key Words

ethos
Warrior Ethos
creed

References

Field Manual 6-22, *Army Leadership: Competent, Confident, and Agile.* 12 October 2006.

Pullen, R. (10 August 2005). Great Raid on Cabanatuan Depicts Warrior Ethos. *Army News Service.* Retrieved 17 August 2005 from http://www4.army.mil/ocpa/read.php?story_id_key=7723

Shinseki, E. K. (n.d.). Warrior Ethos. *Leaders' Perspective.* TRADOC News Service. Retrieved 14 August 2005 from http://www.tradoc.army.mil/pao/Web_specials/WarriorEthos/leaderpersp.htm

ROTC RANK STRUCTURE

Key Points

1 The Purpose of Army Ranks

2 The Cadet Ranks

3 The Cadet Unit Structure

4 The Cadet Chain of Command

As the Continental Army have unfortunately no uniforms, and consequently many inconveniences must arise from not being able always to distinguish the commissioned officer from the non-commissioned, and the noncommissioned from the privates, it is desired that some badges of distinction may be immediately provided. For instance, that the field officers may have red or pink-colored cockades in their hats, the captains yellow or buff and the subalterns green. They are to furnish themselves accordingly. The sergeants may be distinguished by an epaulette or stripe of red cloth sewed upon their right shoulder; the corporals by one of green.

GEN George Washington

Introduction

Your **rank** shows where you fit in the **chain of command**, and the chain of command provides the leadership structure for military **units**.

As a new Cadet, you are responsible for following the directions, guidance, and example of those who outrank you. As you advance through ROTC, you will have the opportunity to lead progressively larger and more complex organizations, from the smallest—the team—through the largest—the ROTC battalion.

Military rank is a critical part of the profession of arms. The Continental Army—the army that won independence from Great Britain—at first had no uniforms or badges of rank. The army was made of farmers, laborers, and shopkeepers who wore their work clothes to drill and battle. Think of the confusion that an army without uniforms and rank might experience.

The Purpose of Army Ranks

Military ranks identify who is in charge, indicate levels of leadership and responsibility, and support fast and effective decision making and problem solving.

The Continental Army drew its rank structure—lieutenant, captain, major, colonel, and general—from the traditions of Great Britain, and today's structure remains close to that of the Continental Army. Lieutenants and captains are "company grade" officers, majors and colonels are "field grade" officers, and generals are "flag" officers.

The Cadet Ranks

ROTC has six Cadet officer ranks. The ranks themselves come from British tradition, and the insignia resemble British, European, and colonial insignia.

Cadet second lieutenants—the most junior of the officer ranks—wear a single disc or dot. Cadet first lieutenants wear two discs or dots. Cadet captains wear three discs or dots.

The insignia changes at major—the first of the field-grade officers. Cadet majors wear a single diamond (sometimes called a *lozenge*), Cadet lieutenant colonels wear two diamonds, and Cadet colonels wear three diamonds.

ROTC recognizes eight Cadet noncommissioned officer (NCO) ranks. The ranks and the insignia resemble those of the active Army. Cadet corporals—the most junior of the NCO ranks—wear two chevrons (sometimes called *stripes*). Cadet sergeants wear three

  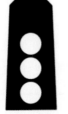   

| CADET SECOND LIEUTENANT | CADET FIRST LIEUTENANT | CADET CAPTAIN | CADET MAJOR | CADET LIEUTENANT COLONEL | CADET COLONEL |

Figure 1.1 Cadet Officer Ranks

Sidebar:

*Military ranks have existed for thousands of years. Attila's horde had ranks. The Roman legions had ranks. The rank of **colonel** originated in Roman times: a Roman colonel was in charge of a column—in Latin, **columna**—of soldiers.*

*The rank of **lieutenant** comes from the French words **lieu** and **tenant**: **Lieu** means "place" (think of "in lieu of"). **Tenant** means "holding a position" (think of the landlord/**tenant** relationship). So a lieutenant is someone acting for a superior: someone acting in place of the person holding the position.*

rank
official position or grade

chain of command
the system by which authority passes down from the top through a series of military ranks in which each person is accountable to a superior—the top of the chain of command is the president of the United States, the commander in chief

unit
an Army group or organization ranging in size from a field army to a squad

Note that the plural form of sergeant major is **sergeants major**.

**Abbreviations for
Army Enlisted Ranks**
PVT—private
PFC—private first class
SPC—specialist
CPL—corporal
SGT—sergeant
SSG—staff sergeant
SFC—sergeant first class
MSG—master sergeant
1SG—first sergeant
SGM—sergeant major
CSM—command
sergeant major

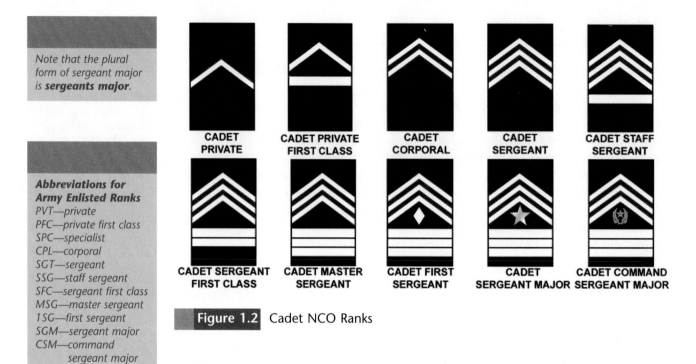

Figure 1.2 Cadet NCO Ranks

chevrons. Cadet staff sergeants wear three chevrons over a bar. Cadet sergeants first class wear three chevrons over two bars, and Cadet master sergeants wear three chevrons over three bars.

Cadet first sergeants wear three chevrons over three bars with a diamond between the chevrons and the bars. Cadet sergeants major wear three chevrons over three bars with a star between the chevrons and the bars. Cadet command sergeants major wear three chevrons over three bars with a star circled by a wreath between the chevrons and the bars.

ROTC recognizes three additional Cadet enlisted ranks, although these are not non-commissioned officer ranks. Basic Cadets wear no insignia. Cadet privates wear one chevron, and Cadet privates first class wear a chevron over a bar.

The Cadet Unit Structure

The Army is made of small units—organizational building blocks—which, when combined, create larger units. Within this organizational structure, leaders command and control the resources necessary to deter conflict and to win when combat is necessary.

Your Cadet battalion and subordinate-unit structure will vary depending upon the size, makeup, and location of your school, but throughout Army Cadet Command, the unit structures will resemble that in Figure 1.3.

Critical Thinking

What would be the effectiveness of an army without ranks? How well would it operate?

Critical Thinking

What advantages and disadvantages are there to the display of rank insignia in a combat zone?

The Cadet Chain of Command

The Cadet chain of command is formed from the MSL IV class at the beginning of each school year. Performance in ROTC, performance at the Leader Development and Assessment Course (LDAC), academics, and overall accomplishments dictate the appointment criteria.

The Cadet chain of command does two things:

1. It helps the professor of military science (the PMS) and other cadre accomplish battalion missions and responsibilities
2. It trains and develops subordinates.

The Cadet chain of command includes four unit levels: battalion, company, platoon, and squad.

The explanation below will include the responsibilities of commanders and staff officers, who help the unit accomplish its missions.

At the Battalion Level—

1. The Cadet Battalion Commander:
   a. Commands the corps of Cadets, sets the example, and leads the way
   b. Coordinates with the battalion staff to supervise leadership labs and other events to ensure the training is effective, motivating, and safe
   c. Conducts meetings and leads battalion formations, such as weekly battalion training meetings to coordinate and confirm all training, logistical, and administrative requirements
   d. Trains and evaluates other Cadets—officers, NCOs, and enlisted ranks.

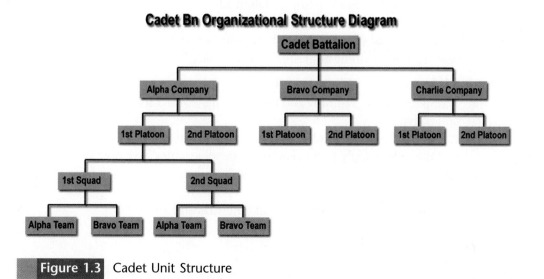

Figure 1.3 Cadet Unit Structure

2. The Cadet Battalion Executive Officer (XO):
   a. Supervises and coordinates all staff functions
   b. Commands the battalion in the absence of the battalion commander
   c. Assists the battalion commander in the performance of his or her duties
   d. Attends the weekly battalion training meeting
   e. Provides instruction and evaluation as required.

3. The Cadet Battalion Command Sergeant Major (CSM):
   a. Advises the Cadet battalion commander
   b. Maintains Cadet accountability during training
   c. Checks the Cadet NCOs for job knowledge, military appearance, and knowledge of their subordinates' strengths and weaknesses
   d. Conducts and supervises training to ensure it meets the Cadet battalion commander's intent
   e. Attends battalion training meetings.

4. The Cadet Battalion S1 (administrative officer):
   a. Is responsible for all Cadet administration and accountability
   b. Ensures Cadet promotions and absences are documented and managed
   c. Coordinates, publishes, and executes all Cadet social functions and award ceremonies
   d. Helps the cadre with sponsorship programs
   e. Provides Cadet status reports at each weekly Cadet training meeting.

5. The Cadet Battalion S3 (operations officer)—
   a. Is responsible for operations and training in the battalion
   b. Prepares weekly training meetings and publishes weekly training schedules
   c. Coordinates all training with the cadre operations officer
   d. Ensures that all instructors conduct rehearsals and back briefs
   e. Provides a training status report at each weekly Cadet training meeting
   f. Coordinates with the cadre operations officer for all required MSL IV Cadet evaluations of MSL III Cadets
   g. Publishes all operations orders (OPORDs) and memorandums of instruction (MOIs) on projects, training, and Cadet activities.

6. The Assistant Cadet Battalion S3:
   a. Is the primary assistant to the battalion S3
   b. Assists with instruction for each lab and coordinates with other staff, lab instructors, and cadre to maintain training standards
   c. Assists in maintaining all training records, aids, and references.

7. The Cadet Battalion S4 (logistics officer):
   a. Is responsible for planning and coordinating logistics for projects, training, and activities
   b. Coordinates with the Cadet operations officer, the cadre operations officer, and the cadre supply technician to ensure all logistics have been coordinated
   c. Coordinates with the cadre supply technician to ensure 100 percent accountability of battalion property
   d. Prepares the logistical portion of all OPORDs and MOIs.

8. The Cadet Battalion Public Affairs Officer (PAO):
   a. Coordinates all PAO activities with the cadre S1, university PAO, and community PAO
   b. Coordinates advertising campaigns, news releases, and feature articles to increase public awareness of ROTC
   c. Assists in activities involving the ROTC Advisory Council, the ROTC Alumni, the ROTC Hall of Fame, and others.

At Company, Platoon, and Squad Levels—

1. The Cadet Company Commander:
   a. Commands the company and is responsible for its day-to-day operations
   b. Reports directly to the Cadet battalion commander on the morale, welfare, accountability, training, and discipline of the company
   c. Plans, organizes, and executes company training
   d. Is responsible for ensuring that the MSL I and II Cadets are prepared for their follow-on years of ROTC.

2. The Cadet Company Executive Officer (XO):
   a. Commands the company in the absence of the company commander
   b. Assists the company commander in the performance of his or her duties.

3. The Cadet Company First Sergeant:
   a. Holds company formations in accordance with Field Manual (FM) 3-21.5 and receives an accurate report from the Cadet platoon sergeants
   b. Supervises Cadet accountability during training
   c. Checks Cadet NCOs for job knowledge, military appearance, and knowledge of their subordinates' strengths and weaknesses
   d. Conducts and supervises training to ensure it meets the Cadet company commander's intent.

4. The Cadet Platoon Leader:
   a. Is responsible for the platoon's day-to-day operations
   b. Is responsible to the Cadet company commander on all matters concerning the morale, welfare, accountability, training, and discipline of the platoon
   c. Plans, organizes, and executes platoon training.

5. The Cadet Platoon Sergeant:
   a. Assists the platoon leader and supervises and coordinates with the squad leaders
   b. Holds platoon formations in accordance with FM 3-21.5 and maintains accountability for personnel at all times during military functions
   c. Conducts and supervises training
   d. Works with the Cadet first sergeant on the issue, receipt, and accountability of all equipment and supplies for the platoon
   e. Acts on the platoon leader's behalf during the platoon leader's absence.

6. The Cadet Squad Leader:
   a. Holds squad formations in accordance with FM 3-21.5
   b. Checks uniforms and equipment
   c. Knows each squad member's strengths and weaknesses
   d. Conducts and supervises training.

Abbreviations for Army Officer Ranks

GEN—general
LTG—lieutenant general
MG—major general
BG—brigadier general
COL—colonel
LTC—lieutenant colonel
MAJ—major
CPT—captain
1LT—first lieutenant
2LT—second lieutenant

CONCLUSION

Effective organization requires both leaders and followers. In the Army, fast and effective decision making requires leadership and teamwork. In combat, there can be no hesitation about who is leading and who is following. Rank takes away the guesswork about who is in charge of what, so leaders and followers can do their jobs.

Learning Assessment

1. What purpose does the division of the Army into officers, noncommissioned officers, and enlisted ranks serve?
2. List the following in order of size: a squad, a company, and a platoon.
3. What is the Cadet battalion chain of command?
4. List the Cadet ranks.

Key Words

rank
chain of command
unit

References

All Empires: An Online History Community. Retrieved 10 August 2005 from http://www.allempires.com/empires/huns/huns1.htm

AR 670-1, *Wear and Appearance of Army Uniforms and Insignia*. 3 February 2005.

Long, O. F. (1895). *Changes in the Uniform of the Army: 1774-1895*. (Army and Navy Regulation). Washington, DC: Army Quartermaster Corps.

US MILITARY CUSTOMS AND COURTESIES

Key Points

1 Military Customs and Courtesies: Signs of Honor and Respect

2 Courtesies to Colors, Music, and Individuals

3 Military Customs: Rank and Saluting

4 Reporting to a Superior Officer

The courtesy of the salute is encumbent on all military personnel, whether in garrison or in public places, in uniform or civilian clothes. The exchange of salutes in public places impresses the public with our professional sincerity, and stamps officers and enlisted men as members of the Governmental instrumentality which ensures law and order and the preservation of the nation.

GEN Hugh Drum

Introduction

A custom is a social convention stemming from tradition and enforced as an unwritten law. A courtesy is a respectful behavior often linked to a custom. A **military courtesy** is such behavior extended to a person or thing that honors them in some way.

Military customs and courtesies define the profession of arms. When you display military customs and courtesies in various situations, you demonstrate to yourself and others your commitment to duty, honor, and country.

As a Cadet and future Army leader, you must recognize that military customs and courtesies are your constant means of showing that the standard of conduct for officers and Soldiers is high and disciplined, is based on a code akin to chivalry, and is universal throughout the profession of arms.

military courtesy

the respect and honor shown to military traditions, practices, symbols, and individuals

military customs

those time-honored practices and outward signs of military courtesy that create a formal atmosphere of respect and honor

Military Customs and Courtesies: Signs of Honor and Respect

Every branch of the armed services has a variety of characteristic customs established long ago and still in use today. Army customs and courtesies lend color, distinction, and ceremony to your daily life as a Soldier.

Courtesies are the outward signs of your respect for your nation, your flag, your comrades, and our country's fallen heroes. They engender mutual respect, good manners, politeness, and discipline.

Customs include such things as responding to a senior officer's presence, recognizing the officer's rank or position of honor, correctly using military titles, wearing headgear, saluting appropriately, reporting correctly, and honoring national and Army symbols and music.

Courtesies to Colors, Music, and Individuals

Courtesies to Colors

National and organizational flags that fly from flagstaffs equipped with finials (the decorative top pieces), are *Colors*. When not in use, Colors are furled and encased to protect them. The military detachment assigned to protect, carry, and display them is called a *color guard*. When you pass an unfurled, uncased national Color, salute at six steps' distance, and hold the salute until you have passed six steps beyond the flag. Similarly, if the uncased Color passes by, salute when the flag is six steps away and hold the salute until it has passed six steps beyond.

You shouldn't salute small national flags carried by individuals, such as those carried by civilian spectators at a parade or printed on solid objects. It's also improper for you to salute while you have any object in your right hand or a cigarette, cigar, or pipe in your mouth.

Courtesies to Music

Military music dates back to the early Roman times when such music called military formations together. Now military music establishes a sense of alertness, urgency, attention to detail, self-discipline, and confidence.

Outdoors, whenever and wherever the United States National Anthem, "To the Color," "Reveille," or "Hail to the Chief" is played, at the first note, all Soldiers in uniform and not in formation face the flag—or the music, if the flag is not in view—stand at attention,

The National Colors and the Army Colors are followed by organizational colors.

and give the prescribed salute. Hold the salute position until the last note of the music sounds. Military personnel not in uniform will stand at attention, removing headgear, if any, and place the right hand over the heart. Vehicles in motion come to a halt. Soldiers riding in a passenger car or on a motorcycle dismount and salute. Occupants of other types of military vehicles and buses remain in the vehicle; the individual in charge of each vehicle dismounts and renders the hand salute. Tank and armored car commanders salute from the vehicle.

Indoors, when honoring the US flag, national anthem, and bugle calls, officers and Soldiers stand at attention and face the music or the flag, if one is present.

Other songs worthy of respect and honor include "The Army Song," "Stars and Stripes Forever," "America the Beautiful," and "God Bless America."

Bugle calls are another form of military music to which you should respond with attention. These include:

- Attention, Assembly, Adjutant's Call
- Carry On, Mess Call, Recall
- Taps, Tattoo
- To the Color, National Anthem
- Sound Off, 1st Call
- Reveille and Retreat.

Courtesies to Individuals

You show respect for people by standing when they enter a room or enter a conversation. When not at attention or saluting, you allow officers the position of honor at a table. These informal gestures demonstrate your character and respect for Army Values.

The expression "under arms" means carrying a weapon in your hands, by a sling, or in a holster.

Uncovering—removing a beret, hat, or headgear—isn't just good manners; it's a sign of respect to others. You should remove your headgear indoors, unless you are under arms. Officers and enlisted Soldiers uncover when they sit as a member of or in attendance on a court or board, when entering places of divine worship, and during attendance at an official reception.

Figure 2.1 Military Rank Progression

Outdoors, you should not remove your military headgear nor raise it as a form of salutation.

Military Customs: Rank and Saluting

Military Rank

For thousands of years, in almost all cultures, leaders have worn or held symbols of their position and authority. In ancient Rome, magistrates carried the *fasces*, a bundle of rods with an axe protruding, as a symbol of their power. Native American chiefs donned eagle feathers to represent their bravery and status in the tribe.

So it's natural for the Army to have rank: Insignia of rank identify who is in charge. The US Army adapted much of its rank structure from the British military tradition. Military rank—unlike a pay grade, which is an administrative feature—is a visible mark of responsibility and leadership meriting recognition and respect. The customary way you recognize an officer of superior rank is to salute him or her.

The Military Salute

The origin of the **military salute** is uncertain, but it probably began as a gesture of trust to show that a person was not holding a weapon. Some historians believe saluting began in Roman times when assassinations were common. A citizen who wanted to see a public official had to approach with his right hand raised to show that he did not hold a weapon. Knights in armor raised their visors with the right hand when meeting other knights. This practice gradually became a way of showing respect and, in early American history, sometimes involved removing one's hat. By 1820, the motion had become touching the hat and, since then, the gesture has evolved into the hand salute used in the military today.

military salute

a formal, one-count military gesture of respect given at attention, in which a subordinate acknowledges a superior officer by bringing the hand to the brim of the cap or to a point slightly above the right eye— Soldiers salute in greeting, leaving, reporting, and other military situations to publicly show respect for the superior's rank

When to Salute

A salute is a public sign of respect and recognition of another's higher rank. When in uniform, you salute when you meet and recognize an officer entitled to a salute by rank except when inappropriate or impractical. Generally, in any case not covered by specific situations, a salute is the respectful, appropriate way to acknowledge a superior officer.

Times you should salute include:

- When the US National Anthem, "To the Color," "Hail to the Chief," or foreign national anthems are played
- When you see uncased National Colors outdoors
- On ceremonial occasions
- At reveille and retreat ceremonies during the raising or lowering of the US flag
- During the sounding of honors
- When the Pledge of Allegiance is being recited outdoors
- When relieving an officer or turning over control of formations
- When rendering reports
- When greeting officers of friendly foreign countries
- When you see officers in official vehicles.

When *Not* to Salute

You don't have to salute indoors, except when you report to a superior officer. If either person is wearing civilian clothes and you do not recognize the other person as a superior officer, salutes are unnecessary.

Use common sense. If you are carrying something with both hands or doing something that makes saluting impractical, you are not required to salute a senior officer or return a salute to a subordinate. A simple greeting of the day, "Good morning, Sir (Ma'am)," is acceptable and encouraged.

Use your judgment. You don't have to salute in an airplane, on a bus, when driving a vehicle, or in public places such as inside theaters or other places of business. The driver of a moving vehicle does not initiate a salute.

Sometimes saluting is inappropriate. Soldiers participating in games and members of work details do not salute. Soldiers reporting to an NCO do not salute.

How to Salute

The hand salute is a smart, one-count movement at the command "Present, arms." When wearing headgear with a visor with or without glasses, on the command of execution "arms," raise the right hand sharply, fingers and thumb extended and joined, palm facing down. Place the tip of the right forefinger on the rim of the visor slightly to the right of the right eye. The outer edge of the hand barely cants downward, so that neither the back of the hand nor the palm is clearly visible from the front. The hand and wrist are straight, the elbow inclined slightly forward, and the upper arm horizontal.

A well-executed salute is crisp, quick, and immediate, with both subordinate and senior officer making the movement in a professional gesture of respect and recognition of that respect. Saluting should become a reflex to you.

Saluting People in Vehicles

You should practice the appropriate courtesy of saluting officers in official vehicles, recognized individually by grade or by identifying vehicle plates and/or flags. You don't salute officers or return salutes from subordinates who are driving or riding in privately owned vehicles.

Greeting an officer

Saluting in Formation

In formation, you don't salute or return salutes except at the command "Present, arms." An individual in formation at ease or at rest comes to attention when addressed by an officer. In this case, the individual in charge salutes and acknowledges salutes on behalf of the entire formation. Commanders of units that are not a part of a larger formation salute officers of higher grade by bringing the unit to attention before saluting. When under battle or simulated battle conditions, you should not call your unit to attention.

Saluting Out of Formation

When an officer approaches a group of individuals not in formation, the first person noticing the officer calls everyone present to attention. All come sharply to attention and salute.

If you are in charge of a work detail, but not actively engaged, you salute and acknowledge salutes for the entire detail.

A unit resting along a road does not automatically come to attention upon the approach of an officer. If the officer speaks to an individual or the group, however, the individual or group comes to attention and remains at attention—unless otherwise ordered—until the conversation ends, at which time the individual or group salutes the officer.

Reporting to a Superior Officer
Reporting Indoors

When **reporting** to a superior officer in his or her office, the Cadet, officer, or Soldier removes headgear, knocks, and enters when told to do so, approaches within two steps of the officer's desk, halts, salutes, and reports, "Sir (Ma'am), Cadet Jones reports." Hold the salute until your report is complete and the officer has returned your salute. At the end of the report, you salute again, holding the salute until it is returned. Then you smartly execute the appropriate facing movement and depart. When reporting indoors under arms, the

reporting

the procedure for approaching and speaking to a superior officer that includes approaching, standing at attention, saluting, politely addressing the officer, waiting for recognition, and concisely giving the necessary report, message, or briefing

Critical Thinking

What could be one practical purpose of the reporting procedure? Why might such formal address be necessary to good order, clarity, and precision in the field?

procedure is the same, except that you don't remove your headgear and you render the salute prescribed for the weapon you are carrying.

When a Soldier reports to an NCO, the procedures are the same, except that the two exchange no salutes.

Reporting Outdoors

When reporting outdoors, you move rapidly toward the senior officer, halt approximately three steps from the officer, salute, and concisely make your report, as you do indoors. When dismissed by the officer, you exchange salutes again. If under arms, you should carry your weapon in the manner prescribed for saluting with that weapon. (See FM 3–21.5, Appendix A.)

CONCLUSION

The disciplined exercise of military customs and courtesies in an organization is a clear indicator of the morale and leadership of that organization. It also indicates an organization's ability to function under stress as a team of professionals bound by a warrior ethos and mutual respect.

As an ROTC Cadet, you acknowledge your place in the profession of arms through your crisp, professional exercise of customs and courtesies—smartly saluting, properly reporting, and otherwise showing appropriate signs of honor and respect.

Learning Assessment

1. While listening to Army music, songs, and bugle calls, demonstrate your ability to stand at attention, salute, report, and uncover at appropriate times by role-playing with classmates.

2. Name three times when you are required to salute a superior officer and three times when saluting is unnecessary.

3. What is the difference between a flag and a Color?

4. What is the difference between a courtesy and a custom? Give an example of each.

5. Explain the purpose of military rank.

Key Words

military courtesy
military customs
military salute
reporting

References

AR 600–25, *Salutes, Honors and Visits of Courtesy*. 24 September 2004.

Field Manual 3–21.5, *Drill and Ceremonies*. 7 July 2003.

Field Manual 670–1, *Wear and Appearance of Uniforms & Insignia*. 3 February 2005.

US Army Military History Institute. (November 1989). The Hand Salute: A Working Bibliography of MHI Sources. Carlisle, PA. Retrieved 18 July 2005 from http://carlisle-www.army.mil/usamhi/Bibliographies/ReferenceBibliographies/customs/salute.doc

OFFICERSHIP AND THE ARMY PROFESSION

Key Points

1 **The Concept of a Profession**

2 **The Three Characteristics of a Profession**

3 **Professionalism and the Military**

Yours is the profession of arms, the will to win, the sure knowledge that in war there is no substitute for victory, that if you lose, the Nation will be destroyed, that the very obsession of your public service must be duty, honor, country.

GEN Douglas MacArthur

Introduction

The Army requires that you—as a Cadet and future officer—accept responsibilities not just for doing a job, but also for assuming a way of life. In other words, the Army requires you to become a professional as stated in FM 1, *The Army*:

> The purpose of any profession is to serve society by effectively delivering a necessary and useful specialized service. To fulfill those societal needs, professions—such as medicine, law, the clergy, and the military—develop and maintain distinct bodies of specialized knowledge and impart expertise through formal, theoretical, and practical education. Each profession establishes a unique subculture that distinguishes practitioners from the society they serve while supporting and enhancing that society. Professions create their own standards of performance and codes of ethics to maintain their effectiveness. To that end, they develop particular vocabularies, establish journals, and sometimes adopt distinct forms of dress. In exchange for holding their membership to high technical and ethical standards, society grants professionals a great deal of autonomy. However, the profession of arms is different from other professions, both as an institution and with respect to its individual members.

As in so much else, GEN George Washington set the example for the Army professional at a time of crisis in our young republic:

GEN Washington at Newburgh

Following its victory at Yorktown in 1781, the Continental Army set up camp at Newburgh, New York, to wait for peace with Great Britain. The central government formed under the Articles of Confederation proved weak and unwilling to supply the Army properly or even pay the Soldiers who had won the war for independence. After months of waiting, many officers, angry and impatient, suggested that the Army march on the seat of government in Philadelphia, Pennsylvania, and force Congress to meet the Army's demands. One colonel even suggested that GEN Washington become King George I.

Upon hearing this, GEN Washington assembled his officers and publicly and emphatically rejected the suggestion. He believed that seizing power by force would have destroyed everything for which the Revolutionary War had been fought. By this action, GEN Washington firmly established an enduring precedent: America's armed forces are subordinate to civilian authority and serve the democratic principles that are now enshrined in the Constitution. GEN Washington's action demonstrated the loyalty to country that the Army must maintain in order to protect the freedom enjoyed by all Americans.

The Concept of a Profession

When you think about professions, what comes to mind? Credentials, years of study and training, a code of ethics, status in the eyes of the community? Think of the medical caregiver, the legal specialist, the accountant, the architect, the teacher, the law enforcement officer, or the clergy member. What do they have in common with the profession you are training for and are about to enter—the military profession? To truly understand your role as a military professional, you must first understand what people mean when they talk about a *profession*.

A profession is a calling—a vocation. It's a livelihood, yes, but it goes far beyond a simple occupation or "what you do" for a living. A profession is a way of being, a way of thinking, a way of behaving, and a way of growing. In short, it's a *way of life*, not just a job or a lifestyle.

Most professionals would probably tell you that they do what they do because they love their work, that they couldn't do anything else, that they would do it even if they didn't make money at it. The Army is just such a profession. That's why it's important to realize the difference between an occupation—a job—and a profession.

The job of Army officer is the highest embodiment of the profession of arms. When you become a commissioned officer in the US Army, you join an elite body of leaders with a long, proud tradition of service to the country and a commitment to high ideals.

The Three Characteristics of a Profession

One of the outward distinctions of a uniformed profession is to display distinctive clothing. In previous sections, you've read about the importance of military rank, insignia, and the uniform.

Another characteristic of a profession is dedication to service. You perform your service in the military within a profession.

Three characteristics distinguish a profession as a special type of work: expertise, responsibility, and corporate culture.

Expertise

Professionals are who and what they are because they acquire **expertise**—a special kind of knowledge and a context for that knowledge. Expertise can be of at least three types: *technical*—based on training and study; *theoretical/intellectual*—based on education and study; and *liberal*—based on broad reading, interactions with colleagues, and a focus on lifelong learning.

expertise

what you know (theoretical), what you know how to do (technical), and what the value of that knowledge is to the greater society (broad liberal application)

Technical Expertise

Professionals know how to operate the hardware of their professions. They are technically expert. For the doctor, it is an in-depth knowledge of medicines and drugs, laboratory testing, imaging equipment, and surgical procedures. For the architect, it is a well-defined knowledge of loads, stresses, materials tolerances, and coefficients. For the military professional, it is an intimate knowledge of the technology of field weapons, aircraft, tank, artillery, computers, telecommunications, or other specialized equipment.

Theoretical (or Intellectual) Expertise

This is the "how" and "why" of the technical component. In our example of medicine, technicians can perform the tests, but may not know the how and why behind the intricate functions of the human body. A construction worker knows how to pour cement for a reinforced foundation, but may not understand how or why the foundation will hold up the building. The same is true of the Soldier who knows the basic functions of the Army's equipment. It's not necessary for him or her to understand the theoretical concepts behind the tactical or strategic use of the equipment. This component of the professional officer's job is what enables him or her to comprehend and apply new techniques.

Life or death decisions come from an officer's ability to understand the greater mission and apply tactical skills to fulfilling the mission. The only information an officer may receive is the commander's intent. He or she must move forward and deduce the how and why, especially during combat and in today's Contemporary Operating Environment.

Broad Liberal Expertise

This is probably the most complex and the most important component of expertise. Liberal knowledge is a professional officer's ability to understand the role of his or her profession and its unique expertise within society. It includes the knowledge of behavior, human relationships, standards of conduct, and the structures of human organizations. A professional needs to know when and how to offer his or her services to achieve the most desirable and effective results. You could call this the *philosophy* of arms or the doctrinal grounding of military science.

Military Expertise

What expertise does the Army expect you, as an officer in training, to master? The Army expects you to learn how to organize, equip, and train the force—your Soldiers. The Army also expects you to plan the activities of the force with clarity of mission. You also must know how to execute the mission, a task critical to the military's success. Finally, the Army expects you to be expert in directing operations—engaging in the many kinds of Army activities during both war and peace. Directing operations is a core responsibility of a professional military officer.

Responsibility

Professional Responsibility

As you've seen, professionals require intensive education in a particular service or skill that most members of society do not have. Along with all of this expertise are some distinct **responsibilities**. As an Army professional, you must be aware of them.

By definition, a professional offers a service that is vital to society. This service is performed for a person or group of people commonly referred to as clients.

By definition, professional expertise is so complex that laymen are usually not capable of understanding what the professional does or how he or she does it. Therefore, the professional has exclusive possession of a certain skill set, and the client agrees to accept the professional's application of those skills. This relationship creates certain expectations. Just as the professional expects the client to place affairs completely within his or her hands, the client expects the professional to observe certain ethical standards of behavior. Society expects the Army professional to fulfill three key obligations:

- Not exceed professional competence (no "Custer's Last Stands")
- Act only in the nation's best interest
- Maintain integrity with the American people.

Clearly the professional has most of the leverage in this relationship, at least until proven otherwise, and he or she is accepted as the unquestioned authority.

Two major motivating factors prevent abuse of this power. The *first* is the vocation or "calling" aspect of the profession discussed earlier. Most people enter a profession because of an abiding desire to serve society and their fellow man. Many endure great personal hardship to meet the standards of their "calling." Consider the medical student who graduates with hefty student loans after spending many years as a full-time student—or your own sacrifices to attend college and become a military professional.

The *second* motivator is autonomy. Most professionals desire to maintain their ability to control their profession. They realize that only as long as the profession as a whole abides by ethical standards will society allow it to keep functioning autonomously.

Responsibility of Officership

The military officer is responsible for the military security of the United States. Most Americans accept the idea of allowing Army professionals to safeguard and carry out the business of protecting the nation. Most would not know how to fight a war and, when placed in a situation of grave danger, would quickly defer to the military officer for that expertise.

Today, the Army spends billions of dollars and huge amounts of time building competence in the military profession. The structure of the Army rests on ensuring that military professionals do not assume command positions until they are capable of doing so. The US Constitution, the Soldier's Creed, and the Army Leadership Framework are all sources of the ethical authority and moral obligation to which military professionals adhere in maintaining the trust of the American people and our allies. You will study the Soldier's Creed, Army Values, and Army Leadership Framework in other sections of this textbook.

Corporate Culture

In the Army, the **corporate culture** for military professionals is found, in part, in its customs and courtesies you have already studied, and in the "Warrior Ethos" introduced earlier in this textbook.

What does corporate culture mean? It refers to a group of people experiencing a sense of belonging or a common bond. Among Army professionals, corporate culture tends to result from the following factors:

- A common bond of mission, shared customs and courtesies, and comradeship
- A desire to remain autonomous
- A unique professional knowledge and expertise.

These factors tend to lead to standard professional practices. Among them are:

1. *A desire to police the profession.* The military has specific doctrine to follow; it also has codes and its own military justice system.

2. *Control of entry.* You must pass the numerous tests used to place military professionals into positions, and you must also go through extensive training and education to receive your commission. A commission is to the officer what a license or certification is to a doctor, attorney, or accountant.

3. *The need to promote professional knowledge.* The key focus is to develop leaders who can fulfill the mission. This requires continuous, extensive training and education.

4. *A desire to represent the profession.* Every action taken by a military professional is representative of the military, down to the uniform he or she wears or the language he or she uses.

Professionalism and the Military

You exhibit professionalism as an Army officer and leader when you respect the Constitution and the military's civilian leadership; when you live the Soldier's Creed and Army Values; and when you can apply the elements of the Army Leadership Framework—Be, Know, Do—in all of your daily activities, no matter what your rank, your current job, or where you are assigned.

While most professionals serve an individual client, the Army officer's client is the nation—whether helping in disaster recovery, protecting national security, or defeating an enemy. As GEN MacArthur notes in the quotation at the beginning of this section, the military's professional failure would be catastrophic. Army officers—like their counterparts in the other armed services—study, work, and train throughout their professional careers to ensure that the military profession will not fail when duty calls.

CONCLUSION

The Army officer is the cornerstone of the nation's military. As George Washington, Douglas MacArthur, and other leaders have asserted, without a strong officer corps, the Army lacks the basis of professionalism critical for national security. Being an Army officer is not just another job. It's a proud profession with a rich history of serving the nation. Army training and leader development are unrivaled in the world. Your ROTC program aims to help you become the kind of Army officer—to reach a degree of professionalism—of which you, your family, and your country can be proud.

Learning Assessment

1. Define the concept of a profession.
2. List and define the three characteristics of a profession.
3. Discuss how a doctor, lawyer, and military officer each approach their vocations with the same mindset.

Key Words

expertise
responsibility
corporate culture

References

Field Manual 1, *The Army*. 14 June 2005.

Field Manual 6-22, *Army Leadership: Competent, Confident, and Agile*. 12 October 2006.

ORIENTEERING

Key Points

1 Understanding Orienteering

2 Using a Map

3 Finding Your Way

4 Orienteering Terms and Techniques

Today, the complexities of tactical operations and deployment of troops are such that it is essential for all Soldiers to be able to read and interpret their maps in order to move quickly and effectively on the battlefield.

FM 3–25.26

Introduction

As an officer and a Soldier, one of your most important pieces of equipment will be a map.

Knowing how to read that map, knowing where you are, and knowing where you are going allows you to call for indirect fire (for example, artillery support), close air support (such as Army aviation assets), and medical evacuation. Using that map is critical to your survival, your Soldiers' survival, and the success of your mission.

This section has three goals:

- To introduce you to some basic concepts and techniques of orienteering
- To introduce you to some basic map-reading and land-navigation skills that will help you find your way in unfamiliar territory, such as your college campus or around your ROTC training area
- To give you a foundation for success as you further develop your map reading and land-navigation skills throughout the ROTC program.

In the following vignette, LTC Robert Ballard studied the terrain features of the French countryside while in flight prior to parachuting into Normandy. His ability to terrain associate and navigate became critical to his survival. As soon as he parachuted to the ground, he compared what he had seen during his flight and descent with his map, determined his location, and continued his mission.

On the Ground in Normandy

It had been the practice of Second Battalion [501st Parachute Infantry Regiment, 101 Airborne Division] to use a large bell and a green electric lantern for assembly following the drop. Coming into Normandy [in France, the night before D-Day, 6 June 1944], these two markers were jumped with personnel. But both of the men were lost and so the assembly ground went unmarked.

LTC Robert A. Ballard came to earth right on the drop zone, which put him about 600 yards to the southeast of Les Droueries. His experience was unique among the battalion commanders of 101st Division in that he knew from the beginning that he was in the right spot. He wasn't quite sure why he knew except that the ground looked as he had expected to find it. Too, he had carefully noted the river courses and roads on the flight in, and when he had jumped, he had felt certain that the calculation had been about right.

Now, lying on the ground, he thought back over the drop and he figured he had probably drifted a little bit. But it was still only a question of being a few fields distant from the point he had been seeking. Mortar and machine gun fire was enlivening the neighborhood; the closest shells were dropping 50 to 75 yards away.

Ballard [had] landed within 25 yards of a hedgerow but he didn't crawl to it immediately. He lay perfectly still for about three or four minutes except for getting a grenade ready while thinking out his next move. He had seen tracer fire follow him during the descent and he strained to know whether he had been spotted. He freed himself at last and ran to a ditch.

There he took out a map and a flashlight and from his reading he knew his location for certain within a few hundred yards; the map checked with what he had remembered of the land picture as he came to earth.

History Section, US Army European Theater of Operations

Understanding Orienteering

FM 3–25.26, *Map Reading and Land Navigation*, describes orienteering as:

> . . . a competitive form of land navigation suitable for all ages and degrees of fitness and skill. It provides the suspense and excitement of a treasure hunt. The object of orienteering is to locate control points by using a map and compass to navigate through the woods. The courses may be as long as 10 kilometers (FM 3–25.26).

The American Heritage Dictionary defines orienteering as "a cross-country race in which competitors use a map and compass to find their way through unfamiliar territory."

Orienteering began in Scandinavia in the 19th century as a military event and a part of military training. It became a competitive sport in the early 20th century in Sweden and came to the United States after World War II.

The object of an orienteering competition is to find a series of specific locations (often called *control points* or *targets*) on the ground. Each participant gets a topographic map with the control points circled. The terrain is usually wooded and uninhabited, and allows for different levels of competition. The course setter (the person who plans the course) tries to keep the course interesting, but not so complicated that the competitors can't complete it.

There are several types of orienteering events. The most common are:

- *Route orienteering.* A master competitor leads a group as it walks a route. Beginners trace the route on the map as they walk it on the ground and circle the control points. In another variation, a route is laid out with markers for individual competitors to follow. The winner is the competitor who has successfully traced the route and accurately plotted the most control points.
- *Line orienteering.* Competitors trace their route from a master map and then walk it, circling the control points as they locate them on the ground. The course usually contains five or more control points.
- *Cross-country orienteering.* This most common type of orienteering event is also called *free* or *point* orienteering. Competitors start at one-minute intervals and visit the control points in the same order. The contestant with the fastest time around the course wins. The course usually contains six to 12 control markers.
- *Score orienteering.* Control points are scattered around the competition area. Those near the start and finish point have a low point value, while those farther away have a higher value. Competitors locate as many control points as they can within a specified time, often 90 minutes. Competitors earn points for hitting the control points and lose points for exceeding the specified time. The contestant with the most points wins.

Like any competitive event, an orienteering competition has officials, scorecards, and a start and finish area. Control points are indicated with markers and have some kind of device so that contestants can prove they have visited the control point. The device may be different-colored crayons, punch pliers, letter or number combinations, or stamps or coupons.

To help develop your map-reading and navigation skills, your ROTC instructor may set up an orienteering course using a combination of orienteering course types and rules in order to cater your orienteering lesson to your campus and to your freshman experience. You and your fellow Cadets, working in teams, should attempt to locate as many control points on your campus map as possible in the time allotted. Below are some of the skills you'll need to successfully complete the course and to prepare for instruction on map reading and land navigation later in your ROTC studies.

Using a Map

The basic tool of orienteering, of course, is a **map**.

Some of the oldest maps still survive on clay tablets archeologists have unearthed in digs of ancient Babylonian cities—present-day Iraq—and date from 2500 to 2300 B.C.E. Demands for better maps came from military necessity. The first tribes needed to map the lay of the land around their villages so they could defend them from other tribes.

Today, maps are everywhere. But for a map to be useful, you must know how to use it.

Orient the Map

Your first step is to orient your map to the north. Almost all modern maps, including most tourist maps, display a north secant arrow somewhere on the map. If a north arrow is not used, as a general rule most maps will show north as "up" or at the top of the map. East is right. West is left. South is "down" or at the bottom of the map. If a north arrow is not used, and the map does not indicate which side of the map is north, then you must orient your map to the lay of the land; that is, you must turn your map so that key buildings, intersections, or terrain features align in the same direction that you are holding your map. This technique is called terrain association, and you will learn more about terrain association in this section as well as in future land-navigation lessons.

1. Unfold your map, preferably on a solid flat surface. Familiarize yourself with the map: its size, scale, features, and colors. Read the legend. Locate the north arrow on your map.

2. Open your **compass** and lay it on top of the map. Let the dial of the compass swing freely. (Many compasses lock as you close them. This protects the moving parts.) The magnetic arrow will point north. Rotate your map under your compass until the map's north arrow points in the same direction as the compass arrow. If you do not have a north arrow on your map, and the map legend indicates that north is to the top of the map, then rotate your map until the side

map

graphic representation of a portion of the earth's surface drawn to scale, as seen from above—it uses colors, symbols, and labels to represent features found on the ground

compass

a navigation tool that uses the earth's magnetic field to determine direction

Critical Thinking

How does learning about a fun and competitive cross-country sport help prepare you to become a better officer?

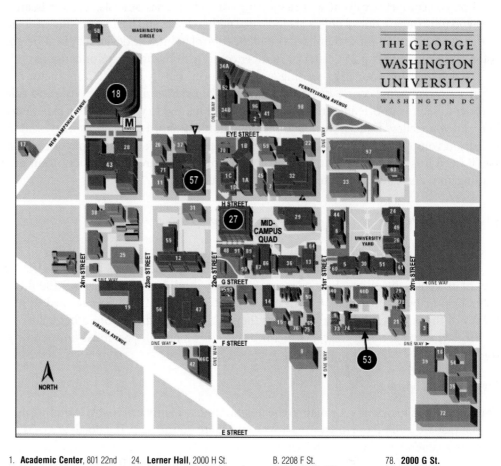

1. **Academic Center**, 801 22nd St.
   A. Phillips Hall
   B. Rome Hall
   C. Smith Hall of Art
   D. Visitor Center
2. **John Quincy Adams House**, 2129-33 Eye Street
3. **Alumni House**, 1925 F St.
4. **Horlense Amsterdam House**, 2110 G St.
5. **Bell Hall**, 2020 G St.
6. **Corcoran Hall**, 725 21st St.
7. **Crawford Hall**, 2119 H St.
8. **Dakota**, 2100 F St.
9. **Davis-Hodgkins House**, 609 21st St.
10. **Abba Eban House**, 607 22nd St.
11. **Fulbright Hall**, 2223 H St.
12. **Funger Hall**, 2201 G St.
13. **Government, Hall of**, 710 21st St.
14. **GSEHD**, 2134 G St.
15. **Guthridge Hall**, 2115 F St.
16. **The George Washington University Club**, 1918 F St.
17. **The George Washington University Inn**, 824 New Hamphsire Ave.
18. **Hospital, GW**, 900 23rd St.
19. **Ivory Towers Residence Hall**, 616 23rd St.
20. **Kennedy Onassis Hall**, 2222 Eye St.
21. **Key Hall**, 600 20th St.
22. **Lafayette Hall**, 2100 Eye St.
23. **Lenthall Houses**, 606-610 21st St.
24. **Lerner Hall**, 2000 H St.
25. **Lerner Framily Health and Wellness Center**, 2301 G St.

Libraries
26. **Jacob Burns (Law)**, 716 20th St.
27. **Melvin Gelman (University)**, 2130 H St.
28. **Paul Himmelfarb Health Sciences (Medical)** 2300 Eye St.
29. **Lisner Auditorium**, 730 21sst St.
30. **Lisner Hall**, 2023 G St.
31. **Madison Hall**, 735 22nd St.
32. **Marvin Center**, 800 21st St.
33. **Media & Public Affairs**, 805 21st St.
34. **Medical Faculty Associates**, 2150 Pennsylvania Ave.
   A. H.B. Burns Memorial Bldg.
   B. Ambulatory Care Center
35. **Mitchell Hall**, 514 19th St.
36. **Monroe Hall**, 2115 G St.
37. **Munson Hall**, 2212 Eye St.
38. **New Hall**, 2350 H St.
39. **Old Main**, 1922 F St.
40. **Quigley's**, 619 21st St.
41. **Rice Hall**, 2121 Eye St.
42. **Riverside Towers Hall**, 2201 Virginia Ave.
43. **Ross Hall**, 2300 Eye St.
44. **Samson Hall**, 2036 H St., 729 21st St.
45. **Schenley Hall**, 2121 H St.
46. **Scholars Village Townhouses**
   A. 619 22nd St.

B. 2208 F St.
C. 520-526 22nd St.
D. 2028 G St.
E. 605-607 21st St.
47. **Smith Center**, 600 22nd St.
48. **Staughton Hall**, 707 22nd St.
49. **Stockton Hall**, 720 20th St.
50. **Strong Hall**, 620 21st St.
51. **Stuart Hall**, 2013 G St.
52. **Student Health Services**, 2150 Pennsylvania Ave.
53. **Support Building**, 2025 F St.
54. **Thurston Hall**, 1900 F St.
55. **Tompkins Hall of Engineering**, 725 23rd St.
56. **Townhouse Row**, 607 23rd St.
57. **University Garage**, 2211 H St.
58. **Warwick Bldg.**, 2300 K St.
59. **The West End**, 2124 Eye St.
60. **Woodhull House**, 2033 G St.
61. **700 20th St.**
62. **812 20th St.**
63. **814 20th St.**
64. **714 21st St.**
65. **600 21st St.**
66. **609 22nd St.**
67. **613 22nd St.**
68. **615 22nd St.**
69. **617 22nd St.**
70. **837 22nd St.**
71. **817 23rd St.**
72. **9957 E St.**
73. **2033-37 F St.**
74. **2031 F St.**
75. **2101 F St.**
76. **2109 F St.**
77. **2147 F St.**

78. **2000 G St.**
79. **2002 G St.**
80. **2008 G St.**
81. **2030 G St.**
82. **2106 G St.**
83. **2108 G St.**
84. **2112 G St.**
85. **2114 G St.**
86. **2125 G St.**
87. **2127 G St.**
88. **2129 G St.**
89. **2129 G St.** (rear)
90. **2131 G St.**
91. **2131 G St.** (rear)
92. **2136 G St.**
93. **2138 G St.**
94. **2140 G St.**
95. **2142 G St.**
96. **2129-2133 Eye St.** (rear)
97. **2000 Pennsylvania Ave.**
98. **2100 Pennsylvania Ave.**
99. **2136 Pennsylvania Ave.**
100. **2140 Pennsylvania Ave.**
101. **2142 Pennsylvania Ave.**

All addresses are in Northwest Washington.

For assistance or information call the GW Information Center (202) 994-GWGW.

For information on accessibility, call (202) 994-8250 (TDDevice).

Parking
Marvin Center (See #32)
University Garage (See #57)

P Visitor parking entrance

Figure 1.1 Map of The George Washington University
© George Washington University

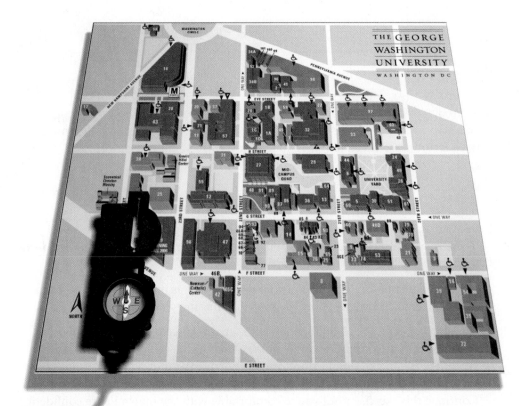

Figure 1.2 Orienting the GWU Map

of your compass is parallel with the side of your map. You have now *oriented* your map to magnetic north. If you have no way of knowing which way on your map is north, then orienting your map to your compass is useless and you must orient your map to the terrain (terrain associate).

Look, for example, at the map of The George Washington University (GWU) in Washington, DC (Figure 1.1). In the lower left-hand corner, you'll see an arrow pointing to north. Using your compass as outlined above, you orient the map so that this north arrow on the map and the compass point in the same direction (see Figure 1.2).

Find Your Location

Now that you have oriented your map, the next step is to figure out where on the map you are located. Doing so is very similar to how you may have determined your location using the maps provided in an amusement park or a shopping mall.

Critical Thinking

Your compass points north because Earth's magnetic field attracts it. Sometimes, however, a compass might not point to true north, or might point a few degrees away from true north. Why would that happen? (You will learn more about the three norths in Section 5.)

Critical Thinking

There are different primitive or "field expedient" methods that you can research on your own as to how to determine your direction both day and night if you do not have a compass. These primitive methods will work, but why is using a compass better?

1. Face north. Look around. Find some identifying features of the area around you. These may be streets and intersections, large buildings (the campus library or the town hall), or hills and streams.

2. Find these identifying features on your map. Spend as much time as you need with this. Be comfortable using the map and finding your location.

3. Compare what you read on the map with what you see on the ground. Locate other features in your area, work from the map to the ground and from the ground to the map. Look in front of you (north). What do you see? What's on the map? Look to your left (west). What do you see? What's on the map? Continue this exercise until you're comfortable with the map and are confident that you have pinpointed your location.

On the GWU map, assume that you have just come up out of the Washington Metro (subway) at the station marked with an "M" in a square—next to Building 18 in the upper left corner of the map. Standing on 23rd Street facing east, you look to your left (north) and see that the building you are looking at is the GWU Hospital. Looking at the legend underneath the map, you see that Building 18 and the GWU Hospital are the same building. Now you know that you are in the northwest corner of the campus. You further confirm your location by correctly identifying that Building 28 is to your south and Building 20 is to your east. You have pinpointed your location as being at the intersection of 23rd and I (Eye) Street.

Finding Your Way

Once you know where north is and where you are, you're ready to find where you want to go and determine how to get there.

1. *Identify the control points.* (Control points are your targets or the locations you want to go to.) These may be already printed on your map or on a plastic (or thin paper) overlay. If the control points are on an overlay, transfer the control points to your map. Mark and identify them with a thin-lead pencil or a thin-point pen. (Keeping the map and the overlay together as you move across campus or through town will be cumbersome.) Ensure that you do not mark over important or identifying features on your map. Your control points may also be named or listed on a separate sheet of paper. If so, you must use your map legend or find your control points on the map using building names, street names, etc. Once you have found your named control points, you can mark them on your map with a light circle or X.

Looking at the GWU map, assume your first control point is at the Support Building. That is your control point. Looking at the alphabetical listing of buildings on campus, you find that it is at 2025 F Street, Building 53. Looking at the map, you find that Building 53 is in the southeast corner of campus. You also notice that the north-south cross streets are numbered (20th, 21st, 22nd, etc.) with the numbers increasing as you move west. The east-west cross streets are lettered (F, G, H, etc.) with the letters deeper in the alphabet as you move north. The diagonal streets are named after states (Pennsylvania, Virginia, New Hampshire).

2. *Plan your route.* Most orienteering events will be timed; the individual or team that returns within the prescribed time with the most correct control points will be determined the winner(s). Because of this, it is crucial for you to correctly plot (mark) your control points accurately on your map and determine the most time-efficient route to take to find as many control points as possible, while still allowing time to return within the time limit. In some orienteering competitions, the sequence in which you must locate your control points may be dictated for you. Plan the course you intend to take to get to each of the control points. You can write down the sequence you wish to take, or you can write your route on your map. One technique to prevent confusing the many routes to control points is to number each "leg" of the route.

   On the GWU map, you have a number of options. You could take I (Eye) Street east two blocks to 21st Street, then turn right (south) and go three blocks to F Street, turn left (east again) and walk to the Support Building. Or, you could walk three blocks south down 23rd Street to F Street, turn left, and walk two and a half blocks east. (Note that the blocks are not all the same size.)

3. *Consider time, distance, crowds, and traffic.* Weigh straight-line routes against ease of passage. (Cutting across the football field may be a good idea as long as the band isn't practicing on the field. You may need to go around.) Also keep safety in mind. Crossing a four-lane highway may be the most direct way to reach a control point, but the risk far outweighs the time you will save.

   Looking at the GWU map, you see the Mid-Campus Quad on H Street between 21st and 22nd Streets. You see that you could cut over from H Street through the Quad to 21st Street and save yourself a few steps. Note also that some of the streets through the campus are one-way streets. You'll want to remember that if you have to drive around campus.

4. *Calculate rough distances.* If your map has a graphic bar scale (similar to a ruler), or some other method to measure distance, you can compute the distance on the map to the distance on the ground. This can be useful in deciding which route to take if there are many possible routes to a control point. If your map has no method to scale distance (the map is not to scale), then you will need to terrain associate to get a good feel to the scale of your map compared with the actual terrain.

   The GWU map doesn't have a scale, but after you've walked one block, you'll have a feel for the distance on the ground compared with the distance on the map.

5. *Follow your route.* The fastest way to navigate on an orienteering course is to terrain associate. As you move across the ground, compare your map with key features on the ground and keep your pace with the distance on your map. Compare the buildings and terrain around you with the markings on your map.

   As you walk across campus, you turn or rotate your map to keep it oriented toward your direction of travel. If you are traveling north, then your map should be oriented north. If you take a right turn, then you should rotate your map to the right so your map is now oriented east—the direction of your travel. This way, the buildings you see in front of you and alongside will be the same as those shown on the map. The time to use your compass is when you have forgotten to maintain your map's orientation to the lay of the land, or if you are uncertain of your location, or if you simply want to double-check yourself. Pull out your compass and orient your map to your compass just as you did when you first began. Once your map is oriented, you can pick up where you left off. If your map does not have a north arrow, and you are uncertain of your location, you must back track to your last confirmed or known point on the map, or the most prominent feature that you can identify (such as an intersection, bridge, or a major building). Once you have your bearings, continue along your planned route to your next control point.

6. *Locate the control point.* For your ROTC orienteering exercise, your control points may be important campus buildings or facilities that may be easily identifiable as you approach the control point. However, in orienteering competitions, control points aren't always the obvious landmarks that are easily identifiable from a distance. If this is the case with one of your control points, then you must navigate to a landmark or feature—such as a hilltop—as a checkpoint (sometimes called an attack point) to find your nearby control point. Find the control point on your map. Find a nearby checkpoint on your map. Move quickly to the checkpoint, which will be more easily identifiable than the control point. Then find and move to the control point. Checkpoints may be major buildings, stream junctions, bridges, or road intersections.

   The Quad itself is a good checkpoint. You can also compare the street signs at each corner with the names of the streets on the map. As you walk east along H Street, check to see that you pass the University Garage (Building 57) on your left. Then, just after you cross 22nd Street, look for the Melvin Gelman University Library (Building 27) on your right. These serve as additional checkpoints. The Quad is just east of the library.

7. *Complete the course and return to the start or rally point.* As described earlier, if your orienteering event is a timed event, you may find yourself in a time crunch and unable to find some of your final few control points. If this is the case, you must adjust your final route(s) in a manner that allows you to find as many of your remaining control points but still arrive back at the finish point within the time limit. In order to adjust your final route(s), you may begin at your last control point, or at an easily identifiable checkpoint. From this location, you must consider distance and time remaining to determine which control points you can find and still return before time runs out. You plan your route (or legs) to those remaining control points that you can find within the prescribed time.

   You arrive at the Support Building; check the address and the sign outside the building to make sure you've arrived at the right place.

Congratulations—you're an orienteer!

Orienteering Terms and Techniques

To improve your orienteering skills, learn and use these terms and techniques:

Dead reckoning is moving a set distance along a set line. Generally, it involves moving so many yards or meters in a specific direction, usually a compass reading in degrees.

dead reckoning

a navigation technique by which you travel a set distance (usually in meters) along a set line (usually a compass reading in degrees)

("Move 350 meters due north" or "Move 1,500 meters on an azimuth [or reading] of 220 degrees.")

As you move along your set line, you may want to identify **steering marks** to guide you. Find a point in the distance—a building, a hilltop, a large tree—on your line and move toward that point.

Dead reckoning has two advantages: It is easy to teach and learn, and it is an accurate way of moving from one point to another over short distances.

Handrails. Find existing linear features—trails, fences, roads, streams, power lines— that parallel your route. Use these "handrails" as a check between control points. On the GWU map, the streets are your handrails.

Pacing. You need to know how to measure distance on the ground. Measure out a (or use an established) 100-meter pace course. Walk the course. Count the number of paces it takes for you to walk the 100 meters. This number is your pace count. Some people use a double-pace count: they step off on their left foot and count every time their left foot hits the ground. It is easier to use a double-pace count because you are counting half the number of steps. Everyone's pace count is different, so never rely on a friend's pace count. The longer your legs, the shorter your pace count, and vice versa. Your pace count (double-pace count) may be 73; that is you reach 100 meters on the 73rd alternate footstep. Your friend, who may be just a few inches taller, may have a much longer stride and may be able to cover the same 100 meters in just 67 paces. It is also important for you to know your pace count for the fractions of 100 meters, such as 25 meters and 33 meters. Knowing paces for these distances will allow you to easily figure out fractions of 100 meters such as 25, 33, 50, 66, and 75 meters without a lot of mental computing.

Terrain association is movement by landmarks. You compare what you see on the ground with what you see on your map as you move. When navigating by terrain association, you must constantly orient your map as you change directions. Moving by terrain association is more forgiving than dead reckoning. If you make a mistake by dead reckoning, many times you must move back to your last known position and begin the dead reckoning over again. With terrain association, you can always quickly find your location by comparing what you see around you with what you see on the map. In most cases, you can identify your location without ever having to backtrack at all. Because of this, terrain association is often less time-consuming than dead reckoning. The example in this section used terrain association to travel across campus using the GWU map.

Thumbing. Thumbing is a technique used in terrain association in which you fold your map small enough to put your thumb next to your start point. Do not move your thumb from your start point. To find your new location, look at your map and use your thumb as a reference for your start point. That way, you don't have to keep looking over the entire map.

steering marks

landmarks located on the azimuth to be followed in dead reckoning—steering marks are commonly on or near the highest points visible along the azimuth line and are selected based on what you see on the actual terrain, not from a map study. They may be uniquely shaped trees, rocks, hilltops, posts, towers, and buildings— anything that can be easily identified

terrain association

a navigation technique by which you move from one point to another using landmarks and terrain features

Critical Thinking

What do you think are the advantages and disadvantages of dead reckoning compared with the advantages and disadvantages of terrain association?

CONCLUSION

Orienteering is a fun way to learn the different land navigation methods and techniques available to you. Your ROTC orienteering lesson is an enjoyable way to introduce you to using a map and a compass to navigate from one point to another. Your ROTC orienteering lesson should allow you to become more familiar with offices and organizations on your campus that can help you during your transition as a college student. As you continue with ROTC, you will apply the knowledge from this orienteering lesson to more advanced skills in map reading, navigation, and terrain analysis. If you enjoyed this lesson on orienteering, you may want to consider further research on competitive orienteering that may be available at or near your college or university by visiting http://www.us.orienteering.org/

While orienteering can be an enjoyable pastime, the map-reading and land-navigation skills it teaches are important life skills for Soldiers and the officers who lead them. In the vignette at the beginning of this section, LTC Ballard knew that he had drifted from his original drop zone or point. His use of orienteering skills—linking what was on the ground to what was on the map—made a difference in his ability to carry out his mission in the crucial first hours of the D-Day invasion.

Learning Assessment

1. Explain how to orient a map to the north.
2. Explain how to relate the points on a map to the points on the ground.
3. Describe how to find a control point on campus, in town, or nearby.

Key Words

map
compass
dead reckoning
steering marks
terrain association

References

Field Manual 3–25.26, *Map Reading and Land Navigation*. 18 January 2005.

History Section, US Army European Theater of Operations. (n.d.). Regimental Unit Study 2. *The Fight at the Lock*. File No. 8-3.1 BB 2. Retrieved 30 June 2005 from http://www.army.mil/cmh-pg/documents/wwii/lock/lock.htm

INTRODUCTION TO TACTICS I

Key Points

1 The Elements of a Fire Team

2 The Elements of a Rifle Squad

Soldiers with sharply honed skills form the building blocks of combat effective squads and platoons. They must maintain a high state of physical fitness. They must be experts in the use of their primary weapons. They must be proficient in infantry skills (land navigation, camouflage, individual movement techniques, survival techniques, and so forth). Finally, they must know and practice their roles as members of fire teams, squads, and platoons.

Introduction

The Army's smallest maneuver element controlled by a leader is the **fire team**. The fire team is the building block for all Army tactical operations. Fire teams make up **squads**; squads make up **platoons**. Army lieutenants lead platoons as part of an infantry rifle company.

This section explains the elements, weapons, roles, and responsibilities of the fire team and rifle squad. Success in tactical operations depends on Soldiers at all levels understanding their tactical mission and the steps necessary to accomplish it.

SGT Tommy Rieman led his rifle squad in a firefight in Iraq in 2003. These Soldiers faced enormous odds—and won.

fire team

an infantry element of four Soldiers: a fire team leader, an automatic rifleman, a grenadier, and a rifleman

squad

a nine-Soldier infantry unit made up of the squad leader and two fire teams

platoon

an infantry unit led by a lieutenant consisting of three rifle squads and a headquarters element

Beating 10:1 Odds, Soldier Earns Silver Star

August 26, 2004—In a fight, two against one is bad odds. Ten against one is a recipe for disaster. Yet those were the odds SGT Tommy Rieman and his squad faced and beat when they were ambushed by more than 50 anti-American insurgents in Iraq last December.

Rieman, 24, a team leader in Company B, 3rd Battalion, 504th Parachute Infantry Regiment, 82nd Airborne Division, was awarded the Purple Heart and the Silver Star for his heroic actions [that] December day during a ceremony at Devil Brigade Field August 6. He was also awarded the Army Commendation Medal with a "V" device for valor for a separate reconnaissance mission that took place in March 2003.

Rieman was in charge during the patrol that garnered him the Silver Star because he had scouted the area before and knew the terrain. His eight-man patrol was in three light-skinned Humvees with no doors when the first rocket-propelled grenade hit.

"The thing I remember most was the sound of the explosion. It was so loud," said Rieman.

They were hit by three RPGs [rocket-propelled grenades] and a barrage of small arms fire coming from 10 dug-in enemy fighting positions. Staying in the kill zone meant certain death, so the vehicles never stopped moving. Rieman knew he had to return fire. Bullets whizzed after them as the vehicles sped away from the ambush and the Soldiers found themselves caught in another ambush.

There were maybe 50 enemy attackers blasting away at him with small arms fire from a grove of palm trees nearby. Injuries to his men were beginning to pile up. Out of [Rieman's] squad, SGT Bruce Robinson had lost his right leg in the RPG attack and SPC Robert Macallister had been shot in the buttocks. Rieman himself had been shot in the right arm and chest, and had shrapnel wounds to his chest, stomach, and ear. Worst of all, they were almost out of ammo.

He began firing away with his M203 grenade launcher, raining round after round down on the attackers. After being battered by 15 of Rieman's 40mm grenades, the enemy's guns were silent.

Soldier Stories

The Elements of a Fire Team

SGT Rieman led an infantry rifle squad of eight other Soldiers. That nine-Soldier squad fought as two four-Soldier fire teams, plus the squad leader, SGT Rieman.

A squad's fire teams are referred to as the Alpha Team and Bravo Team. Each fire team has four Soldiers—a fire team leader, a rifleman, an automatic rifleman, and a grenadier. The team members' rank and experience will range from a private (E-1) straight out of Initial Entry Training (IET) and Advanced Individual Training (AIT) to a specialist (E-4) who may have anywhere from one to four years of experience. The team leader is generally a sergeant (E-5) with three to five years of experience.

The team members' positions (rifleman, automatic rifleman, and grenadier) are based on their assigned weapons (rifle, squad automatic weapon [SAW], and M203 grenade launcher). The platoon leader and platoon sergeant consider each Soldier's experience, skill with the weapon, and longevity in the unit before assigning the Soldier a position on the fire team. The rifleman, team leader, and squad leader carry rifles from the M16/M4 family of weapons, based on the table of organization and equipment (TO&E) for various units.

Rifleman

The *rifleman* carries an M16/M4 rifle, a night-vision device, and an infrared (IR) aiming device. Riflemen carry close-combat optic devices and reflexive fire optics. Their role is to engage targets within the range and capability of their weapon. They may also serve as pace man, compass man, near- or far-side security, en route recorder, or ammo bearer.

The M4 Carbine is the fourth generation of the Army's M16 rifle, which was introduced during the Vietnam War. It fires a 5.56 mm round. The M4 has been a part of the Army inventory since 1997. It uses a 30-round magazine and offers the rifleman two firing modes: semiautomatic (a single shot every time the rifleman pulls the trigger) and three-round burst (three shots every time the rifleman pulls the trigger). It has a shorter barrel than

If the platoon does not have enough sergeants to fill all the platoon's team leader positions, the most experienced specialist with the best leadership qualities will be promoted to the leadership rank of corporal and will lead a fire team. The corporal remains at the pay grade of a specialist (E-4), but has the additional leadership responsibilities of a sergeant. The corporal will remain the fire team leader until promotion to sergeant, or until the platoon receives a new sergeant.

Fire Team

Team Leader

Rifleman   Automatic Rifleman   Grenadier

Figure 2.1 Fire Team

Figure 2.2 M4/M4A1 Carbine

Figure 2.3 M4 MWS Carbine

Figure 2.4 Mounting the M68 Close Combat Optic to the M16A1/A2/A3

Figure 2.5 M68 Close Combat Optic Mounted on M16A4/M4-Series Weapons

Figure 2.6 Thermal Weapons Sight for M16A1/A2/A3

the M16 and a collapsible stock, making it lighter and easier for Soldiers to use in close quarters, such as inside a building or in an urban area. Its enhanced upper rail allows Soldiers to mount various day and night sighting devices to improve their effectiveness.

The M4 weighs about seven and a half pounds. A bayonet can be attached for hand-to-hand fighting. It can reach out—accurately—to 600 meters—or more than a quarter-mile away.

Automatic Rifleman

The *automatic rifleman* carries an M249 Squad Automatic Weapon (SAW), a night-vision device, and an IR aiming device. The automatic rifleman's role is to use his or her weapon to maximum effect.

The M249 Squad Automatic Weapon delivers accurate, lethal, and direct automatic fire. Like the M4, it fires a 5.56 mm round. It has been part of the Army inventory since 1987.

TABLE 2.1	Characteristics of the M16-/M4-Series Weapons			
Characteristic	**M16A1**	**M16A2/A3**	**M16A4**	**M4**
WEIGHT (pounds):				
Without magazine and sling	6.35	7.78	9.08	6.49
With sling and loaded:				
20-round magazine	6.75	8.48	9.78	7.19
30-round magazine	7.06	8.79	10.09	7.50
Bayonet knife, M9	1.50	1.50	1.50	1.50
Scabbard	0.30	0.30	0.30	0.30
Sling, M1	0.40	0.40	0.40	0.40
LENGTH (inches):				
Rifle w/bayonet knife	44.25	44.88	44.88	N/A
Overall rifle length	30.00	39.63	39.63	N/A
Butterstock closed	N/A	N/A	N/A	29.75
Butterstock open	N/A	N/A	N/A	33.0
Operational Characteristics:				
Barrel rifling-right hand 1 twist (inches)	12	7	7	7
Muzzle velocity (feet per second)	3,250	3,100	3,100	2,970
Cyclic rate of fire (rounds per minute)	700-800	700-900	800	700-900
Maximum Effective Rate of Fire:				
Semiautomatic (rounds per minute)	45-65	45	45	45
Burst (3-round bursts)(rounds per minute)	N/A	90	90	90
Automatic (rounds per minute)	150-200	150-200 A3	N/A	N/A
Sustained (rounds per minute)	12-15	12-15	12-15	12-15
RANGE (meters):				
Maximum range	2,653	3,600	3,600	3,600
Maximum effective range:				
Point target	460	550	550	500
Area target	N/A	800	600	600

Figure 2.7 M249 Squad Automatic Weapon

Figure 2.8 M4 Carbine With M203A1 Grenade Launcher

The M249 SAW uses 30-round M4 magazines or 200-round preloaded plastic magazines. It weighs a little more than 16 pounds, or twice the weight of an M4. The M249 has a maximum effective range of 1,000 meters—a full kilometer or more than half a mile away.

Grenadier

The *grenadier* carries an M203A1 grenade launcher attached to an M4. It adds about 11 pounds to the weight of the M4. The grenadier carries the same equipment as the others in the squad.

The M203A1 grenade launcher fires out 40 mm grenade rounds. It can fire high-explosive (HE) rounds, tear gas (CN/CS/OC) rounds, smoke rounds, nonlethal projectiles, signal rounds, and practice rounds. The maximum effective range for the M203A1 is 350 meters—or three-and-a-half football fields.

Fire Team Leader

The fire team leader carries an M4 and leads by example. The leader moves the fire team and controls the rate and placement of its fire. Fire team leaders keep track of their teams and their teams' equipment. They make sure their teams meet unit standards and help their squad leaders as necessary.

Buddy Teams

Fire teams are divided into two-Soldier *buddy teams*. Buddy team members support and watch out for each other during combat or other operations. FM 7-8 states that the leader and the automatic rifleman form one buddy team and the grenadier and rifleman form the other, but this is not always the case. Based on unit standing operating procedures (SOPs) and depending on the mission, many units may place the grenadier with the team

TABLE 2.2	General Data for M249 Squad Automatic Weapon
Ammunition	5.56-mm ball and tracer (4:1 mix) ammunition is packaged in 200-round drums, each weighing 6.92 pounds; other types of ammunition available are ball, tracer, blank, and dummy.
Tracer burnout	900 meters (+)
Length of M249	40.87 inches
Weight of M249	16.41 pounds
Weight of tripod mount M122 with traversing and elevating mechanism and pintle	16 pounds
Maximum range	3,600 meters
Maximum effective range	1,000 meters with the tripod and T&E
Area: Tripod	1,000 meters
Bipod	800 meters
Point: Tripod	800 meters
Bipod	600 meters
Suppression	1,000 meters
Maximum extent of grazing fire obtainable over uniformly sloping terrain	600 meters
Height of M249 on tripod mount M122A1	16 inches
Rates of fire:	
Sustained	100 rounds per minute Fired in 6- to 9-round bursts with 4 to 5 seconds between bursts (change barrel every 2 minutes)
Rapid	200 rounds per minute Fired in 6- to 9-round bursts with 2 to 3 seconds between bursts (change barrel every 2 minutes)
Cyclic	650 to 850 rounds per minute Continuous burst (change barrel every minute)
Basic load, ammunition	1,000 rounds (in 200-round drums)
Elevation, tripod controlled	+200 mils
Elevation, tripod free	+445 mils
Depression, tripod controlled	−200 mils
Depression, tripod free	−445 mils
Traverse, controlled by traversing and elevating mechanism	100 mils
Normal sector or file (with tripod)	875 mils

Note: T&E=traverse and elevation mechanism

TABLE 2.3   **Technical Data for the M203/M203A1 Grenade Launcher**

WEAPON

Length:	
Rifle and grenade launcher (overall)	99.0 cm (39 inches)
Barrel only	30.5 cm (12 inches)
Rifling	25.4 cm (10 inches)
Weight:	
Launcher, unloaded	1.4 kg (3.0 pounds)
Launcher, loaded	1.6 kg (3.5 pounds)
Rifle and grenade launcher, both fully loaded	5.0 kg (11.0 pounds)
Number of lands:	6 right hand twists

AMMUNITION

Caliber	40 mm
Weight	About 227 grams (8 ounces)

OPERATIONAL CHARACTERISTICS

Action	Single shot
Sights:	
Front	Leaf sight assembly
Rear	Quadrant sight
Chamber pressure	206,325 kilopascals (35,000 pounds per square inch)
Muzzle velocity	76 meters per second (250 feet per second)
Maximum range	About 400 meters (1,312 feet)
Maximum effective range:	
Fire-team sized area target	350 meters (1,148 feet)
Vehicle or weapon point target	150 meters (492 feet)
Minimum safe firing range (HE):	
Training	130 meters (426 feet)
Combat	31 meters (102 feet)
Minimum arming range	About 14 to 38 meters (46 to 125 feet)
Rate of fire	5 to 7 rounds per minute
Minimum combat load	36 high-explosive rounds

leader so that the team leader can direct the grenadier to mark targets. Because the M203 can mark targets, some units assign M203s to squad leaders so that they can mark targets for the squad.

Why These Weapons?

At this point, you may be wondering why rifle team members carry different weapons. Why not have everyone carry a grenade launcher, for example?

There are several reasons. The fire team must be able to engage and destroy the many different types of targets they are likely to meet on the battlefield. The different weapons the members carry give the team a balance of firepower, simplify the logistics of supplying ammunition, and vary the load each Soldier has to carry. The heavier the weapon, the less other gear or ammunition a Soldier can bear and the less he or she can maneuver.

Critical Thinking

Considering the characteristics, capabilities, and versatility of the fire team's weapons, what factors must the squad leader or fire team leader take into consideration when deciding which team member to assign to each weapon?

The team uses its M16/M4s to engage individual enemy fighters, especially at close quarters, while the M249 is used to engage a concentration of troops or targets covering a larger area with heavy, continuous fire.

Once you compare the maximum rates of fire, the sustained rates of fire, and the maximum range of the rifle and automatic rifle, you can easily understand the value of an automatic rifle on the fire team. The M249's rate of fire and range allow the gunner to cover fire team members when they are maneuvering on the offensive. It is also the backbone of the team's defense when attacked—leaders position the SAW to protect a unit's front, flanks, and rear. In the defense, leaders assign the M249 a *final protective line* to defeat the enemy's attempts to overrun their defensive position. The automatic rifleman has increased lethality (deadliness) and range over the rifleman, but because of the M249's high rate of fire, the automatic rifleman must also carry more ammunition than the rifleman does.

The M203 grenade launcher is the most versatile of the fire team's weapons. The primary advantage the M203 has over the rifle and automatic rifle is that it provides the fire team with indirect fire capabilities; that is, the grenadier can engage targets that he or she cannot see along a direct line of sight. Because the M203 round travels at a high trajectory, or arch, the rounds can reach enemy soldiers in "dead space" (gullies, ditches, trenches, or other fighting positions), or it can reach enemy fighters taking cover in bunkers or in buildings.

When shooting the high-explosive (HE) round, the grenadier is essentially sending out to 350 meters an exploding round with the lethality of a hand grenade—but at a distance far greater than any Soldier can throw a hand grenade. The dual purpose HE round can penetrate up to two inches of light armor, and therefore can destroy trucks and other lightly armored vehicles. During night operations, the grenadier can illuminate the enemy with the star parachute round, allowing other fire team members to see and engage the enemy. The grenadier can show the team members where the enemy is located by using the marking round. The marking round can also be used to indicate landing zones for helicopters or targets for close air support aircraft to attack. The grenadier can also use the star cluster

I love the infantry because they are the underdogs. They are the mud-rain-frost-and-wind boys. They have no comforts, and they even learn to live without the necessities. And in the end they are the guys that wars can't be won without.

Ernie Pyle, World War II correspondent

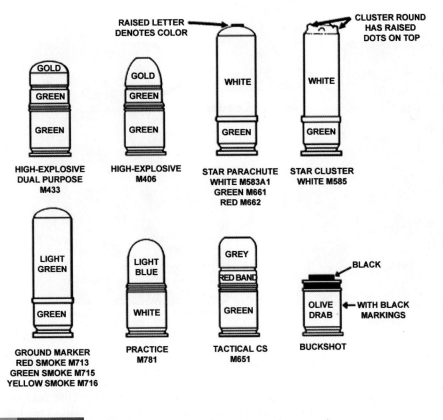

Figure 2.9 Cartridges for the M203 Grenade Launcher

as a prearranged signal to begin a certain tactical action. In urban environments, the grenadier can use tactical CS to flush the enemy out of hiding, or the grenadier can use the buckshot round when entering or clearing rooms or buildings.

As you can see, the various ammunition available for the M203 gives the small fire team a lot of varied firepower and capability that a rifle and an automatic rifle can't provide. The grenadier must also carry a heavier load, however, due to the weight of each round.

The Elements of a Rifle Squad

Two fire teams and a squad leader make up the squad. The rifle squad leader is generally a staff sergeant (E-6) with six to eight years of experience, who came up from the ranks and started as a fire-team rifleman. The squad leader is responsible for everything the squad does—or fails to do. He or she is a tactical leader and leads by example.

Among other things, the squad leader:

- Maneuvers the squad and controls the rate and distribution of its fire
- Trains the squad members in their individual and collective tasks
- Manages the squad's needs, requesting and issuing ammunition, water, rations, and equipment
- Keeps track of the squad's Soldiers and their equipment
- Inspects the squad's weapons, clothing, and equipment and directs their maintenance.

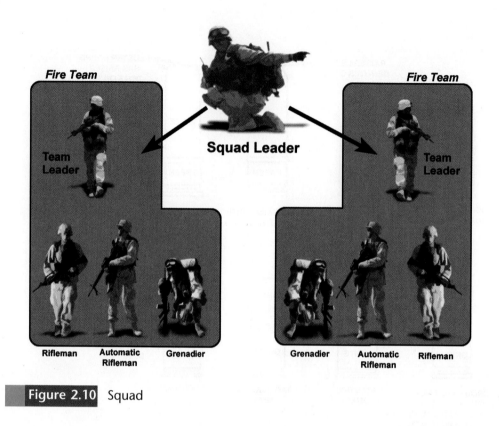

Figure 2.10 Squad

Most of the maneuver and firepower of a rifle platoon derives from the platoon's three rifle squads. Later you will learn more about the infantry rifle platoon and the composition, duties, and responsibilities of the platoon's headquarters element. Together, the rifle squads and headquarters element make up the rifle platoon an Army lieutenant leads. Soon you will study the many types of missions the infantry fire team and squad may be called upon to complete as part of the infantry rifle platoon.

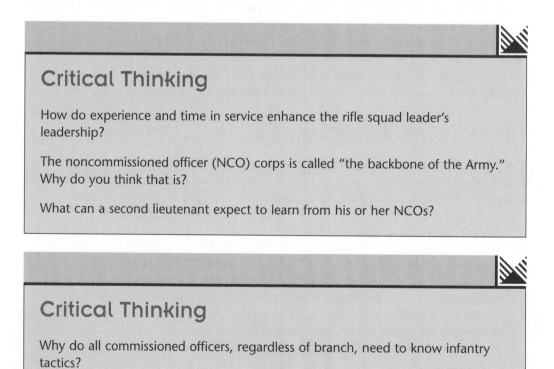

Critical Thinking

How do experience and time in service enhance the rifle squad leader's leadership?

The noncommissioned officer (NCO) corps is called "the backbone of the Army." Why do you think that is?

What can a second lieutenant expect to learn from his or her NCOs?

Critical Thinking

Why do all commissioned officers, regardless of branch, need to know infantry tactics?

CONCLUSION

The infantry is often described as "the tip of the spear." The four Soldiers in a fire team and the nine Soldiers in a rifle squad represent the sharpened tip of that spear. Success in a mission depends on all Soldiers in the fire team and squad understanding the unit's mission—its task and purpose—and how each Soldier's assigned weapon and each Soldier's role and responsibility relate to mission success. Fire teams and squads led by the Army lieutenant form the Army's basic maneuver element—the infantry rifle platoon—the foundation on which all tactical operations rest. Now that you understand the composition and leadership of the fire team and squad, in the next lesson you'll learn how individuals and fire teams move on the battlefield.

Learning Assessment

1. Name the duty positions that make up a fire team.
2. Identify the weapons that each member of the fire team carries.
3. Name four responsibilities of the rifle squad leader.
4. Describe the primary purpose of each weapon in the fire team.

Key Words

fire team
squad
platoon

References

Field Manual 3-21.8, *The Infantry Rifle Platoon and Squad*. 28 March 2007.

Field Manual 3-22.9, *Rifle Marksmanship*. Change 3. 28 April 2005.

Field Manual 3-22.31, *40 mm Grenade Launcher, M203*. 13 February 2003.

Field Manual 3-22.68, *Crew Served Machine Guns, 5.56 and 7.62 mm*. 31 January 2003.

Tobin, J., ed. (1987). *Ernie Pyle's War: America's Eyewitness to World War II*. New York: Simon and Schuster.

US Army. (26 August 2004). Beating 10:1 odds, Soldier earns Silver Star. *Soldier Stories*. Retrieved 15 July 2005 from http://www4.army.mil/ocpa/soldierstories/story.php?story_id_key=6307

INTRODUCTION TO TACTICS II

Key Points

1 The Three Individual Movement Techniques

2 The Two Fire Team Movement Formations

Infantry platoon and squad leaders must be tacticians. They cannot rely on a book to solve tactical problems. They must understand and use initiative in accomplishing the mission. . . . The art of making sound decisions quickly lies in the knowledge of tactics, the estimate process, and platoon and squad techniques and procedures.

Introduction

From the introduction of the muzzle-loaded smoothbore musket until the mid-19th century, infantry units in Europe and the Americas **maneuvered** in long lines and large formations. The idea was to subject the enemy, who stood or knelt in similar formations, to massed fire at short range. Often these formations got off one shot, then charged the enemy with fixed bayonets.

That changed during the American Civil War with the advent of the rifled musket, conical bullet, repeating rifle, and primitive machine gun. Infantry tactics did not keep pace with these advances in weaponry, and this led to the increased carnage at battles like Fredericksburg, Gettysburg, and Cold Harbor.

The bloodbaths on World War I battlefields, where British, French, and German infantry charged futilely into machine-gun and grenade fire with massive losses, showed the gap between increasingly lethal military technology and outdated infantry tactics.

Fortunately for the Soldiers of today, much has changed. The modern, trained Army uses traveling techniques, movement formations, and **cover** and **concealment** to advance on or defend objectives with the fewest possible casualties. In this section, you will learn how to move under fire, as an individual and as part of a fire team.

In his book, *Steel My Soldiers' Hearts*, COL David Hackworth relates how his battalion surgeon, CPT Byron Holley, welcomed a young medic to Vietnam:

maneuver

employment of forces in the battlespace through movement in combination with fires to achieve a position of advantage in respect to the enemy in order to accomplish the mission

cover

protection from the effects of direct and indirect fires

concealment

protection from observation and surveillance

Learning to Crawl

Holley couldn't help remembering his own baptism by fire and told Billy how when he heard the bullet snapping by barely a foot above his head, "it was the first realization I had that, hey, a guy can get killed pretty easy over here. I looked up at the moon and prayed, 'God, please don't let me die in this hellhole.' And it was just like I heard a voice saying: Relax, everything's going to be just fine, just remember what you learned in basic training—when the lead's flying, get your butt down. It was like a protective shield came around me and I lost any fear. And I learned fast that you can cover a lot of territory crawling.

David H. Hackworth

The Three Individual Movement Techniques

As Holley learned, knowing how to move on the battlefield is the key to staying alive. But before you move, you must know where you want to move to next. Stay on the route that your leader selects for the team. Then identify the next covered or concealed position that is nearby. Select your route to your next position so you are exposed to the least amount of enemy fire. And don't forget—you don't want to cross in front of your other squad members' fires, either.

To protect yourself, it's important to consider the difference between *cover* and *concealment*. Cover will afford you a degree of protection from enemy direct or indirect fire. Depending on the type of cover, cover can also provide concealment from enemy observation. Concealment means the enemy can't see you, but concealment doesn't protect you from enemy direct or indirect fire.

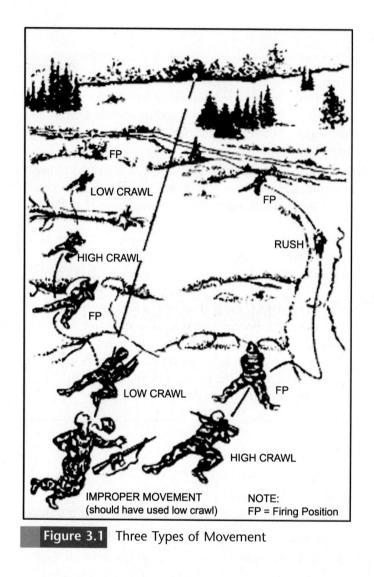

Figure 3.1 Three Types of Movement

There are varying degrees of cover and concealment. Tall grass or dense vegetation will help conceal your movement, but will not stop a bullet or shrapnel from direct or indirect fire. Getting behind a tree or a wall will help stop bullets, and may improve your concealment, but will not afford much protection from indirect fire. Occupying a position inside a building will improve your cover from direct and indirect fire and may offer better concealment from enemy observation.

So now you have identified your next covered position, and you know which route provides the best cover or concealment. You have three options for movement: the *high crawl*, the *low crawl*, and the *3–5 second rush*. You choose which one to use depending on the conditions you face—such as the terrain and the likelihood of enemy contact—or, if you are already receiving enemy fire, on the enemy fire's degree of accuracy. Features such as a gully, ditch, ravine, or wall can provide cover and concealment when you use the low or high crawl. Features such as hedgerows or lines of thick vegetation offer concealment only when you use the low or high crawl. (Remember that high grass or weeds only partially conceal you, since the movement of the grass as you crawl could give away your position.) Large trees, rocks, stumps, folds or creases in the ground, or vehicle hulks can give you cover and concealment in a temporary position.

If the enemy fire you are receiving is from a great distance or is inaccurate fire, it may be best for you to move quickly out of the enemy's line of fire by conducting 3-5 second rushes. If the enemy's fire is close, and somewhat accurate or effective, you may need to high crawl out of the enemy's fires or to a covered position. If you are receiving close, accurate, or effective enemy fire, then in order to survive, you must give the enemy the smallest possible target by low crawling to the nearest cover.

An exception to this would be if you were the target of a close ambush. In this case, you would immediately return fire and assault through the ambush in order to get out of the kill zone and survive. This technique is known as a *battle drill*. You will learn more about battle drills later in ROTC.

The Low Crawl

The low crawl offers you the greatest protection with the slowest movement. Use the low crawl when you do *not* have to move quickly and you have less than a vertical foot of cover and concealment (or when the enemy has good visibility).

With the low crawl, you hug the ground:
1. Keep your body as flat as possible.
2. Grab the upper sling swivel of your weapon and let the weapon trail behind you (see Figure 3.2). The hand guard will rest on your forearm and the butt of the weapon will drag on the ground. Keep the muzzle off the ground.
3. Push both arms forward and pull your right leg forward. Move forward by pulling with your arms and pushing with your right leg. Continue to push, pull, and move. Switch legs as you get tired. *Stay low.*

The High Crawl

Use the high crawl when you have to move quickly and your route offers cover and concealment (or when poor visibility limits enemy observation).

The high crawl is a modified version of crawling on your arms and legs:
1. Keep your torso off the ground and rest your weight on your forearms and lower legs—or your elbows and your knees.
2. Cradle your weapon in your arms and keep the muzzle off the ground (see Figure 3.3).
3. Keep your knees behind your buttocks so your buttocks stay low.
4. Move forward on your right elbow and left knee, then follow with your left elbow and right knee.

Figure 3.2 The Low Crawl

Figure 3.3 The High Crawl

The 3-5 Second Rush

The 3-5 second rush—as the name implies—offers you the fastest movement with the least protection. *You will be exposed*. Use the rush when you have no cover or concealment, and breaks in enemy fire allow you to expose yourself *briefly*.

1. Roll or crawl away from your fighting position.
2. Push up with your arms. Spring to your feet. Carry your weapon at a modified position of port arms. Be ready to fire—or return fire—on the run.
3. *Run* to your next position. Run a short distance. Keep your exposure time to no more than 3-5 seconds. Do not let the enemy fire on you. Speed and surprise are your best friends.
4. Just before you hit the ground, plant both feet and fall forward. As you fall forward, slide your hand to the heel of the butt of your weapon, and use the butt of your weapon to break your fall.
5. Take up a good prone firing position and cover your buddy's movement.

In the last section, you learned that you work with a buddy on your fire team. Always move as a team. Cover one another. Never move without your buddy covering your movement. Never let your buddy move without you covering his or her movement with your weapon.

Figure 3.4 The 3-5 Second Rush

Communicate with your buddy. Make sure you and your buddy understand who moves when and where and when to provide covering fires to protect each other's movement. More important, in order to prevent fratricide (your buddy accidentally shooting you or vice versa), you and your battle buddy must also communicate when you will cease your covering fire.

The Two Fire Team Movement Formations

Fire teams, squads, and platoons use movement formations because:

- they allow the leader to maintain control over the Soldiers
- they allow the Soldiers to protect each other
- they allow the Soldiers to react flexibly when making contact with the enemy
- they make the best use of the team, squad, or platoon's firepower.

In both of the following fire team formations, the fire team leader moves at the front of the formation. This allows the fire team leader to lead by example, allows each fire team member to see the leader, and allows the fire team leader to fire and maneuver the fire team by using hand and arm signals.

Fire teams have two options for movement formations: the wedge formation and the file formation.

The Wedge Formation

The wedge is the basic fire-team formation. The Soldiers are spaced about 10 meters apart, depending upon the terrain. The team leader moves at the point of the wedge. Behind the leader and to his or her sides are the automatic rifleman and the grenadier. The rifleman trails the automatic rifleman or the grenadier in the wedge (see Figure 3.5). If the fire team is moving independently, or is the last element in part of a squad or platoon movement,

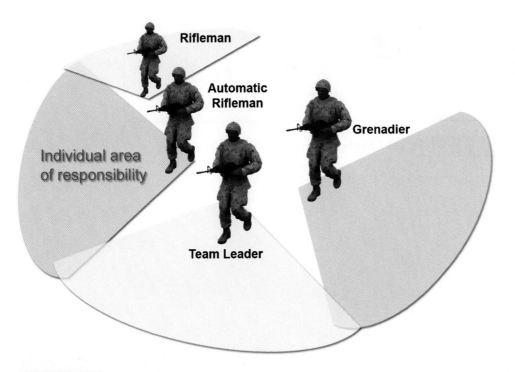

Figure 3.5 The Wedge Formation

the rifleman will occupy the center rear of the wedge formation and the wedge will resemble a diamond shape (see Figure 3.6).

The fire team leader adjusts the distance between Soldiers based on the terrain and the chance of enemy contact. If the terrain becomes restrictive, or if enemy contact is not likely, the fire team leader will contract, or collapse, the wedge formation by closing up the distance and dispersion between Soldiers. This allows easier command and control over the fire team. In severely restricted terrain or very low visibility, the fire team leader may collapse the wedge to the point where the wedge looks like a single-file formation. If the terrain is more open, or if enemy contact is likely or expected, the fire team leader expands the wedge formation by increasing the distance between Soldiers. This increases the difficulty of command and control, but also increases the protection and security of the fire team from enemy contact. In all cases, the fire team leader modifies the formation by reducing or increasing the interval—while still allowing each team member to see the fire team leader and the fire team leader to see the squad leader.

The wedge is easy to control, is flexible, provides good security, and allows the team members to fire immediately in all directions.

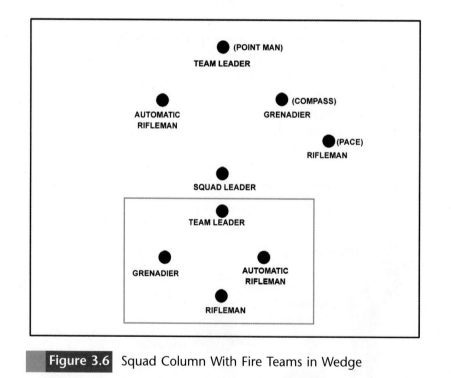

Figure 3.6 Squad Column With Fire Teams in Wedge

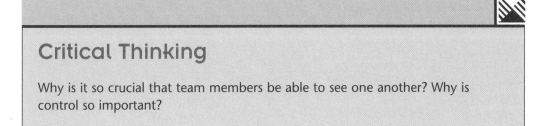

Critical Thinking

Why is it so crucial that team members be able to see one another? Why is control so important?

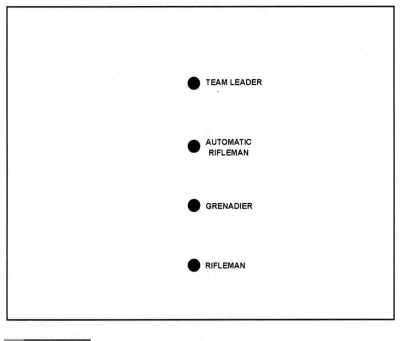

TEAM LEADER

AUTOMATIC RIFLEMAN

GRENADIER

RIFLEMAN

Figure 3.7 The File Formation

The File Formation

If terrain or visibility prevents the team members from using the wedge, they use the file formation. The team leader walks at the point, followed by the automatic rifleman, the grenadier, and the rifleman. They walk about 10 meters apart.

While the file provides the team leader greater control than the wedge does, it is less flexible, less secure, and prevents the team from firing to the front and rear.

| TABLE 3.1 | A Comparison of the Wedge and File Formations |

| CHARACTERISTICS | | | | | |
Movement Formation	When Normally Used	Control	Flexibility	Fire Capabilities/ Restrictions	Security
Fire Team Wedge	Basic fire team formation	Easy	Good	Allows immediate fires in all directions	Good
Fire Team File	Close terrain, dense vegetation, limited visibility conditions	Easier	Less flexible than the wedge	Allows immediate fires to the flanks, masks fires to the front and rear	Not as good

Critical Thinking

Using Table 3.1, compare and contrast the characteristics of the fire team wedge and file. Why is the file easier to control than the wedge? How is it that the file is easier to control than the wedge, but is less flexible than the wedge? Consider fire capabilities and dispersion. Why does the wedge afford better security than the file?

CONCLUSION

An Army adage dictates, "The more you sweat in training, the less you bleed in battle." In the opening vignette, Holley was reminded to "just remember what you learned in basic training—when the lead's flying, get your butt down."

The Army has developed individual movement techniques and movement formations through years of experience in infantry tactics during combat. Just as Holley discovered, if you are to survive in combat, your training must become natural, instinctive, and automatic. The better you learn these techniques, the better your chances of surviving and prevailing in combat. You learned about individual movement techniques and moving as a buddy team in this section. In later ROTC courses, you will learn how small units use movement techniques and formations to survive on the battlefield.

Learning Assessment

1. Describe the advantages and disadvantages of the low crawl.
2. Describe the advantages and disadvantages of the high crawl.
3. Describe the advantages and disadvantages of the 3-5 second rush.
4. Describe the advantages and disadvantages of the wedge formation.
5. Describe the advantages and disadvantages of the file formation.
6. Which Soldier takes point in a fire-team formation?

Key Words

maneuver
cover
concealment

References

Field Manual 1-02, *Operational Terms and Graphics*. 21 September 2004.
Field Manual 3-21.8, *The Infantry Rifle Platoon and Squad*. 28 March 2007.
Hackworth, D. (2002). *Steel My Soldiers' Hearts*. New York: Simon and Schuster.
STP-21-1-SMCT, *Soldier's Manual of Common Tasks*. 31 August 2003.

INTRODUCTION TO MAP READING

Key Points

1 Marginal Information

2 Topographic Symbols

3 Terrain Features

4 Determining Four- and Six-Digit Grid Coordinates

With our military forces dispersed throughout the world, it is necessary to rely on maps to provide information to our combat elements and to resolve logistical operations far from our shores. Soldiers and materials must be transported, stored, and placed into operation at the proper time and place. Much of this planning must be done using maps. All operations require a supply of maps; however, the finest maps available are worthless unless the map user knows how to read them.

FM 3-25.26

Introduction

In Section 1, you learned how to navigate using information from a civilian-style map and a compass. In doing so, you learned that in order to navigate accurately, the map is one of your most important pieces of equipment. In this section, you will examine a military map, study its parts, and learn more about its uses. To be safe in a battle zone, you must know how to read a map, plot your location, and move in the right direction. If you can't navigate correctly, you risk getting lost—or worse, stumbling into dangerous territory. Consider the experience of MAJ Robert K. Wright Jr., historian for XVIII Airborne Corps. MAJ Wright accompanied the Corps in Operation Just Cause, the American liberation of Panama in 1989.

Lost in Panama

I had one last interview to do on [January] 13th[, 1990].... So I went over and got that interview; they were off at a different location, so I'd gotten a driver to take me over, and I got one of their drivers to take me back to Fort Clayton, to the battalion headquarters. And I'd really gotten to know that battalion ... very, very well while I was down there. So I asked the S-3 could he get me a ride to the airport. So he gave me an NCO and a driver and a 'Hummer' [HMMWV; M-998-series High Mobility Multi-Wheeled Vehicle] and said "Sure, just take the Doc out."

So we swung by, picked up my gear. I cleared post. And off we went. And we're driving and driving and driving, and I know it isn't that far. Plus, we're going through the jungle. We're going up a paved highway and everything, but passing traffic and whatnot, which is taking forever. And then we went past this one area and I recognized it from aerial recon that I had done in the helicopter photography missions—this was Cerro Tigre, the PDF [Panamanian Defense Force] supply depot. Which was about 120 degrees in the wrong direction from the airport.

So at that point I casually inquired of the driver "Do you know where we're going?" And he said, "Why no, sir, I thought you knew where we're going." And I turned around and looked at the NCO, and he said "Don't look at me, I don't have a map either." So I said "Oh, O.K., well, hang a right and we'll keep going until we find the ocean or something and we get oriented." And we literally wandered around.

And I remembered thinking at the time, yeah, I've got seven rounds in my .45 . . . . So here we are, traveling through the countryside and had . . . I mean, we were out in the boonies. And had there been a disgruntled PDF guy still running around loose, it was me and my seven rounds from the .45, and that's all we had to protect us.

Department of the Army, XVIII Airborne Corps

Critical Thinking

What mistake did MAJ Wright, his driver, and the NCO make? Who was responsible for the mistake: MAJ Wright, the driver, or the NCO?

Marginal Information

The Army defines a map as "a graphic representation of a portion of the earth's surface drawn to scale, as seen from above."

Because the map is a *graphic* representation, you'll need a written explanation of the graphic elements. You'll find that explanation in the margins of the map: the *marginal information*. (Chapter 3 of FM 3-25.26 explains all the marginal information in detail.)

Figure 4.1 Scaled Representation of the Earth's Surface

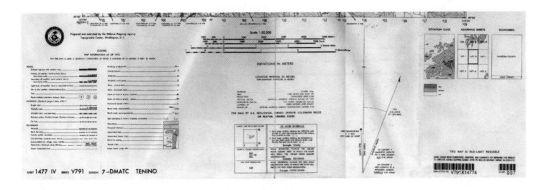

Figure 4.2 The Bottom of a Map

The map **legend** identifies the symbols used to depict the prominent natural and man-made objects that exist on the ground. These symbols are not the same on every map, especially foreign maps. Check the legend to avoid making serious mistakes. The legend from the bottom of the map in Figure 4.2 is shown enlarged in Figure 4.3.

The *sheet name and number* provide the title and the reference number for the map. Maps usually take their sheet names from the largest settlement or natural feature on the map. For example, the "Tenino Map" includes the community of Tenino, Wash.

The sheet number is in bold print in the upper right and lower left areas of the margin (Figures 4.2 and 4.3). At the lower right margin on the map is a diagram that shows adjoining map sheets. Your map sheet will always be depicted in the center of this diagram. You will learn later in your military studies how to link adjoining map sheets to operational overlays, operation orders, and operation plans.

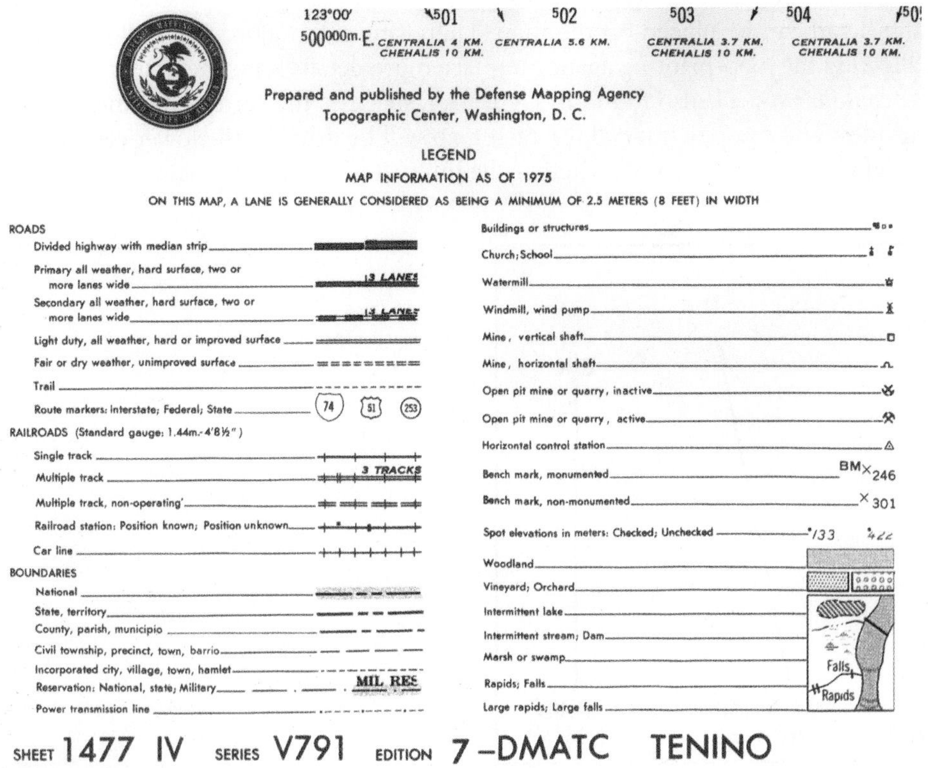

legend

the section on a map that contains the symbols you need to read the map

123°00' ⬈501 ↘ 502 503 ↗ 504 ⬈50!
500 000m.E. CENTRALIA 4 KM. CENTRALIA 5.6 KM. CENTRALIA 3.7 KM. CENTRALIA 3.7 KM.
CHEHALIS 10 KM. CHEHALIS 10 KM. CHEHALIS 10 KM.

Prepared and published by the Defense Mapping Agency
Topographic Center, Washington, D. C.

LEGEND
MAP INFORMATION AS OF 1975
ON THIS MAP, A LANE IS GENERALLY CONSIDERED AS BEING A MINIMUM OF 2.5 METERS (8 FEET) IN WIDTH

ROADS
Divided highway with median strip
Primary all weather, hard surface, two or more lanes wide ___ 13 LANES
Secondary all weather, hard surface, two or more lanes wide ___ 14 LANES
Light duty, all weather, hard or improved surface
Fair or dry weather, unimproved surface
Trail
Route markers: Interstate; Federal; State ___ (74) (91) (253)
RAILROADS (Standard gauge: 1.44m.-4'8½")
Single track
Multiple track ___ 3 TRACKS
Multiple track, non-operating
Railroad station: Position known; Position unknown
Car line
BOUNDARIES
National
State, territory
County, parish, municipio
Civil township, precinct, town, barrio
Incorporated city, village, town, hamlet
Reservation: National, state; Military ___ MIL. RES.
Power transmission line

Buildings or structures
Church; School
Watermill
Windmill, wind pump
Mine, vertical shaft
Mine, horizontal shaft
Open pit mine or quarry, inactive
Open pit mine or quarry, active
Horizontal control station
Bench mark, monumented ___ BM×246
Bench mark, non-monumented ___ ×301
Spot elevations in meters: Checked; Unchecked ___ ·/33 ·//
Woodland
Vineyard; Orchard
Intermittent lake
Intermittent stream; Dam
Marsh or swamp
Rapids; Falls ___ Falls
Large rapids; Large falls ___ Rapids

SHEET **1477 IV** SERIES **V791** EDITION **7–DMATC TENINO**

Figure 4.3 Map Legend

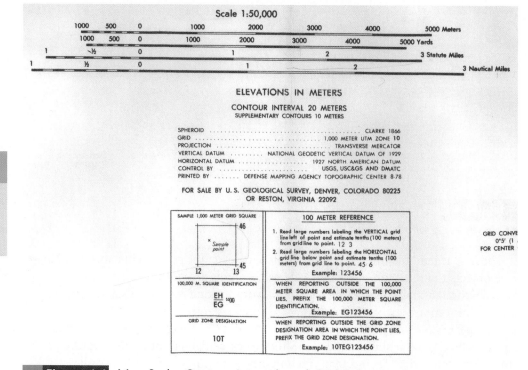

Figure 4.4 Map Scale, Contour Interval, and Grid Reference Box

scale

the ratio of the map distance to the corresponding distance on the earth's surface

The **scale** gives you the ratio of the distance on the map to the distance on the ground. For example, a scale of 1:50,000 (Figure 4.4) indicates that one unit of measure on the map equals one unit of measure on the ground. In other words, one inch on the map equals 50,000 inches on the ground, or approximately 8/10ths of a mile or 1.27 kilometers. The larger the ratio, the less detail can be placed on the map. Likewise, the smaller the ratio, the more detail can be placed on the map. Therefore, a 1:25,000 map will have larger grids, allowing the map-printing agency to place more details onto the map.

The *contour interval*, also found in Figure 4.4, specifies the vertical distance between contour lines. The contour interval for each map will be listed in the lower center of the map margin. Make sure you note whether the interval is in meters or feet.

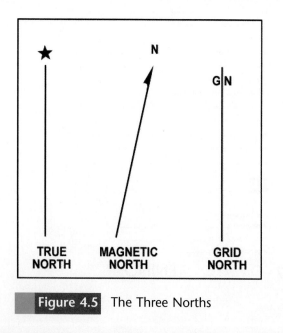

Figure 4.5 The Three Norths

The **declination** *diagram* depicts the three norths on your map: **true north**, **magnetic north**, and **grid north** (Figure 4.5). The declination diagram also lists the grid to magnetic angle (**G-M angle**) in degrees. The G-M angle is the angular difference between grid north and magnetic north. The closer to the poles you go, the greater this angle becomes. Understanding the G-M angle is critical. In order to use a grid map and compass to navigate, you must know how to convert a magnetic azimuth from your compass to a grid azimuth onto your map (or vice versa). You'll learn more about azimuths in the next section.

The *adjoining sheets diagram* tells you the sheet numbers of the adjoining sheets (Figure 4.6). You'll see a checkerboard-like display with the square in the center of the display representing the map you are reading. For example, if you need the map to the east of the map you're reading, look at the adjoining sheets diagram, identify the sheet number of the adjoining map, and request the map.

The *notes* tell you—among other things—the references the mapmakers have used in determining vertical and horizontal distances and the agencies responsible for the map information.

Mapmakers have divided the world into 60 grids and given those grids short letter- and-number (alpha-numeric) designators called *grid zone designators*. The grid zone designator for your map sheet is located at the bottom center of the map inside the *grid reference* box (Figure 4.4). The information in this box gives you the grid zone designation and the 100,000-meter square identification for your map sheet. You need to know the grid zone designator and the 100,000-meter square identification in order to convey information to others about your location or accurately call for indirect fire or close air support.

declination
the angular relationships between grid north and true north or magnetic north measured in degrees or mils east or west—a circle has 360 degrees or 6400 mils

true north
a line from any point on the earth's surface to the North Pole

magnetic north
the direction to the north magnetic pole, as indicated by the north–seeking needle of a magnetic instrument, such as a compass

grid north
the north that is established using the vertical grid lines on a map

G-M angle
the angular distance between grid north and magnetic north

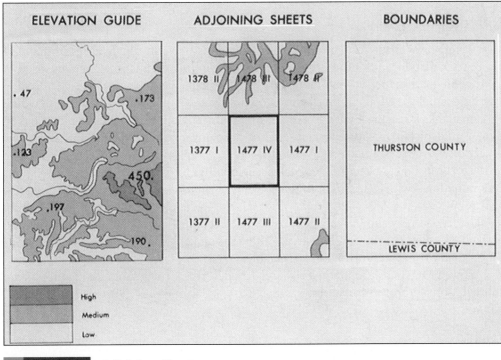

Figure 4.6 Adjoining Sheets

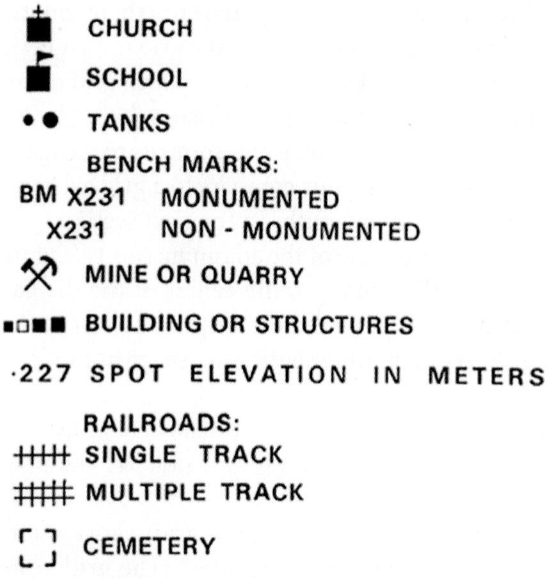

Figure 4.7 Topographic Symbols

topographic symbols

symbols on a map that represent natural and man-made features found on the earth's surface

*The word **topography** comes from two Greek words: **topo**, meaning "place or region," and **graphos**, meaning "to write." So a topographic symbol or a topographic map is a detailed and precise description of a place or region.*

In order to maintain operational security and your night vision, you will use a red-lens flashlight when conducting operations during limited visibility. Older maps printed major roads and built up areas in a red ink that "disappeared" in red-filtered light. Imagine the difficulty of navigating at night when your major roads and built up areas disappeared after you turned on your red-lens flashlight! Mapmakers have recognized the problem and now print military maps with a red-brown ink color that is red-light readable.

Topographic Symbols

Military maps show various man-made and natural features using **topographic symbols** and different colors.

Topographic Symbols

Mapmakers draw maps so you can visualize the landscape with the features in the right place. Your map legend defines the topographic symbols the mapmakers have used to identify the man-made and natural features on the map (Figure 4.7).

For example, the topographic symbol used on your map to represent a school would be a small, black rectangle with a pennant drawn on the top. Another example would be a vineyard depicted on your map as a series of close tiny green dots. The legend may show a place of worship as a small rectangle with a cross, an upward arrow, or a crescent drawn on the top. Most maps of the United States will identify churches—no matter the religious denomination—with a cross. This practice will vary in foreign areas. Check the legend to be sure.

The legend may show a cemetery as a small rectangle drawn with dotted lines and marked "Cemetery." In foreign areas, the mapmakers may indicate the religious denomination, if that information is available.

Army FM 21-31, *Topographic Symbols*, describes the symbols, features, and abbreviations approved for military maps. Do *not* assume that all maps use the same symbols.

Colors

Imagine the difficulty of using a map printed only in black and white. Roads and rivers would look the same—probably with disastrous consequences. As early as the 15th century, mapmakers were coloring their maps. The use of color has become standardized, but check the legend to be sure.

1. *Black* indicates cultural (man-made) features such as buildings, railroads, and roads

2. *Red and brown* combinations identify cultural features (such as major roads), relief features, and contour lines on red-light readable maps

3. *Blue* identifies water: lakes, swamps, rivers, and coastal waters

4. *Green* identifies vegetation such as woods, orchards, and vineyards

5. *Brown* identifies cultivated land on red-light readable maps—on older maps, brown represents relief features and elevation such as contours

6. *Red* was used on older maps to mark populated areas, main roads, and boundaries

7. *Other colors* may show special information. Check the legend.

Be aware of how the seasons and climate may affect the presence or depth of intermittent water sources. Maps will display intermittent water sources as blue, but water may not actually be present at the time you are navigating.

Terrain Features

As you look at the land around you, you will notice different **terrain features**: the hills, valleys, and other features on the ground. Maps represent these features in specific ways.

The Army divides terrain features into three groups: major, minor, and supplementary terrain features.

Major terrain features include *hills, saddles, valleys, ridges,* and *depressions.*

a. A *hill* is an area of high ground. If you stand on a hilltop, the ground slopes away from you in all directions. A map represents a hill with contour lines forming concentric circles. The inside of the smallest circle is the hilltop (Figure 4.8).

b. A *saddle* is a dip or a low point between two areas of higher ground. If you stand in a saddle, you have high ground in two opposite directions and lower ground in the other two directions. The contour lines on a map representing a saddle are shaped like an hourglass (Figure 4.9).

c. A *valley* is a groove in the land, usually formed by a stream or a river. A valley usually begins with high ground on three sides and has a course of running water through it. If you stand in a valley, you will have higher ground in three directions and lower ground in one direction. Depending on the size of the valley and where you are standing, you may not see the higher ground in the third direction, but the stream or the river will flow from higher to lower ground (Figure 4.10).

terrain features

characteristics of the land, such as hills, ridges, valleys, saddles, depressions, and so forth

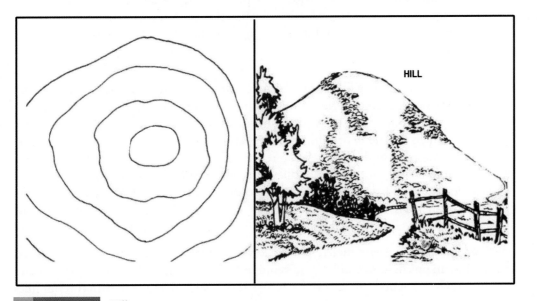

HILL

Figure 4.8 Hill

Figure 4.9   Saddle

To the untrained eye, the contour lines of a valley and a draw (Figures 4.10 and 4.13) look very similar on a map. From a military consideration, a valley will afford a degree of maneuver room for troops and equipment, whereas a draw may only accommodate a small maneuver element, such as a squad or platoon.

Figure 4.10   Valley

Not too long ago, the military term for a ridge was **ridgeline**. Many older Soldiers will still refer to a ridge as a ridgeline, as ridges will generally join a series of hills along a line.

A map represents a valley with U-shaped or wide V-shaped contour lines. Look at the contour lines to determine the direction the stream or the river is flowing. The closed end of the contour lines (the U or the V) points upstream and toward higher ground.

d. A *ridge* is a sloping line of high ground. Think of a ridge as the high ground that runs along a hill. A series of hills connected forms a ridgeline. If you stand on the centerline of a ridge, you will normally have low ground in three directions and high ground in one direction. If you cross a ridge, you will climb to the crest and descend to the base. A map represents a ridge with U-shaped or V-shaped contour lines, but, unlike a valley, the closed end of the contour lines point to lower ground. A ridge can be easily confused with a spur (see Figure 4.14). The difference is that a spur will generally run perpendicular to a ridge or ridgeline, while a ridge will run directly off a hill or a series of hills (Figure 4.11).

e. A *depression* is a sinkhole, a pit, or a low point in the ground. Think of a depression as an upside-down hill. If you stand in the center of a depression, you will have higher ground in all directions. A map represents a depression with contour lines forming concentric circles; tick marks point to the lower ground (Figure 4.12).

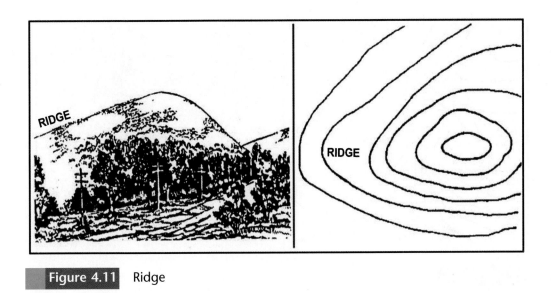

Figure 4.11   Ridge

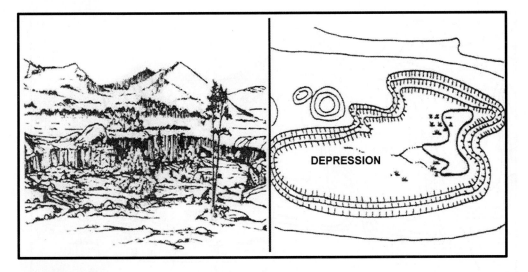

Figure 4.12   Depression

Minor terrain features include *draws, spurs,* and *cliffs* (Figures 4.13 through 4.15).

a. A *draw* is a small valley. A draw has essentially no level ground and little or no maneuver room. If you are standing in a draw, the ground slopes upward in three directions and downward in the other direction. You could consider a draw to be the initial formation of a valley. A valley will usually have many draws feeding into the valley with streams or intermittent streams feeding into the body of water flowing through the valley. On a map, the contour lines depicting a draw are sharply V-shaped, pointing to higher ground. In most cases, a draw will be situated to the left or right of a spur or lying between two spurs (Figure 4.13).

b. A *spur* is a short ridge. The ground will slope downward in three directions and upward in one direction. On a map, the contour lines depicting a spur are U-shaped pointing away from higher ground. In most cases, a spur will have draws to the left or right, or a spur is situated between two draws (Figure 4.14).

c. A *cliff* is a vertical or near-vertical feature. On a map, the contour lines for cliffs are nearly touching or the contour lines come together to form one contour line depicting the edge of the cliff. Newer maps may also depict a cliff with the

Figure 4.13 Draw

Figure 4.14 Spur

Figure 4.15 Cliff

same type tick marks used in depicting a depression, with the tick lines facing downward representing the vertical face of the cliff (Figure 4.15).

Supplementary terrain features include *cuts* and *fills* (Figure 4.16).

a. A *cut* is a man-made feature that cuts through raised ground. You may see a cut on a map forming a level bed for a road or railroad track.

b. A *fill* is a man-made feature that fills a low area. Again, you may see a fill on a map forming a level bed for a road or railroad track.

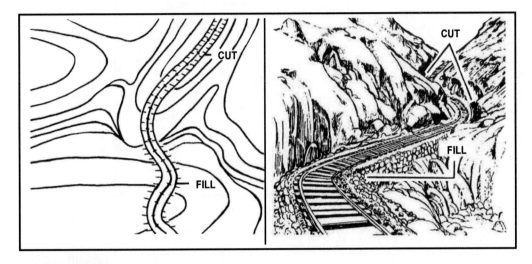

| **Figure 4.16** | Cut and Fill |

Using Four- and Six-Digit Grid Coordinates

Grid coordinates are very important to the daily life of the Soldier. Soldiers use grid coordinates to find locations or convey locations on maps to others. They use grid coordinates to navigate, report enemy activity, request medical evacuation, or call for additional supplies and ammunition. Soldiers use grid coordinates to request indirect fire support from field artillery and naval gunfire. They also use grid coordinates to request close air support from fixed- and rotary-wing aircraft. As you read earlier, you'll find the grid reference box at the bottom center of the map. This gives you the grid zone designation and the 100,000-meter square identification for your map sheet. With more-exact grid coordinates you can more precisely plot or convey a location on the map. An important tool for doing so is your protractor.

Protractor

A protractor is a tool for working with maps. Protractors have an index mark in the center and divide a 360-degree circle into units of angular measure that are marked on two scales (degrees and mils) along the outside edge. The index mark is the center of the protractor circle, from which you measure all directions.

The Army protractor is Graphic Training Aid (GTA) 5-2-12, 1981 (Figure 4.17). It has four major parts:

1. A cross-hair in the middle, which you use to reference the north-south and east-west grid lines on a map

grid coordinates

letter and number designations that allow you to locate a point on a map

Think about the coordinates on the map at a multistory shopping mall. The directory might tell you that the store is at F23. You examine the map and find that Section F is located on the third floor. Store 23 is in a side corridor at a right angle to the main shopping corridor, just before you reach the food court. Once you've located the store on the map, you find the nearest escalators and you're on your way. Using grid coordinates on a military map is quite similar.

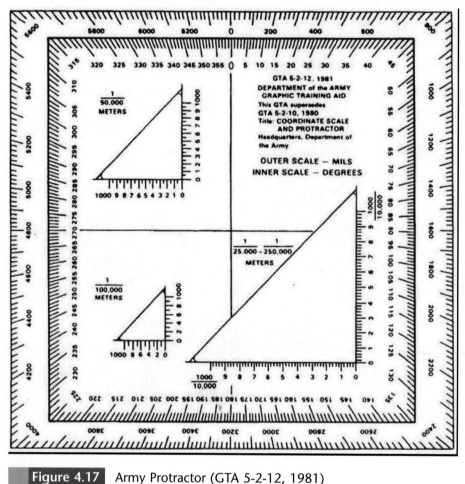

Figure 4.17 Army Protractor (GTA 5-2-12, 1981)

2. Three scales—1:100,000; 1:50,000; and 1:25,000

3. An inner scale of 360 degrees, which you use to plot azimuths (You'll learn more about azimuths in the next section.)

4. An outer, mils scale. (There are 6400 mils in a circle. You'll learn to use this scale for indirect fire.)

Using Four-Digit Grid Coordinates to Determine a Location

Earlier in this section you learned that mapmakers break down the earth's surface into 60 grid zone designators. The grid zone designator for your Tenino map, for example, is 10T. Each of these grid zone designators covers very large areas of the earth's surface. Because grid zones are not manageable in size when navigating, the mapmakers further break down each grid zone into 100,000-meter squares to make the grid zones more manageable. This means that the distance between each grid line is 100,000 meters.

For example, the area on your Tenino map covers portions of two 100,000-meter squares, and their identification is EH and EG. Unless you are flying, you will never need to navigate over an area as large as a 100,000-meter square. So mapmakers break down the earth's surface within the 100,000-meter squares into 10,000-meter squares (Figure 4.18) and then into even smaller, 1,000-meter squares (Figure 4.19) and number them beginning with 00 and ending in 99 (see Figure 4.4). Between each number, 01 and 02 for example, the distance is 1,000 meters.

Now imagine you are behind enemy lines and you are in satellite radio contact with your rescue aircraft, which is in another part of the world. You cannot simply give your

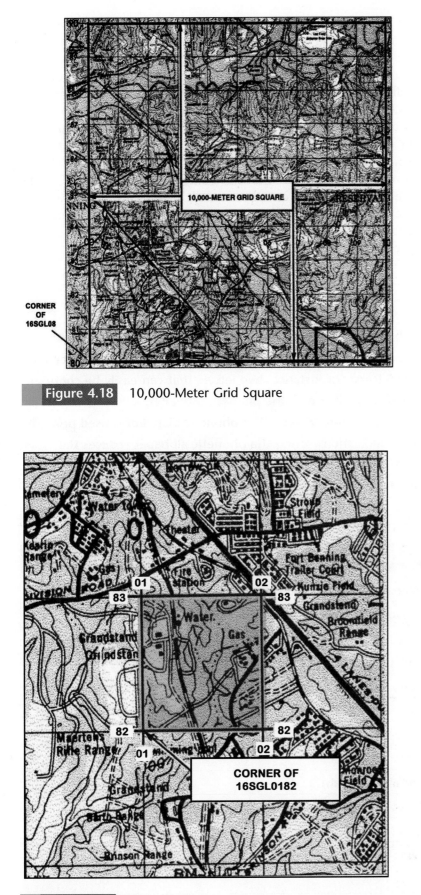

Figure 4.18 10,000-Meter Grid Square

Figure 4.19 Four-Digit or 1,000-Meter Grid Square

rescuers the four-digit grid to your location because every one of the 60 grid zones has thousands upon thousands of similar four-digit grids. You radio the aircraft, "Rescue 6 this is Lost Sheep 3—I am in grid zone Sixteen-Sierra." With this information, your rescuers can now narrow down your location on the earth to one of the 60 grid zones around the world. They begin to fly toward your area of the world, but need to narrow their search. You radio in your 100,000-meter square identification, "Rescue 6, I am at Sixteen-Sierra, Gold Lima." Your rescuers now know where you are within a 100,000-meter square. This is still too large of an area to search, so they ask you for more detailed coordinates. You radio back, "Rescue 6, I am at Sixteen-Sierra, Golf Lima, Zero One, Eight Two (Figure 4.19)." With this information. The pilots have to search only a 1,000-meter square, or one grid square on your map. Aided by your complete four-digit grid, your rescuers are able to spot your infrared emergency beacon and rescue you in a short period of time.

The pairs of numbers on the horizontal (east-west) and vertical (north-south) grid lines on your map are used to identify grid squares. Every set of grid coordinates will

The Phonetic Alphabet

The phonetic alphabet is used to spell out letters in place of just saying the letter itself. By using a word for each letter, there is less chance that the person listening will confuse letters. For instance, two letters that can easily be confused are "D" and "B." When a speaker uses the phonetic alphabet, a listener can easily distinguish between "*Delta*" and "*Bravo*." The phonetic alphabet is used primarily in two-way radio communications. Using the phonetic alphabet reduces the effects of noise, weak signals, distorted audio, and radio operator accent. Maritime units, aircraft, amateur radio operators, and the military around the world use this system of spelling letters.

Letter	Pronunciation	Letter	Pronunciation
A	Alpha (AL fah)	N	November (no VEM ber)
B	Bravo (BRAH VOH)	O	Oscar (OSS cah)
C	Charlie (CHAR lee)	P	Papa (pah PAH)
D	Delta (DELL tah)	Q	Quebec (keh BECK)
E	Echo (ECK oh)	R	Romeo (ROW me oh)
F	Foxtrot (FOKS trot)	S	Sierra (see AIR rah)
G	Golf (GOLF)	T	Tango (TANG go)
H	Hotel (hoh TELL)	U	Uniform (YOU nee form)
I	India (IN dee ah)	V	Victor (VIK tah)
J	Juliet (JEW lee ETT)	W	Whiskey (WISS key)
K	Kilo (KEY loh)	X	X Ray (ECKS RAY)
L	Lima (LEE mah)	Y	Yankee (YANG key)
M	Mike (MIKE)	Z	Zulu (ZOO loo)

Note: Stress the syllables printed in capital letters.

have an even set of numbers. In a four-digit grid, the first half of the grid coordinate numbers represents the horizontal, "left-to-right" or "easting" reading. The second half of the grid coordinate numbers represents the vertical, "bottom-to-top" or "northing" reading. For example, grid coordinate 16SGL0182 in Figure 4.19 would identify all of the area within the grid square to the right of line 01 and above line 82.

The *critical* rule is to read *right* and then *up*. Notice how the example reads *right* and then *up*: Grid square 0182 was to the *right* of line 01 and above—*up* from—line 82.

Using Six-Digit Grid Coordinates to Determine a Location

Submitting a four-digit grid location may be acceptable for large-scale operations or large-scale units. For example, a one-grid-square location might be sufficient for identifying the location of a brigade combat team forward operating base or a zone reconnaissance for a company-sized element. There are other situations, however, where your grid locations must be narrowed down in order to be more accurate than a 1,000-meter square For situations in which you need to be within a 100-meter square—such as calling for indirect fire or close air support, or calling for an emergency resupply or medical evacuation— you will need to know how to determine and plot six-digit grid coordinates.

Think back to the earlier search-and-rescue scenario. Imagine you are hunkered down in hiding because enemy forces are actively searching for you. It is crucial to your survival that your rescuers find you quickly. Rather than have them search an entire grid square for you, you radio your rescuers, "Rescue 6, this is Lost Sheep 3, I am at grid Sixteen-Sierra, Golf Lima, Zero-One-Two, Eight-Two-Eight (Figures 4.20, 4.21, and 4.22). Rather than searching for an hour, your rescuers hover within 100 meters of your location within a matter of minutes.

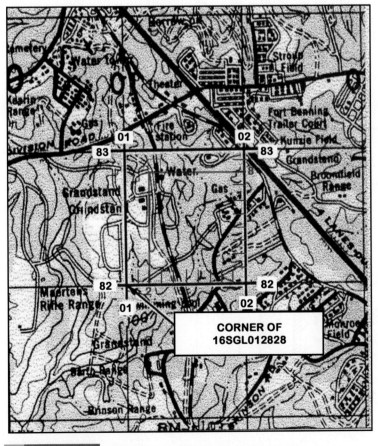

Figure 4.20 Six-Digit or 100-Meter Grid Square

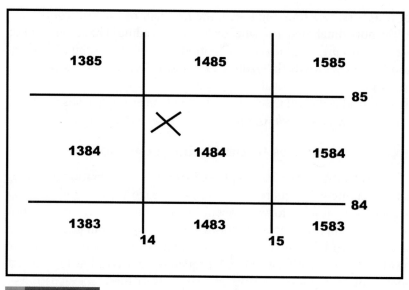

Figure 4.21 Plotting a Specific Point

Follow these five steps to identify a more specific location:

1. Make sure you are using the appropriate scale (check the scale in the map's marginal information) and make sure the scale is right side up

2. Place the protractor scale with the zero-zero point at the lower left corner of the appropriate grid square

3. Keep the horizontal line of the protractor's scale directly on top of the horizontal, left-to-right, or "easting" grid line, and slide the protractor—and its scale—to the right until the left vertical line of the grid square touches the point on the protractor scale for the coordinate you want

4. Read up the vertical scale until you reach the coordinate you want

5. Mark the location.

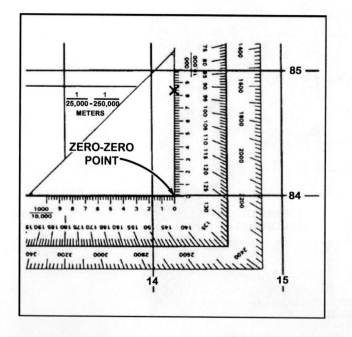

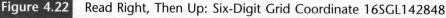

Figure 4.22 Read Right, Then Up: Six-Digit Grid Coordinate 16SGL142848

Make sure the horizontal line of the protractor's scale is lined up with the horizontal, left-to-right, or "easting" grid line, and the vertical line of the scale is parallel with the vertical, bottom-to-top, "northing" grid line.

Remember to write coordinates as one continuous number without spaces, parentheses, dashes, or decimal points. Write them as an even set of numbers so that whoever uses your coordinates knows where to make the split between the *right* and *up* readings.

Be *very* careful not to misidentify or transpose the grid numbers. Double- and triple-check the numbers. Ask someone else to review your numbers. If you send wrong or transposed numbers, the rescuers may not find you or the artillery rounds will not fall where you want them to—they may fall on your position.

Critical Thinking

Discuss some consequences (other than those discussed in the text) of misidentifying or transposing grid coordinates. Think about how far off your grid coordinates will be if you just make one numerical error.

How could you make sure your grid coordinates are accurate in a pressure situation?

CONCLUSION

MAJ Wright, his driver, and an NCO wound up "out in the boonies" because none of them had looked at a map before leaving for the airport. Knowing how to read a map and plot coordinates are essential military skills. In this section, you learned how to determine and plot a grid coordinate with 100-meter square accuracy. In later sections, you will learn how to plot and determine grid coordinates within a 10-meter square by using eight- and 10-digit grid coordinates. During any mission you must always know where you are and where you are going. If you are to be a credible leader, your Soldiers must be confident that you are proficient in map reading and land navigation. Take the time now to gain and polish your map-reading skills. Not only are they important to your Army career—they can save your life or your Soldiers' lives in combat.

Learning Assessment

1. Describe and explain in your own words the five major terrain features of hill, valley, saddle, ridge, and depression.
2. Explain the difference between a draw and a valley; and between a spur and a ridge.
3. Define man-made and natural objects depicted on a military map by topographical symbols.
4. Which is more precise—a four-digit or six-digit grid location?
5. Explain how to determine a four-digit grid location of an object on a military map.
6. Explain how to determine a six-digit grid location of an object on a military map.
7. Describe how to identify a four-digit grid coordinate on a military map.
8. Describe how to identify a six-digit grid coordinate on a military map.

Key Words

legend
scale
declination
true north
magnetic north
grid north
G-M angle
topographic symbols
terrain features
grid coordinates

References

Department of the Army, XVIII Airborne Corps. (6 April 1990). Joint Task Force South in Operation Just Cause. *Oral History Interview JCIT 046.* Fort Bragg, NC. Retrieved 8 July 2005 from http://www.army.mil/cmh-pg/documents/panama/jcit/JCIT46.htm

Field Manual 1-02, *Operational Terms and Graphics.* September 2004.

Field Manual 3-25.26, *Map Reading and Land Navigation.* 18 January 2005.

Field Manual 21-31, *Topographic Symbols.* Change 1. December 1968.

INTRODUCTION TO LAND NAVIGATION

Key Points

1 Understanding Azimuths

2 Converting Azimuths

3 Determining Elevation

4 Calculating Distance on a Map

Introduction

To accomplish your mission, you must be in the right place at the right time. Being in the right place requires you to navigate well. Knowing how to read a map is one thing—knowing how to use a map to navigate requires that you understand how to use azimuths, elevation, and map distance.

In the previous section, you learned how to identify and interpret topographic symbols, colors, contour lines, and marginal information found on a military map. You also learned about the military grid reference system and how to plot grid coordinates using a military map and protractor.

This section will expand your map-reading skills and introduce you to how the military navigates using a map, compass, and protractor. You will learn what an azimuth is and how to convert azimuths in order to navigate using a compass and map. You will also learn how to determine the elevation of the terrain by analyzing the contour lines and contour interval data from the marginal information on a military map. Lastly, you will learn to compute straight-line and road distance using the scale in the margin of the military map. Coupled with your learning from your orienteering and map reading lessons, you will have the basic knowledge to navigate from one point to another and arrive safely at your destination.

In the following vignette, COL John Zierdt Jr., commander of the 1st Support Command during the first Gulf War, remembers how a group of Soldiers paid a serious price when they decided to rely on familiarity rather than put into practice basic map-reading and land-navigation skill required of all Soldiers.

Captured During Desert Storm

The driver had been on a particular route two or three times and thought he knew where he was going. Then instead of turning left, he kept going straight. They even saw the water on their right, which was a dead giveaway that they were going north rather than west. There were two HETs [heavy trucks] following each other. The guy, the one that was eventually captured, was in the lead vehicle, and stopped. And the guys behind him said, "You're going the wrong way and we need to turn around." He said, "I am not." He says, "I'm going straight. You can follow me or turn around if you want."

So, they kept going straight. The next thing you knew they were in the middle of a firefight. The second vehicle got turned around in time [and] got out of there; the [first] vehicle got stuck and didn't get turned around, and the two of them got captured.

Department of the Army, XVIII Airborne Corps and
US Army Center of Military History

Critical Thinking

If the drivers of the two vehicles had looked at and oriented their maps, what might have told them they were headed in the wrong direction?

What would you have done if you were in the second vehicle? Would you have continued to follow the first vehicle after you decided it was going the wrong way?

What could you have said over the radio to the Soldiers in the first vehicle that may have triggered in their minds that they were, in fact, going in the wrong direction?

Understanding Azimuths

azimuth

the horizontal angle, measured clockwise by degrees or mils between a reference direction and the line to an observed or designated point—there are three base (reference) directions or azimuths: true, grid, and magnetic azimuth

The terms **azimuth** and **direction** are interchangeable.

Everything in land navigation begins with an **azimuth**. An azimuth is a horizontal angle measured clockwise by degrees or mils between a reference direction and a line to an observed or designated point. There are three base directions or azimuths: true, grid, and magnetic.

The Army uses azimuths to express direction. Direction is determined from your start point, or where you are, outward toward your desired destination, or your intended target. Because you use north (0 or 360 degrees) as your base line, 270 degrees away from north will always be due west.

Think of yourself as standing in the middle of a Nebraska cornfield. You are facing north. The horizon stretches around you in a great 360-degree circle. If you travel an azimuth of zero degrees—or 360 degrees—or due north—you will wind up in Canada.

If you turn to your right and travel on an azimuth of 90 degrees—due east—you will wind up in the Atlantic Ocean, probably off the coast of New Jersey.

An azimuth of 180 degrees—due south—will take you into Mexico, and an azimuth of 270 degrees—due west—will take you to the Pacific, just off the coast of Northern California.

Determining a Grid Azimuth Using a Protractor

There are two ways you can determine an azimuth. You can use a map to determine a grid azimuth, or you can use a compass to determine a magnetic azimuth. Regardless of the technique, you will learn in this chapter how to convert a grid azimuth to a magnetic azimuth and a magnetic azimuth to a grid azimuth. You will first use a map and learn how to determine a grid azimuth. The steps in this process should be very familiar if you have ever taken a geometry class.

To begin, select a start point on the map. Mark it as point A. Identify an end point on your map. Mark it as point B. Using the edge of your protractor, draw a straight pencil line between points A and B. The line is your azimuth. Now you must determine the **grid azimuth** of that line—the angle between the line and grid north.

When you lay your protractor down on your map, make sure you place it right side up; verify this by checking to see that the writing on the protractor is not backward. If your protractor is wrong side up, you will get grid azimuths that are 180 degrees off from the

grid azimuth

the angle between grid north and a line drawn on the map

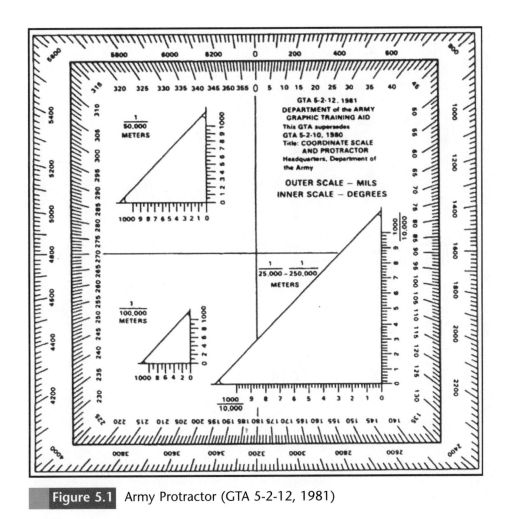

Figure 5.1 Army Protractor (GTA 5-2-12, 1981)

Although having the mils scale on the outside of the protractor may seem confusing now, don't get into the habit of cutting the mils scale off your protractor. Later in your military career, your military occupational specialty (MOS) may require you to state azimuths in mils as well as degrees.

correct grid azimuth. Also, make sure the 0- or 360-degree mark of your protractor is toward the top (or north) of your map, and make sure the 90-degree mark is toward the right (or east) of your map. *If you place your protractor down incorrectly on your map, the grid azimuth that you determine will be a minimum of 90 degrees off and as much as 270 degrees off the actual azimuth.*

Follow these three steps to determine your grid azimuth from the arbitrary points A and B (Figure 5.2):

1. Place the index of your protractor (the place where the etched vertical line and the etched horizontal line meet) at the point where the line you drew on your map crosses a vertical, north-south grid line.

2. Keeping the index at this point, line up the 0-to-180-degree line, or base line, of the protractor on the vertical, north-south grid line.

3. Follow your line outward to the degree scale of your protractor. Read the value of the angle from the protractor. This is your grid azimuth from point A to point B expressed in degrees.

Next, you will plot an azimuth from a known point on a map. Imagine you receive an order to move from your current position in a given direction. Plotting the azimuth on your map will allow you to see the terrain and objects you will need to navigate through along the entire length of your azimuth. The steps are as follows:

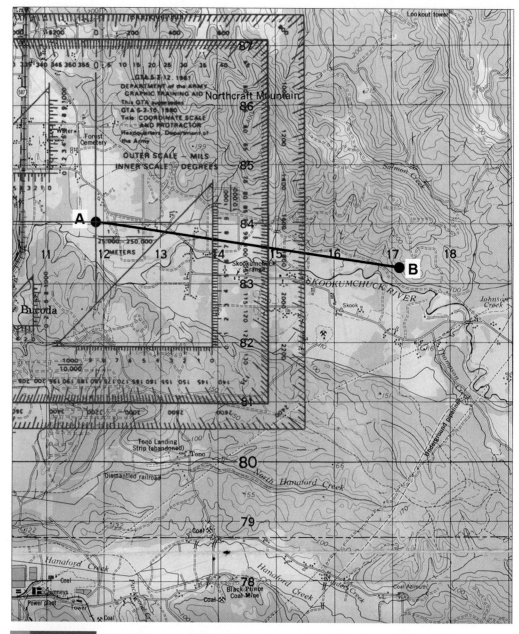

Figure 5.2 Measuring an Azimuth

This is the same method you will use to determine the grid azimuth between any two points on the map.

1. Place your protractor on the map with the index mark at the center of the known point and the base line parallel to a vertical, north-south grid line.

2. Using your pencil, make a small tick mark on the map at the edge of the protractor at the desired azimuth. Remember that your protractor will have degrees on the inner scale and mils on the outer scale. Ensure the tick mark on the map is beside the desired azimuth in degrees and not mils.

3. Lift and reposition the protractor so you can use its side as a straightedge. Draw a line connecting the known point and the tick mark on the map. This is your grid direction line—your azimuth.

Determining a Back Azimuth

A **back azimuth** is simply the opposite direction to your azimuth. A simple example is when you get on the interstate going north when you wanted to go south. At the next exit, you get off the interstate, turn around, and get back on the interstate going south. You just took a back azimuth, or in slang, you just "did a 180."

To compute a back azimuth from an azimuth, simply add or subtract 180 degrees to or from your original azimuth. Remember that a circle has 360 degrees, so if your azimuth is greater than 180 degrees, adding 180 degrees to determine your back azimuth will give you an azimuth that is more than 360 degrees. For example, if your azimuth were 200 degrees, adding 180 degrees would result in a back azimuth of 380 degrees, whereas subtracting 180 degrees would result in a back azimuth of 20 degrees. The back azimuth 380 degrees is obviously greater than the number of degrees in a circle—20 degrees greater. Sure, you could subtract 360 degrees from 380 degrees and still get the same correct back azimuth of 20 degrees. But this simply adds another step to the process. So, subtracting 180 degrees from azimuths greater than 180 degrees simplifies determining back azimuths.

back azimuth

the opposite direction of an azimuth—to obtain a back azimuth from an azimuth, add 180 degrees if the azimuth is 180 degrees or less, or subtract 180 degrees if the azimuth is 180 degrees or more

Determining a Magnetic Azimuth to an Object

A *magnetic azimuth* is an azimuth determined using magnetic instruments, such as a compass. The Army uses two types of compasses: the M2 compass and the lensatic compass. Soldiers use the M2 compass primarily for positioning indirect fire weapons such as mortars. The lensatic compass, pictured in Figure 5.3, is the compass the Army uses for land navigation.

To determine a magnetic azimuth using a compass:

1. Open your compass to its fullest so the cover forms a straightedge with the base. Move the lens (the rear sight) to the rearmost position. This allows the dial to float freely.

2. Place your thumb through the thumb loop, form a steady base with your third and fourth fingers, and extend your index finger along the side of the compass.

3. Place the thumb of your other hand between the lens (rear sight) and the bezel ring; extend your index finger along the remaining side of the compass, and your remaining fingers around the fingers of your other hand. Tuck your elbows into your sides. This will place the compass between your chin and your belt.

4. Turn your body toward the object that you wish to get an azimuth to, pointing your compass cover directly at the object.

5. Look down and read the azimuth from beneath the fixed black index line on the compass face.

Critical Thinking

1. Why is it important for you to understand how to determine a back azimuth?

2. When would you use a back azimuth?

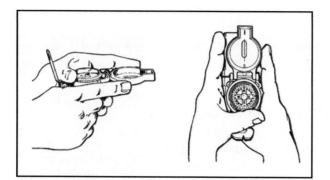

Figure 5.3 Centerhold Technique With a Lensatic Compass

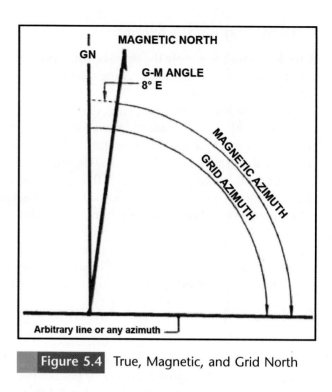

Figure 5.4 True, Magnetic, and Grid North

Shooting an Azimuth with a Compass

When you already know the magnetic azimuth that you want to navigate along, you follow the above steps, but reverse steps 4 and 5. You look down at the compass bezel and slowly turn your body until you see the azimuth you wish to take. Once you see your azimuth on the bezel, look up, and identify an easily recognizable object off in the distance that is in line with your azimuth. Once you have identified the object on your azimuth, you can put your compass away and move to that object. As long as you continue to move to your identified object, you will be on your desired azimuth. This method is known as "shooting an azimuth."

Converting Azimuths

Two problems complicate your easy use of a map and compass:

First, the surface of the earth is curved, while the surface of your map is flat. This creates problems between what your map shows as north (grid north) and what really is north (true north).

Second, the earth's magnetic pole is not the same as the earth's axis. This creates a difference between what your compass shows as north (magnetic north) and what really is north (true north).

Your map contains information to help you overcome these problems. The **declination diagram** in your map's legend gives you the information you need to compensate for the differences—declination—between grid north, true north, and magnetic north.

The declination diagram (Figure 5.4) shows you the difference in angle between any of these norths. Since you will navigate with a magnetic compass and a grid map, your primary concern is the difference between grid north and magnetic north. The difference between grid north and magnetic north is known as the G-M angle (grid-magnetic angle).

declination diagram

the chart in the map legend that tells you the differences in angle between true north, grid north, and magnetic north

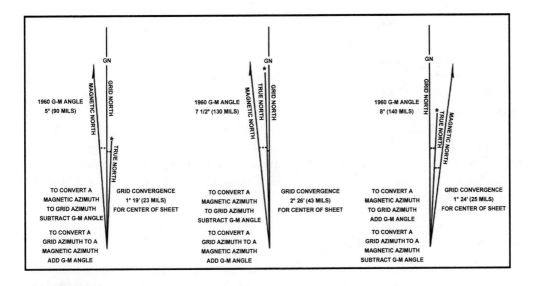

Figure 5.5 Map Declination Diagram

The G-M angle will be shown in the declination diagram and will be expressed in degrees. The G-M angle will either be to the west of grid north (westerly G-M angle) or to the east of grid north (easterly G-M angle). To reduce the confusion of converting easterly and westerly G-M angles from grid to magnetic or magnetic to grid, the mapmakers now include easy-to-understand instructions on the declination diagram so you can quickly convert azimuths without remembering formulas (Figure 5.5).

The three vectors that make up the declination diagram (true north, grid north, and magnetic north) are not drawn to scale. Use the written value for the G-M angle and do not try to measure the vectors to determine the G-M angle.

Most military maps will display the declination diagram in the lower margin. Some maps may not display the declination diagram and will only list the declination information as a note in the map margin.

Adjusting for the Grid-Magnetic (G-M) Angle

The G-M angle value is the size of the angle between grid north and magnetic north. You will see it as an arc, indicated by a dashed line, connecting the grid-north and magnetic-north vectors.

The G-M angle is important because if you don't adjust for the G-M angle, your grid azimuth translated from your map to your compass will be wrong by the size of the angle and vice versa. For example, if your G-M angle is 8 degrees *and you don't adjust for that angle*, your grid or magnetic azimuth will be off by 8 degrees. The farther you move away from your start point on your incorrect azimuth, the farther off you will be from your objective. The angular error increases the farther you move. Not using the G-M angle when converting from a grid azimuth to a magnetic azimuth can cause you to miss your objective. Likewise, if you forget to use the G-M angle when you convert a magnetic azimuth to a grid azimuth, you will plot the wrong azimuth on your map. This could result in passing on incorrect information or calling in inaccurate indirect fire missions.

Look at the notes that accompany the G-M angle diagram (Figure 5.5). One note tells you how to convert your magnetic azimuth to a grid azimuth; another tells you how to convert your grid azimuth to a magnetic azimuth.

A typical note may read "To convert a magnetic azimuth to grid azimuth, subtract G-M angle." If you have a magnetic azimuth of 270 degrees, and the G-M angle is 8 degrees, your grid azimuth will be 262 degrees.

The conversion (whether to add or subtract) depends on whether your map has an easterly or westerly G-M angle. If your magnetic north is to the right (east) of the grid north, then your map has an easterly G-M angle. If your magnetic north is to the left (west) of the grid north, then your map has a westerly G-M angle.

You will learn more about azimuths and land navigation as you progress through ROTC. By the end of your MSL III year, you must master land navigation in order to succeed at the Leader Development and Assessment Course (LDAC), which you will attend at Fort Lewis, Wash., after your MSL III year.

Determining Elevation

You can determine the elevation of any location on your map without any special equipment using two things on your map that you learned about in the previous Map Reading section—contour lines and the contour interval. Before you can determine the elevation of any point on your map, you must first know the contour interval for the map you are using. As you read previously, you can find the contour interval in the margin of your map—usually in the middle of the lower margin. Recall that the contour interval is a measurement of the vertical distance between adjacent contour lines.

Refer to Figure 5.7 to learn how to determine the specific elevation of a point on a map:

1. Identify the contour interval and the unit of measure used (feet, meters, or yards) from your map's marginal information at Figure 5.6 (most military maps use meters).

    Using the map example at Figure 5.7, if you wanted to determine the elevation to point A, you would find the numbered index contour line nearest point A. In Figure 5.7, the closest numbered contour line to point A is the 500-meter contour interval.

    Determine if point A is above (higher in elevation) the 500-meter contour line, or if point A is below (lower in elevation) than the 500-meter line. Since point A lies between the 500-meter contour line and the 600-meter contour line, moving from the closest contour line (500-meter) to point A would be traveling uphill to a higher elevation.

2. Determine the elevation of point A by starting at the index contour line numbered 500 and counting the number of intermediate contour lines (the unmarked contour lines) to point A.

    Point A is on the second intermediate contour line above the 500-meter index contour line. Since the contour interval is 20 meters (Figure 5.6), each intermediate contour line crossed to get to point A adds 20 meters to the 500-meter index contour line. The elevation of point A is 540 meters.

3. Determine the elevation of point B by going to the nearest index contour line. In this case, it is the upper index contour line, numbered 600. Point B is located on the intermediate contour line immediately below the 600-meter index contour line.

    Therefore, point B is located at an elevation of 580 meters. Remember, if you are increasing elevation, add the contour interval to the nearest index contour line. If you are decreasing elevation, subtract the contour interval from the nearest index contour line.

123°00'   ′501   ′502   503   504   ′50!

500000m·E. CENTRALIA 4 KM.   CENTRALIA 5.6 KM.   CENTRALIA 3.7 KM.   CENTRALIA 3.7 KM.
            CHEHALIS 10 KM.   CHEHALIS 10 KM.   CHEHALIS 10 KM.

Prepared and published by the Defense Mapping Agency
Topographic Center, Washington, D. C.

LEGEND
MAP INFORMATION AS OF 1975
ON THIS MAP, A LANE IS GENERALLY CONSIDERED AS BEING A MINIMUM OF 2.5 METERS (8 FEET) IN WIDTH

ROADS
    Divided highway with median strip
    Primary all weather, hard surface, two or
        more lanes wide _____ 13 LANES
    Secondary all weather, hard surface, two or
        more lanes wide _____ 13 LANES
    Light duty, all weather, hard or improved surface
    Fair or dry weather, unimproved surface
    Trail
    Route markers: Interstate; Federal; State   (74) (51) (253)
RAILROADS (Standard gauge: 1.44m.-4'8½")
    Single track
    Multiple track   3 TRACKS
    Multiple track, non-operating
    Railroad station: Position known; Position unknown
    Car line
BOUNDARIES
    National
    State, territory
    County, parish, municipio
    Civil township, precinct, town, barrio
    Incorporated city, village, town, hamlet
    Reservation: National, state; Military   MIL RES
    Power transmission line

Buildings or structures
Church; School
Watermill
Windmill, wind pump
Mine, vertical shaft
Mine, horizontal shaft
Open pit mine or quarry, inactive
Open pit mine or quarry, active
Horizontal control station
Bench mark, monumented   BM×246
Bench mark, non-monumented   ×301
Spot elevations in meters: Checked; Unchecked   ·'133   ·222
Woodland
Vineyard; Orchard
Intermittent lake
Intermittent stream; Dam
Marsh or swamp
Rapids; Falls   Falls
Large rapids; Large falls   Rapids

SHEET 1477 IV   SERIES V791   EDITION 7–DMATC   TENINO

Figure 5.6 Example of a Contour Interval Note

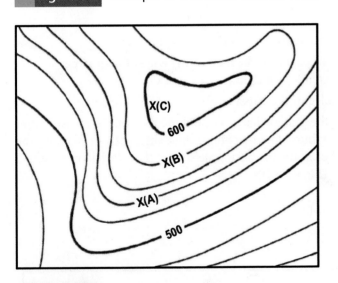

Figure 5.7 Points on Contour Lines

Critical Thinking

Why is it important for you to know how to determine elevation on a military map? Think about the azimuth you will plot on your map in order to travel from point A to point B. How will knowing elevation help you when navigating from point A to point B? Can knowing the elevation help you decide which azimuths or routes to take to your destination?

4. Estimate the elevation of the hilltop, point C, by adding one-half of the contour interval to the elevation of the last contour line. In this example, the last contour line before the hilltop is an index contour line numbered 600. Add one-half the contour interval, 10 meters, to the index contour line. The elevation of the hilltop would be 610 meters. You use the same process to estimate the elevation of a depression, except you subtract half of the contour interval to estimate the elevation at the bottom of the depression.

Calculating Distance on a Map

Now you know how to plot and determine azimuths on your map, and you understand how to determine elevation on your map or along your plotted azimuth. But how far is it from your start point to your destination? The marginal information on your map allows you to determine both straight-line distance and road distance. You can use the graphic scale—located in the lower center portion of the map margin—as a ruler to convert distances on the map to distances on the ground (Figure 5.8).

The graphic scale is divided into two parts. To the right of the zero, the scale is marked in full units of measure and is called the primary scale. To the left of the zero, the scale is divided into tenths and is called the extension scale.

Most maps have three or more graphic scales, each with a different unit of measure, such as meters, yards, statute miles, and nautical miles. When you use the graphic scale, be sure that you use the appropriate unit of measure.

Straight-Line Distance

To calculate the straight-line distance between two points on your map:

1. Lay a straight-edged piece of paper on the map so the edge of your paper touches both points and extends past them.
2. Make a tick mark on the edge of the paper at each point (Figure 5.9).
3. Then move your paper to the graphic bar scale, and use the scale to measure the distance between the two points. Note that you should align the tick mark on the right with a printed number in the primary scale so that the left tick mark falls within the extension scale (Figure 5.10).

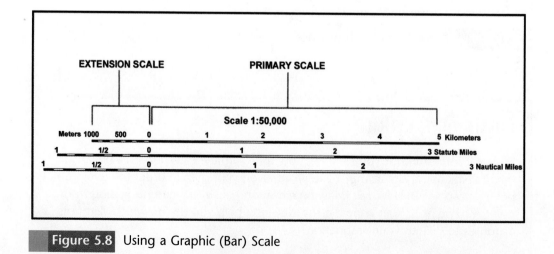

Figure 5.8 Using a Graphic (Bar) Scale

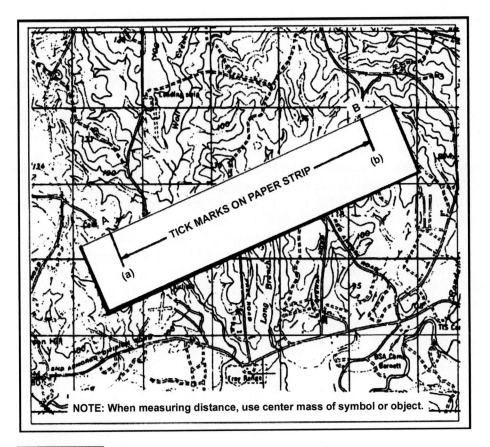

Figure 5.9 Transferring Map Distance to Paper Strip

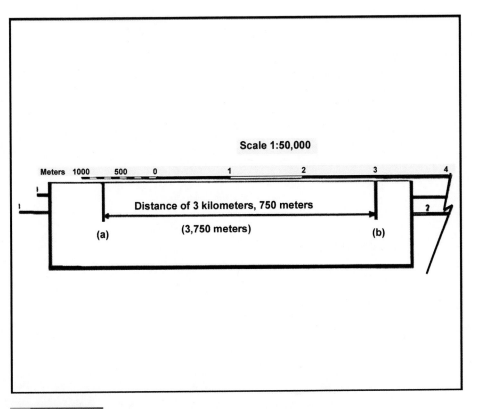

Figure 5.10 Measuring Straight-Line Map Distance

Curved-Line Distance

The more tick marks you make when measuring your curved route, the more accurate your final distance will be. This is especially true when measuring along curves.

To measure the distance along a curved route, such as a road, trail, waterway, or other curved line:

Put a straight-edged piece of paper on your map with the edge next to your starting point. Place a tick mark on the paper and on your map.

Line up the straight edge of the paper with the straight portion of the curved route you are measuring. Make a tick mark on both map and paper when the edge of the paper leaves the straight portion of the line you're measuring. (See View A in Figure 5.11.)

Pivot the paper until another straight portion of the curved line lines up with the edge of the paper. Continue in this manner until you have completed the distance you want to measure. (See View B in Figure 5.11. Notice the number of small ticks on the edge of the paper and that the last is labeled tick mark B.)

Move the paper to the graphic scale to determine the ground distance. The only tick marks you need to measure are tick marks A and B. (See View C in Figure 5.11.)

In order to maintain accuracy when measuring curved distance, it is important to keep the straight edge of your paper on the same side of the curve you are measuring. If you start off measuring a curved road on one side of that road, then keep your paper on that side of the road and mark all of your tick marks on that same side of the road. Do not cross over and start making tick marks on the opposite side of the road.

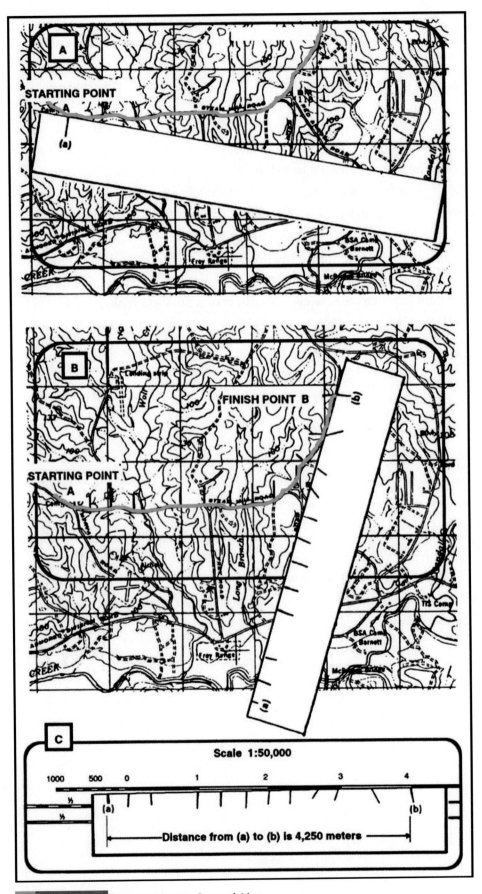

Figure 5.11 Measuring a Curved Line

CONCLUSION

You are a Cadet now. In the not-too-distant future, you may be an Army second lieutenant leading a platoon. Perhaps, in the distant future, you will be a lieutenant colonel commanding a battalion, a colonel commanding a brigade, or even a major general commanding a division. Whatever your position and rank, you will always need to get your Soldiers from one point to another. If you can't do so, you endanger your mission and perhaps the lives of your Soldiers.

It's impossible to overemphasize the importance of map reading and land navigation. They are critical leadership skills. They are also perishable skills—they require constant practice and review, regardless of a Soldier's rank or experience. Start now to develop your expertise and work to keep your skills honed and at the ready.

Learning Assessment

1. What is an azimuth?
2. Explain how to determine a grid azimuth.
3. Explain how to determine a magnetic azimuth.
4. Explain the differences between the three norths.
5. Explain how to use the G-M angle to convert grid and magnetic azimuth.
6. What is a contour interval?
7. Explain how to determine elevation on a map.
8. Explain how to measure the straight line and curved distance between two points on a map.

INTRODUCTION TO LAND NAVIGATION

Key Points

1 **Understanding Azimuths**

2 **Converting Azimuths**

3 **Determining Elevation**

4 **Calculating Distance on a Map**

INDEX

achieving, 65–67
active voice, 105
adjoining sheets diagram, 183
Afghanistan, 77, 87
Aristotle, 46
Army leadership levels, 9
Assistant Cadet Battalion S3, 124
attributes, 6
automatic rifleman, 160, 161, 164, 166, 173
azimuth, 199, 200

Babylonian, 147
back azimuth, 203
back-brief, 124
Baghdad, 49, 51–52
Baker, Vernon J., 2Lt., 25
Ballard, Robert A., Ltc., 145
Bataan, 19, 114
Bataan Death March, 114
Battle of Balaklava, The, 103–104
Be, Know, Do, 3, 4, 5–8, 141
Bleak, David B., Sgt., 23
BLUF, 104
body composition, 78
Body Fat Standards, 78
bottom line up front (BLUF), 104
Bradley, Omar N., Gen., viii, 45
Brewster-Norman, Diane, 106
buddy teams, 161
Bush, George W., 37

Cabanatuan, 114
Cadet Battalion Command Sergeant
    Major (CSM), 124
Cadet Battalion Executive
    Officer (XO), 124
Cadet Battalion Public Affairs Officer
    (PAO), 125
Cadet Battalion S1 (administrative
    officer), 124
Cadet Battalion S3 (operations
    officer), 124
Cadet Battalion S4 (logistics officer), 124
Cadet Command Leadership
    Development Program, The, 11

Cadet Company Commander, 125
Cadet Company Executive
    Officer (XO), 125
Cadet Company First Sergeant, 125
Cadet evaluation report, 13–14
Cadet NCO ranks, 122
Cadet officer ranks, 121
Cadet Platoon Leader, 125
Cadet Platoon Sergeant, 125
Cadet Squad Leader, 125
Cadet Unit Structure, 123
cardio-respiratory (CR) endurance, 78
Cato the Elder, 104
chain of command, 121, 123–125
character, 17–29
Churchill, Winston, Sir, 76, 109
Clark, Mark, Gen., 2
Clarke, Bruce C., Gen., 70
cliff, 187, 188
climate and culture, 62
coaching, 64
colors, 129–130, 132
command, 4, 10
commitment, 57
communication, 102–108
compass, 146, 147, 149, 152–153
competence, 7, 8
compliance, 57
concealment, 169
confidence, 36
Connelly, William, Sgt. Maj., 25
Contemporary Operating
    Environment, 111
Continental Army, 120, 121
contour interval, 182, 207
contour lines, 207
control points, 146–147, 150–152, 153
corporate culture, 138, 140–141
Corregidor, 19, 114
counseling, 64
cover, 169
Crandall, Bruce P., Maj., 36
creed, 27, 113, 114
curved-line distance, 210, 211
cut, 189

dead reckoning, 152–153
Dean, Christopher, 1st Lt., 49
declination, 183
declination diagram, 204–205
depression, 90–91, 186–187
Desert Storm, 199
developing, 61–65
diet, 81–83
direct leadership, 9, 10
distress, 87
diversity, 45
domain knowledge, 48–51
draw, 187, 188
Drucker, Peter, 98
Drum, Hugh, Gen., 128

Edwards, Robert D., Sgt., 65
Eisenhower, Dwight D., 23, 26
elevation, 206
empathy, 26–27
esprit de corps, 8
ethos, 112
eustress, 87
Ewell, Richard S., Ltg., 102
exercise, 76–80
expertise, 138–139

fieldcraft, 48
file formation, 175, 176
fill, 189
final protective line, 164
fire team, 157, 158, 161, 166
fire team leader, 161, 166
FITT, 79–80
flexibility, 78, 79, 80, 81
Food Pyramid, 81–83
France's Argonne Forest, 41

G-M angle, 183, 204–205
Gates, Julius W., Sgt. Maj., 35
George Washington University, The, 148, 149
Gettysburg, 102
goals, 97
Gordon, Gary, MSG, 111
Grant, Ulysses S., Gen., 106
Great Britain, 121
Great Raid, 114
grenadier, 161, 166, 167
grid azimuth, 200–201
grid coordinates, 189

grid north, 183, 204
grid reference, 183
grid zone designators, 183

"Hail to the Chief", 129, 132
handrails, 153
Harvey, Francis, J., 54
Hester, Leigh Ann, Sgt., 3
high crawl, 171
high-explosive (HE) round, 164
hill, 185
Hughes, Christopher, Lt. Col., 51–52

infrared (IR) aiming device, 158
innovation, 44–45
interpersonal tact, 45–47
Iraq, 147, 157

Jackson, Thomas J. (Stonewall), Ltg., 35, 47, 102
Jefferson, Thomas, 16

Kennedy, John F., 22
King, Martin Luther, Jr., Dr., 104, 109
Kingston, Joseph, 1st Lt., 28
Kissinger, Henry, 94
Korea, 23, 28–29
Krueger, Walter, Lt. Gen., 115

Lawrence, T. E., 50
LDP Model, 12
LDRSHIP, 18
Leader Development and Assessment Course (LDAC), 123
leader intelligence, 40, 42–51
leadership, 4–12
leadership presence, 32–36
leadership vs. management, 10–11
leadership requirements model, 56
leading, 56–61
Lee, Robert E., Gen., 101–102
legend, 181
lensatic compass, 203–204
Light Brigade, 103
Lorimer, George H., 72
Louisell, William C., Capt., 46
low crawl, 171

M16 rifle, 158, 160
M16/M4 rifle, 158, 159, 160, 164
M203A1 Grenade Launcher, 161, 163, 165

M249 Squad Automatic Weapon (SAW), 160, 161, 162
M4 Carbine, 161
M4 MWS Carbine, 159
M4/M4A1 Carbine, 159
M68 Close Combat Optic, 159
MacArthur, Douglas, Gen., 19–20, 23, 136
magnetic azimuth, 203
magnetic north, 183, 204
maneuver, 169
map, 147–150, 180–182
Marshall, S.L.A., Brig. Gen., 18
Medal of Honor, 20, 23, 24, 25, 37, 42
Mendonca, Gisela, 2Lt., 87
Mental Agility, 43
Mentoring, 64
Meyer, Edward C., Gen., 12, 64
military bearing, 34–35
military courtesy, 129, 131
military customs, 129, 131
military rank progression, 131
military salute, the, 131–134
mission, 139–141
mission statement, 96–97
Mogadishu, 111
Montgomery, Viscount, Field Marshall, 48
Movement Techniques, 170
Mucci, Henry A., Lt. Col., 115
Murphy, John F., 1st Lt., 115
muscular endurance, 78, 80
My Lai, 17

National Anthem, 129, 132
National Guard, 3
Nein, Timothy, Staff Sgt., 3
noise, 102
Noncommissioned Officer's Manual, 45
Noncom's Guide, 32
Normandy, 132, 145–146
notes, 183

Oath of Office, 9
Operation Just Cause, 179
orienteering, 146–153

pacing, 153
Panama, 179
passive voice, 105
Patton, George S., Gen., 18, 28, 40
personal mission, 96–97
Philippines, 18–19, 114–115
phonetic alphabet, 192

physical fitness, 35, 78–83
Pimentel, Eliel, ILt., 77
platoon leader, 158
platoon sergeant, 158
platoons, 157, 158, 166
POW, 114–115
Powell, Colin, Gen., 46, 65, 95
POWER model, 71, 73
P-R-I-C-E, 80–81
Prince, Robert W., Capt., 115, 116
profession, 138–141
professionalism, 34, 141
protractor, 189, 190, 200–202
P-R-O-V-R-B-S, 78–79
Purple Heart, 157
Pyle, Ernie, World War II correspondent, 164

Raglan, Lord, 103
rank, 9, 121–122, 131
Reagan, Ronald, 104, 109
receiver, 102
reporting, 133–134
resilience, 36
responsibility, 138, 139
"Reveille," 129
Rickenbacker, Eddie, Capt., 24
ridge, 186, 187
Ridgway, Matthew B., Gen., 55
Rieman, Tommy, Sgt., 157
rifleman, 158, 161, 164, 165, 166, 173
Roosevelt, Franklin D., 19, 104, 109

saddle, 185, 186
saluting people in vehicles, 132
scale, 182
Schofield, John M., Maj. Gen., 21
self-awareness, 63
sender, 102
seven Army values, 5, 18–26
Shinseki, Eric K., Gen., 27, 110
Shughart, Randall, SFC, 111–112
signs of major depression, 91
Silver Star, 157
SMART Goals, 72, 97
SMART model, 72
Soldier's Creed, 27, 111, 113, 141
Somalia, 111
sound judgment, 44
spur, 187, 188
squad, 157, 165–166
squad leader, 166

squads, 157, 166
steering marks, 153
straight-line distance, 208
stress, 87
suicide, 91–92

tactics, 48
Target Heart Rate (THR), 79–80
team leader, 158, 161, 166, 173
terrain association, 153
terrain features, 185
Thatcher, Margaret, 109
Thermal Weapons Sight, 159
Thompson, Hugh C. Jr., Warrant
    Officer (WO1), 17
3-5 second rush, 170, 172
thumbing, 153
"To the Color", 129, 132
topography, 184
true north, 183, 204

units, 43, 50
use active voice, 105

valley, 185, 186
values, 17
Vietnam, 17, 33, 36–37
vision, 4, 96
von Moltke, Helmuth, Field Marshal, 100

warning signs of suicide, 92
Warrior Ethos, 27–29, 111, 112–114
Washington, George, Gen., 22, 120, 137
wedge formation, 173, 174, 176
Wright, Robert K. Jr., Maj., 179

York, Alvin, Sgt., 41–42

Zierdt, Jr., John, Col., 199